D0874070

*Policy for the West* is a book of the utmost timeliness, for the problems it discusses are those that leap at us from the front page of our daily papers; a book of the utmost clarity, for no one today surpasses Barbara Ward in the ability to make plain the essential simplicity of apparently confused questions; a book of the utmost hopefulness, for it presents a positive policy to which free men can rally.

At a time when the nature of the Soviet challenge to the free world has become overwhelmingly clear, one of the main means of countering it—the Marshall Plan—is timed to disappear. The need for joint effort is greater, but with the termination of ECA, the machinery for joint action may actually be less.

In this situation, Barbara Ward sees the need for new, more comprehensive, and more unified policies on the part of the Western nations. In *Policy for the West* she examines how these policies can develop and relates them not only to the known hostility of the "Soviet half" but also to the positive vision of a free and united Western world which can enlist the heart and mind and will of us all.

# POLICY *for the* WEST

BOOKS BY BARBARA WARD

*The West at Bay*
*Policy for the West*

# POLICY *for* the WEST

*by* BARBARA WARD

NEW YORK · W · W · NORTON & COMPANY, INC.

All statistics quoted in this book are drawn from three sources: (a) Government publications, (b) Records of the United Nations, (c) Reports from the Organization for European Economic Cooperation (OEEC).



PRINTED IN THE UNITED STATES OF AMERICA

*For R. J.*

# Contents

# PART I · *Containment*

# 1

# *The Fact of Soviet Hostility*

WHEN in 1945 the combined efforts of the Western world and of Soviet Russia had defeated Hitler in the field, there was one hope above all others abroad among the free nations. It was that peace and future security could be based upon a working agreement with the Soviet Union. The heroic endurance of the Russian people and the military feats of the Red Army had created deep enthusiasm for Soviet Russia. Such men as Wendell Willkie and even President Roosevelt himself felt for a time that it might be easier to rebuild the world in alliance with the "progressive" Soviet Union than with the tradition-bound backward-looking Britain of Mr. Winston Churchill. Russia's readiness to co-operate in the United Nations set the seal on the idealists' hope of seeing realized a universal reign of law, and the close agreements reached at Teheran, Yalta and Potsdam seemed to promise that there would be no disastrous wrangling over the peace treaties. A new era would be built on Great Power agreement and upon a steady growing together of the two systems—capitalist and communist. A jocular, and probably apocryphal, remark of Stalin's was widely quoted, to the effect that if America needed more state control, Russia needed more free initiative, and newspapers were glad to publish his impressive assurances that there was no essential hostility between the Soviet and other ways of life: Had he not personally abolished the Comintern in 1943? In short, the general Western atmosphere was one of relief and hope and very genuine good will toward the Soviet people.

A few voices were raised in warning, but they were not heeded. The suggestion was made, for instance, after the victory in Europe that the West should use its overwhelming military advantage to secure the withdrawal of Soviet troops from Europe. Not only was the idea buried as a black heresy, but the West agreed in the arrangements for Berlin to base some of its own crucial military commitments upon blind trust in the word of the Russians. The Western forces drew back, leaving their garrisons in Berlin completely dependent upon Soviet good will for all their communications by land.

This small and total act of confidence reflected the West's general complacency. Their armies virtually flung themselves back into civilian life. The American armed forces which had numbered 11,900,000 in the summer of 1945, had fallen to 2,500,000 a year later, to 1,500,000 six months after that. The United Nations was set enthusiastically to work. The United Nations Relief and Rehabilitation Administration drew most of its income from the West and distributed most of its aid to war-ridden Eastern Europe. There was no lack of optimism or hope in those early days. Difficult as it is today to recapture that atmosphere, most of us felt it at the time and most of us, with deep chagrin and foreboding, have seen it drain away ever since.

How did the vision of "one world" fade—and fade in so short a span? The Communists have, of course, their answer. The will to co-operate with Russia which was so strong in 1945 was, they say, frustrated by the capitalist and imperialist rulers of the Western world. The peoples' desire to work with the Soviet Union was genuine, their leaders' was bluff. Thus from the start these same rulers—the ingenious Attlee, the cunning Truman—set to work to frustrate the "will to peace" of the masses. They refused to give Russia the secrets of the atomic bomb. They intervened in Eastern Europe to undermine the new people's democracies by supporting peasant leaders such as Mikolajczyk, or protesting against the liquidation of "traitors" such as Petkov. They backed the "Monarcho-Fascists" in Greece in their struggle to wipe out the Communist-led left. They refused to reunite Germany and divided the country willfully by setting up a government of their own in the Western half. They brought UNRRA to a premature end and substituted the Marshall Plan for the exclusive help of the West. They backed the forces of reaction and "bourbonism" in the Far East and armed Chiang Kai-shek in his murderous war against the workers. Finally, they threw down the gauntlet, signed the Atlantic Pact, piled up the atomic bombs and armed themselves to the teeth for an encirclement of the Soviet Union. This without much exaggeration is the version which Communist sources give and Communists must believe of the years since the war—a progression of Western hostility and aggression manfully countered by a peace-loving but unterrified Communist front.

How much do the Soviet leaders themselves believe it? Perhaps it is academic to ask. The mentality of the men in the Kremlin is so remote from ours that our guesses are mostly blind. But at least we know that those who mold Russian policy have been trained in an atmosphere precisely calculated to produce in them a deadly mixture of arrogance and suspicion. Many of them—Stalin for instance—have hardly left Russia throughout their lives. The traditional mood of Russian society in which fear of the progressive Western world and contempt for it were equally blended has seeped into their souls. Their conscious minds, meanwhile, have been molded by Marxism and the revolution which gave them at once a recognition and a fear of the technical achievements of Western society and profound scorn for all who do not accept the absolute and eternal truths of Marxist doctrine. Arrogance and fear, contempt and distrust, scorn and inferiority—these are the strands that have been woven together to make the fabric of Soviet thought. We cannot say which has been paramount—genuine fear or equally genuine confidence and contempt. All that we can be sure of is the hostility.

Yet the question of Russian motives must be put. The reason lies not so much in any hope of plucking the heart out of the Soviet mystery. It lies rather in the need to steady and unify opinion in the West. Communism is well aware of the scruples and uncertainties in Western thought. To create division and misunderstanding and to arouse uneasy consciences is one of the steady aims of its propaganda. It is a sobering thought that Hitler may have helped to perfect the technique. What more effective weapon did he use against the Allies than his claim that their Treaty of Versailles was responsible for all Germany's ills? Weakened, divided and uncertain, Hitler's neighbors accepted all his early violent redrawing of the map of Europe on the grounds that perhaps after all it was their fault. Today the Communists attempt to play upon the tender conscience of the West in a way which all too often recalls the effectiveness of Hitler's propaganda. The Communist-inspired "Stockholm peace campaign" of 1950 which was devoted to outlawing the one kind of weapon —the atomic bomb—in which America has the superiority, owed whatever success it had to the Western nations' profound distaste for mass destruction and underlying guilt that they first used the frightful weapon. True, it was used to end a war, not to start one. To judge by the lessons of direct aggression in the last ten years—the Nazi attack upon Poland, the Low Countries or Russia, the Soviet onslaught on Finland or South Korea—the tank is the weapon which must be outlawed if sudden aggression is to be effectively banned. But the peace campaigners will hardly demand such a step so long as Russia's superiority lies in the field of tank warfare.

The "peace campaign" is only quoted here as an example of the importance the Communists attach to playing upon the Western conscience in order to weaken Western unity and determination. It is therefore important to assess squarely the Soviet claim that the catastrophic disintegration in the relations between Russia and the free world since the war has been entirely due to the ill will, hostile pressure and military plotting of the West. Unless our minds are clear on this point, there may be hesitations and confusions in our reaction to the fact of Communist hostility. No nation or group of nations can claim that their policy has been faultless—unless they happen to be Communists. Then, of course, it is infallibly right even if it reverses itself sharply three times in as many weeks. Undoubtedly, the West has made blunders, supported unworthy groups and causes, been inconsistent, put interest before honor and behaved as states have tended to behave ever since the unalienable right of nations to serve their own *sacro egoismo* became an accepted fact in international society. The question here, however, is not the original innocence of the Western Powers but whether they can be fairly blamed for the frightening postwar deterioration in Soviet-Western relations.

There are two general points to be borne in mind. There is first of all the fact that, as Mr. Churchill's own reminiscences [1] of the early days of the Soviet-Western alliance against Hitler remind us, the Soviet Union was a hostile and distrustful ally as far back as 1941. The cry for a second front went up within a few weeks of Hitler's attack and was used with such venom and insistence in the following years that it became a political embarrassment to Russia's comrades-in-arms. Soviet claims to the Baltic States and parts of Poland—upon which the Anglo-Russian talks in 1939 had in part broken down—were revived in the first months of the alliance. At no time was there any genuine sharing of information, any sign of increasing trust, any deviation from the mood of lightly disguised suspicion and hostility. Yet these were the years of the full alliance. It is hard to blame Western behavior after 1945 for a mood which palpably existed long before.

The second point has already been mentioned—the degree of Western disarmament. The British were not much behind their American allies. By 1946, their armed forces had fallen from 5,100,000 to 1,427,000, by 1949 to 716,000. The Russian figures cannot be established accurately but it seems certain that demobilization never reduced the Soviet Army much below three or four million men. Thus while the effec-

[1] Cf. *The Grand Alliance*, Vol. III of Mr. Churchill's history of the Second World War.

tive force of the West in Europe amounted to no more than a few undermanned divisions, the Russians have had fully mobilized on Europe's land frontiers at least a hundred divisions for the last three years. To suggest that the Western nations, signing the Atlantic Pact in a belated attempt to correct this disparity, are offering "provocation" to Russia is to extract all reason from language (a technique, unhappily, perfected by the Communists). What sense is there in, say, the accusation that the Western Powers provoked Russia to clamp down its extreme control upon Eastern Europe, when at the time of this supposed provocation—1945 to 1947—they were without the military means to make any aggressive policy effective, whereas the presence or threat of the Red Army could be felt from Stettin to the Aegean?

Such general arguments may, however, be insufficient to convince the doubter. It is better to take two perfectly specific Soviet accusations and examine them more closely. Communist propaganda, for instance, would have us believe that the process whereby Poland has come to be ruled by a Russian Marshal has been largely a reaction to Western attempts to frustrate "the people's will" in Eastern Europe. What in fact do we find? The first step in the chain of events which gave Poland first a coalition controlled by Communists, then a Communist-run dictatorship and finally a government under the thumb of the Russian Marshal Rokossovsky was taken as far back as 1943 when Soviet Russia broke off relations with the London Government of General Sikorski. The establishment of the Beirut Committee of Communists and Communist sympathizers in Russia, its promotion to become the Lublin government, the Soviet decision not to establish contact with the London-directed Polish Underground in its magnificent rising against the Nazis in Warsaw, even though Soviet tanks and guns were at the gates—all these were steps which preceded by a year and more any Western protests at the disappearance of free government in Poland. Can a policy worked out step by step from 1943—significantly enough, from the first recovery of Soviet strength and confidence after Stalingrad—be fairly attributed to later Western protests or even mistakes? The time table is there for all to study. It certainly shows a Soviet decision to secure control of Poland that antedates the agreements reached at Yalta by nearly two years.

The record in Germany is no different. The decisive factor in frustrating the reunion of Germany has been the transformation of the Soviet Zone into a Communist State. But the process of sovietizing Eastern Germany began not as a reaction to any Western moves but on the very morrow of the Russian occupation. As those who were in Berlin at that time can testify, Social Democrats who would not accept Communist dictation were already in concentration camps by Christmas, 1945. The forced fusion of the Socialists with the Communists to form the Communist-dominated "Socialist Unity Party" took place in the spring of 1946, while there was still four-power administration of Berlin and while the experts of the four occupation authorities were still drawing up joint proposals for reparations. From the day of the fusion, the Socialist Unity Party has steadily usurped all the powers of single party rule. The process was no reaction to Western policy. On the contrary, it was the evident fact of sovietization in the East that changed the occupation line in Germany into a frontier between two opposite ways of life.

The list could be continued at length. Again and again Western policies which now earn Communist attack on the grounds that they are "provocation," turn out on examination to be belated Western reactions to Communist policies undertaken long before. But perhaps a more conclusive proof of the Soviet's major responsibility for the present division of the world lies in the fate of those who have staked everything on securing Russian co-operation and have been prepared to go to very great lengths to secure it. After all, the criticism the Communists make of the Western Powers is in essence that they have not been prepared to accept Soviet policies. No doubt many things—a United Germany or Austria, for instance, or a limited form of atomic control or a Japanese peace treaty—could have been secured if Russian terms had been accepted. The Communist charge is that the West by refusing the Soviet terms has unmasked its hostility and its determination to encircle and defeat the Soviet Union. We are therefore on sure ground if we ask what has happened to those men and those states who have loyally accepted Russia's terms. Have they thereby earned the kind of honorable partnership which the Communists seem to suggest is possible? Have they found that *modus vivendi*, that capacity for living together, that co-operation, which inspired such ardent Western hopes in 1945?

The answer comes to us, unhappily, in large measure from the grave. The men who in Europe preached and practiced the doctrine of full and frank co-operation with communism are most of them dead. Ehrlich and Alter, the two Polish socialist leaders, were shot in Russia before the end of the war. Benes is dead, of despair and disillusion. Jan Masaryk has killed himself. Petkov, the Bulgarian left wing leader, with a valiant record against Hitler, has faced the firing squad. These men believed that alliance between Communist and non-Communist was possible on decent and reasonable terms. They have had their tragic answer.

The trouble goes deeper still. It is not simply that the non-Communist stands little chance unless he identifies himself completely with the Soviet line, as such ex-Socialists as Grotewohl in Germany or Cyrenkiewicz in Poland have contrived to do. The truth is that Communists themselves are suspect unless their submission is complete. In Bulgaria, the Communist leader, Kostov, found that his nationalist feelings, still stirring below the Marxist crust, could not stomach the open economic exploitation of his country by the Soviet Union. His reward was trial and execution. In Hungary, Rajk shared the same fate. Gomulka in Poland may go the same way. They were all Communists but their submission to Moscow was insufficiently total.

It is from Jugoslavia, however, that we have the clearest evidence of Russia's designs and pretensions. Here is the satellite that broke away. No one will accuse Tito of being lukewarm in his Communist faith. He belongs to the old aristocracy of European Marxism—the long exile, the fight in the Spanish war, the sojourn in Moscow, crowned in his case, however, by return and a hero's role in his country's war against Hitler. No state was more quickly transformed after 1945 into a "people's republic." Nowhere did socialization go further. The collectivization of agriculture went forward more speedily than anywhere else. The flaming breach between Tito and the Soviet Union thus occurred not on any issue of dogma or performance. Tito was thrust out from the Soviet paradise because, like Lucifer, he cried: "I will not serve."

In the fascinating and revealing correspondence between Tito, Moscow and the Cominform, we can see in full publicity the real extent of Soviet claims to power and control. They are total. Tito's only sin has been to reject Soviet tutelage, supervision, direction and domination. He has dismissed Soviet "advisers," clapped Soviet sympathizers in jail, lacked respect for Soviet envoys, permitted his picture to appear as large as Stalin's. It would be laughable, were it not so tragic. The tragedy is the totality of Russian pretensions. The tragedy is the impossibility of finding any *modus vivendi* with a power which claims everything and gives nothing. This is the Russia that emerges in monstrous clarity from the Tito-Soviet exchanges.

Can the West believe, in the face of this evidence, that anything it could have done or left undone would have altered or modified Soviet distrust and hostility? If the most abject collaborators are shot for not collaborating enough, if the smallest tinge of national sentiment in a man's view of communism can send him to the firing squad, if the total acceptance and practice of communism cannot save a Tito once he hankers for a hairsbreadth of independence, why pretend that the West, whose sacrifices of national interest and national sovereignty would inevitably have been more moderate, could ever have found a way by sweetness and light and conciliation to make itself acceptable to the dark men of the Kremlin? No Western state could have made the advances of a Petkov, the sacrifices of a Benes, the submission of a Rajk, the Communist parade of a Tito. And they have all been balanced in the

Soviet scales and found wanting. The Western Powers can therefore deplore Soviet hostility. They can fear it, they can seek to understand it, they can look for ways of deflecting it. But there is one thing they cannot do—they cannot take any blame for it. It is self-caused and self-sustained and even if the years since the war had been one long record of Western acceptance, compliance and accommodation, the hostility of the Soviet world would have remained as intense as it is. For one thing only assuages it—the certainty of total control.

# 2

## *Do We Face General War?*

EVER since modern Communism appeared on man's horizon—a hundred years ago in Marx's *Communist Manifesto*—it has been the fundamental belief of Communists that their system would either conquer or destroy the world. The rising power of the workers represented by Marxist Communism would supersede the rule of the bourgeoisie embodied in capitalism. Or else the struggle between them would lead to "the common ruin of the contending classes." Since that prophecy was made, no real change has occurred in strict Marxist thinking. Lenin believed in the inevitability of imperialist war which would destroy the capitalist states and liberate the colonial peoples. Trotsky foresaw a "permanent revolution" by which Communism, first triumphant in Russia, would spread to the whole world. Stalin, preaching "socialism in one country" may seem an exception, but the difference is only one of emphasis and timing. He preached socialism in one country when the outside world seemed unripe for further Communist experiments. Whenever a measure of stability reappeared in non-Communist lands, Stalin was content to speak of the possibilities of the "peaceful coexistence" of the two systems. But the "peaceful coexistence" was only the degree of tolerance a cat offers a mouse when it has temporarily vanished down its hole. When instability and disorder reappear, Communist revolutionary pressure reappears with it.

When the mouse ventures out again, the paw descends. The underlying determination to eat the mouse is absolutely unchanging.

How, then, can we keep the peace? The Soviet Union makes no secret of its hostility. On the contrary the language it uses to express its views of the West have the terrifying ring of paranoic mania.[1] Nor is there much doubt of its scale of military preparedness, nor of the share of Russian resources devoted to the weapons of war. Moreover this state which predicts its own world triumph and is forging at least some of the means necessary to victory is ruled by the most absolute dictatorship known to history, and history itself is our warning that of all types of government it is absolute dictatorship that most easily takes the plunge into war. The reasons are obvious enough. The distaste for war felt by ordinary men and women is, as the Communists shrewdly judge in their peace campaigns, almost infinite. No democratic government can plan aggression or secure from its people the military supplies necessary to carry it out. Government proceedings carried on in the full light of public discussion ensure that, far from planning war, a democracy is normally unready even to fight the wars thrust on it by others.

Dictators work and strike in the dark. Public opinion is told only of the menacing hostility of the outside world and lashed into moods of fear and self-defense. Since access to most other sources of information is denied to the dictator's subjects—Russians may not travel and now a complete net-

[1] This analysis of American policy after Korea was broadcast over Moscow radio: "In what way" (asks *Pravda*) "is President Truman, that sanctimonious hypocrite, perpetrator of so many bloody deeds in all corners of the earth in post-war years, instigator of murderers, traitors, and marauders, to-day's murderer of Korean women and children, better than the mad Führer? . . . Truman, bustling like a haberdashery shopkeeper, scribbling envenomed, man-hating epistles; whispering under cover with the professional butchers, the Bradleys, MacArthurs, and other Forrestals; signing the order for intervention in Korea with an ominously scratching pen—such is the unseemly, disgust-provoking spectacle of the world of imperialist gangsters in the grip of violent insanity."

work of jamming stations prevents even the modest echo of a Western word to cross the Soviet frontiers—the national mood becomes an instrument upon which the dictator can play at will. Armaments can be piled up against the imagined ring of encirclement. Aggression can be launched in the guise of self-defense.

There is another even more sinister aspect of dictatorial rule which, in history, has led again and again to external adventures. If all criticism and opposition are silenced at home, there remains no domestic scapegoat for the evils and irritations inseparable from any form of government but always aggravated in the illegal police state. A cartoon of the thirties showed Hitler face to face with the Father of Lies. Around them lay the massacred bodies of Hitler's opponents—liberals, socialists, Catholics, Lutherans, Jews—and the Devil said sardonically to the Fuehrer: "Take care, little man, soon there will be no one left to blame but you." When this stage is reached, the temptation to find the scapegoat abroad—in the hostility of a neighbor, in the threat of encirclement—is overwhelming. Can we assume that Stalin who has liquidated more "scapegoats" than most dictators is entirely immune?

And is he, for all his experience, equally immune to the other bane of dictators—the desire to see all accomplished within their single span? He is an old man. In the last ten years, the Soviet scramble for control and territory has grown much more intense. Is it simply that Hitler's war gave him unrivaled opportunities for extending his dominion? Or has he begun to be, after all, "an old man in a hurry"?

These are some of the disturbing reflections that come to mind as soon as one asks whether the Soviet Union seeks to precipitate a general war. But it is not the whole story and happily there are as many pointers to a more cautious state of mind in the Kremlin. In the first place, we should not underestimate the effectiveness of the sheer horrors of modern war as a strong discouragement to would-be aggressors. Mr. Churchill has frequently pointed to the likelihood of the terrors of modern warfare acting as a deterrent to aggression, and behind them loom the unknown horrors—the lingering deaths left by radioactivity, the monstrosities known to biological warfare, the destruction of man and soil that may be, as far as the scientists can see, permanent. The Russian people and their rulers are not ignorant of these things. On the contrary, no people in the last war had to withstand so savage an attack or so long an agony. To risk similar horrors within five years of the last great bloodletting seems beyond the bounds of reason. Even if pity does not hold back the Soviet leaders, surely a realistic calculation of their available manpower and the possible degree of popular endurance should have some effect.

But, it may be argued, calculations of this sort would not have held back Hitler. Of this, however, we cannot be sure. Hitler was not made to face the certainty of general war until it was too late. But even if it were so, even if we could prove that no fear of the consequences would have restrained the Fuehrer, Russia is not Germany, Stalin is not Hitler. There is evidence from history to support the view that general war is not the Soviet strategy. The record of Czarist Russia should not be ignored, for there is a tough, lasting quality about national traditions which tends to modify the most radical social and economic revolutions wrought on the surface of a nation's life. Its roots run deeply into the centuries and from this heredity come habits and reactions which change less than the prophets of transformation by environment care to admit. The Russian tradition is certainly not one of willfully launching general war. By inept policies, by fishing in troubled waters, by pursuing limited expansionist aims on the side, the Russians have usually managed to involve themselves in whatever general wars occurred but they have not precipitated them and they have always suffered horribly from them—there is probably no part of Europe that has been as savagely and as frequently invaded and occupied as the Ukraine.

This does not mean that they have been reliable and peaceable partners in Europe. On the contrary, their desire to secure control of the Balkans and Constantinople in succession to the decaying power of Turkey was a permanent source of upheaval in the nineteenth century. Nevertheless, it did not, until Germany came on the scene, lead to general war. The reason was simple and significant. The Russians were left in no doubt by the British that if they did seize Constantinople, the result would be war. This celebrated "Eastern Question," which lived with British politics for nearly a hundred years and could be relied upon at any time to win a by-election or fill in a dreary debate in the House of Commons, showed that Czarist Russia, when faced with the inescapable evidence of armed opposition, did not care to press its cause to the point of war. By the time the struggle for succession in the Balkans did lead to general war—in 1914—it was Germany's "drive to the East" that bore the primary responsibility for the catastrophe.

The old difference between Czarist Russia and imperial Germany has been repeated in the Germany and the Russia that grew up after the First World War. The dictatorship of Hitler in Germany was probably the briefest, gaudiest, and most contemptible essay in destruction ever perpetrated by man. It lasted precisely eleven years, only six of them at peace. From the first day of power to the last day of collapse, only one energy inspired the Nazi system—violent conquest and domination. There was no other *raison d'être* in the whole movement and virtually the first act of policy of the new regime was rearmament and the purposeful preparation for war. The record of Soviet Russia has been very different. The Soviet Union lived at peace with the rest of the world from the moment the postwar stability was restored in Europe—say, about 1924—until the beginning of Hitler's war. During that time, much of Russia's energies were devoted to a herculean effort of economic and social construction. There was no special bent in the system toward militarism, war and conquest. On the contrary, had there been no Nazi onslaught upon Poland and later upon Russia, there is little reason to suppose that the Soviet frontiers today would have been any different from those of 1939. By one of the recurrent ironies of history, it was the man who justified his whole war by the claim of defending Europe against Bolshevism that opened

Europe's gates to it as wide as the sky itself. The Soviet leaders have extorted every political and territorial advantage they could snatch from victory. But the war was none of their making.

How, then, are we to explain the paradox? History tells us that Russia does not launch major wars. Recent events tell us that the Soviet Union can live at peace with its neighbors and cultivate its own immense back garden—another contrast to Hitlerism with its clamor for "living space." Yet we have equally to face the fact that few nations have taken so little time to annex so many territorial possessions or to extend their imperialist control over so many neighbors as have the Russians since the end of the Second World War. In five short years, they have added 179,954 square miles and over 21 million inhabitants to their own empire and exerted their direct control over five sovereign European states. This estimate leaves out their total control of Eastern Germany and the still uncertain extent of their influence in China. But the list is formidable enough in all conscience and, on the fringe of the vast Soviet system, the process of collecting satellites still continues—in Korea, it has led to local war.

The answer lies in the Communist view of history and in Stalin's glosses upon it. All history, in Marx's view, can be explained by the rhythm and counterpoint of the dialectical process—the creation of new forms of society in the bosom of the old, their growing and strengthening until in due time, the old order disintegrates completely and a new order of society emerges to take its place. Slavery gives way to feudalism, feudalism to capitalism. Capitalism is now in process of disintegrating before the rise of communism and its decay and disappearance are as certain as the waning of the moon or the turn of the seasons. In the long view, history will do communism's work for it since the seeds of destruction are self-sown in the capitalist order of society. Its own "inherent contradictions" will bring it down. Its structure of class and property will not permit the full use of the new methods of production made possible by capitalism. The power of the poor to purchase will never catch up with the power of the machines to produce. Gluts will appear at regular intervals, gluts of so-called "overproduction," during which men will go workless and goods will be destroyed. Markets, too, will become more and more hotly contested as the productive power of each national economy increases without corresponding increases in the peoples' ability to earn and buy. The struggle for markets will lead to the imposition of colonial rule on backward peoples and to war, to imperialist war. But as the confusion and the destruction, the exploitation and the misery spread and deepen, the eyes of the workers will be opened. Conscious of their class and of their numbers, they will confront the decreasing group of monopolists who hold them and the vast productive wealth of modern industry in thrall. They will rise and shake off their chains. The "expropriators will be expropriated." The communist age of the world will begin.

The theory clearly expects the capitalist world to do most of the work of destroying itself unaided. Since there are "inherent contradictions" in the core of capitalist society, they will have their effect, just as cancer works inexorably through the human organism. The collapse does not necessarily occur all at once. A period of convulsion, followed by partial recovery, followed by further frightful spasms and even briefer rallies, is quite compatible with an inexorable advance toward destruction. Probably the decisive difference between Trotsky and Stalin after the revolution lay in Trotsky's fear that the capitalist world would turn and destroy Communism in Russia unless the Communist Revolution spread, and Stalin's growing belief that the revolution in Russia could be preserved as a base for future operations when the next crisis in capitalism would occur—as it was bound "objectively" to do.

This, in short, is the Communist view of the present state of world history. On the one hand, the new social order of communism has lodged itself in the bosom of the old society by capturing Russia and making it a firm foundation and starting point for a new world. On the other, the declining and decaying capitalist society can be relied upon to produce at regular intervals crises of economic glut and stagnation, leading to violence and imperialist war. After each crisis, capitalism's will to resist and survive is weakened and communism can expand at its expense. But the final collapse will come only when all capacity for revival and stability has vanished from the West. Then Communist world order will triumph and the end of history come into sight. Only one danger threatens to frustrate this happy consummation. The final struggle between capitalism and communism might lead, as Marx half-prophesied, to the destruction of both.

If this is the historical situation such as it exists in the minds of the men in the Kremlin, one can understand the delicacy of the strategy they believe themselves compelled to pursue. On the one hand, they must snatch every opportunity they can during periods of capitalist crisis in order to extend their control. So long as there are signs of weakness and disintegration that can be exploited, Communist pressure must be maintained and intensified. But to push as far as general war is a risk which "objectively" is unnecessary since capitalism itself will produce its own major upheavals. To attack the West during a period of relative stability is to invite just that danger of common destruction which stands between communism and its goal of world dominion. Once relative strength returns to the Western nations, open provocation is therefore to be avoided; but at the first sign of confusion, the floodgates can be opened again. The strategy is, in short, that of helping history to help itself.

There is thus no contradiction at all between the peacefulness of Russian policy before the Second World War and the violent phase of smash and grab which followed it. Between 1924 and 1929, the capitalist world had recovered some stability. Then followed twenty years of crisis—first economic crisis, then the rise of Hitlerism, then total war, and finally the world-wide upheavals caused by war during which the Soviet leaders have secured whatever extension of power could be salvaged from the catastrophe. It can thus be said of the Soviet Union that while it seeks world power as Hitler did, it does not see in a general war of conquest the chief instrument of its policy. Under certain conditions, as Stalin has often said, there is nothing to prevent peaceful coexistence between communism and capitalism. The Soviets simply bide their time, sure that sooner or later another wave of crisis will be generated by the instability of capitalist society and that, in the ensuing confusion, more of the world will be gained for communism. Meantime, they can afford to wait.

The Western task is therefore to secure the conditions in which the Soviet Union is prepared to wait. But how are the free nations to set about it? One thing they can renounce from the start—they cannot hope to change the Soviet view of history. Marx was still flexible enough to believe that developments he could not foresee might come to alter his predictions. He believed, for instance, that England might produce a collectivist society without violent civil war. He never knew America or he might have made even more considerable modifications in his theory. But there are no thinkers of Marx's caliber in the Soviet Union today. And even if there were, their chances of being listened to would be very slight. The fate of the Soviet Professor Varga illustrates this point. After the war, Professor Varga published a book suggesting, among other things, that the experience of wartime controls might make it simpler for the United States to overcome the instabilities of the trade cycle, that through the British Labour Party the working classes and the trade unions were securing a fuller representation of their interests in Britain, that the granting of Dominion status to India had somewhat modified Britain's imperialist hold on the sub-continent. Such heresy could not be tolerated in Moscow. The Professor was forced to recant and to confess that he had grossly misinterpreted the facts. One should, perhaps, be not too discouraged. Since one Varga has managed to observe and write, others may follow. Intellectual curiosity and an unbiased mind are possible within the Soviet system, even if, at the moment, they must wear a white sheet and carry a candle. But any hope that the Western states themselves might succeed in modifying Soviet orthodoxy, when their own intellectual leaders have so signally failed, must be ruled out for the time being.

It is easy to understand why. Accept a fantastically simplified Marxism and the rest follows. All capitalist states, says the dialectic, become imperialist as they develop. Germany and Japan have already done so. The United States and Great Britain are capitalist states, therefore they will sooner or later follow the example of the Germans and the Japanese. Provided one accepts the view that the economic substructure of society determines all the rest, then capitalist states must by definition behave in the same way. Otherwise the dogma is false. It is therefore useless to explain to the Kremlin that the United States and Great Britain whose political and national life has been molded in a very different tradition from that of Germany and Japan do not in fact behave in the same way, do not become progressively more imperialist, do not launch wars, do not fight each other for the other's markets, do not overtly attack Communist states, do not crush the trade unions, shoot the liberals and gas the Jews. Seen from the Kremlin, seen with the narrowness of minds that know nothing but Marxism and know it is right, the United States and Nazi Germany are indistinguishable and Truman is a second Hitler, Attlee his fascist tool. There is no breaking through such walls of ignorance and prejudice, at least, not by any frontal assault of explanation and propaganda.

What, then, can be done? The only hope lies in creating in the free world conditions of such strength and stability that even the Soviet leaders cannot misunderstand or underestimate them. Such a policy means recreating in the fifties the kind of confidence and cohesion which for a brief time in the twenties persuaded the Russians that it was better to put their own house in order than to try to upset the house the Europeans had managed to rebuild. The task is more difficult today for the degree of strength and stability which the Communists will respect needs now to be much greater than was the case thirty years ago when Russian confidence in their own system had not yet survived such grueling tests as the first Five Year Plan, the collectivization of agriculture or the Nazi invasion. It is, moreover, a dual strength that is required. On the one hand, the West needs sufficient military strength to deter the Russians from thinking they can manage a local aggression too speedily for effective counteraction to be possible. On the other, they need a social strength and cohesion that can discourage the Communists from trying out their favorite contemporary weapon—the fomenting of civil war. To build up these "positions of strength," as Mr. Dean Acheson has called them, will not do away with Communist hostility and pressure. But it will make it possible for the West to hold them back. No Dutchman expects the sea miraculously to abandon its ceaseless attack upon the shores of Holland. He mans the dykes instead. So it is with Communism. Like a force of nature it will continue, for some time at least, to pour through the world, lapping at the free world's defenses and seeking by every tactic of infiltration to trickle through the barriers, to crumble the earth that is soft and suck down the wood that has grown rotten. But where the dykes are strong and the banks well built, the pressure will be made in vain. The floods can be controlled and deflected, the menace contained. This—the policy of containment—may make formidable calls upon Western resources and Western patience, but in so far as it is given to us to see the future, it offers a chance and a hope of peace.

# 3

# *The Theory of Containment*

IF WE accept—as we must—the fact of Soviet hostility and Soviet pressure, our first need, if we are to contain them effectively, is to be sufficiently armed ourselves. There is no secret about the necessary scale. Russia has some 175 divisions in readiness and presumably at least 125 would be available for work in Europe. If the ratio of strength needed by defenders to hold off an attack is as one to three, the Western Powers need between 40 and 50 divisions to hold them in check. This is the minimum line of security and it should be said at once that in spite of pressing dangers elsewhere in the world, Europe remains the crucial front in the whole free world. Elsewhere, it would be possible to retreat, to buy time by ceding space, to regroup for the attack after initial withdrawals. But in Europe, there is no space left for maneuver. To lose the Rhine, to see Rome under Soviet occupation or Paris taken over by the Communists would mean the extinction of some of the most vital centers of the Western civilization which we are attempting to preserve. The fate of the active liberals, socialists and Catholics in Eastern Europe shows how little there would be left of Europe's spirit to liberate once any prolonged Soviet occupation had taken place.

The defense of Europe is the West's front line, but Europe is not the only threatened area. Soviet Russia occupies a very favorable strategic position as the core of a vast land mass, fringed round either with its own satellites or with states whose independence can be easily threatened by pressure outward from the Soviet center. If we could make the mental revolution of looking at the world from Moscow, we would realize what ridiculous appendages to the solid mass of the Soviet empire appear such tips of the continent as Western Europe, Greece, Turkey and Persia, the whole Southeast Asian peninsula from Indo-China to Singapore or Korea and Japan. The mere weight of concentrated geographical power seems to press down upon them. From its central position, the Soviet Union can thrust now in this direction, now in that. In many places, a satellite can be used as the spearhead of pressure. Feints can be made and as quickly disowned. It is the perpetual advantage of the aggressor. He can pick the time and the place of the attack. Russia's policy today would no doubt be very different if the tables were turned and it genuinely feared what it claims to fear—a Western attack say, on the Baku oil fields or a Western seizure of the lower reaches of the Danube. In fact, of course, the Russians fear nothing of the kind and their whole policy confirms it. The Western Powers, on the contrary, are faced with the problem of defending the gigantic periphery of the free world, knowing all the time that they, as defenders, cannot pick the scene of action. Their only expedient is, therefore, to create small, highly mobile, highly armed police units which can be dispatched with sufficient speed to any point of conflict in time to reinforce the resistance of local forces.

These commitments—an effective defense system in Europe and mobile forces for use along the Soviet perimeter—need to be underpinned not only by a sizable effort of rearmament but by plans held always in readiness for the total mobilization which would be necessary if the Russians, in folly or miscalculation, took the plunge into general war.

Clearly, defense on this scale is a much more formidable burden than the democracies normally expect to shoulder when war has not actually broken out. It is far heavier than the level of defense they have actually supported since 1945.

It must be admitted, too, that there are immense psychological barriers in the way of the realization of a sensible defense policy. To liberal thought in the West, to arm at all seems the equivalent of preparing for war. The Communists are shrewd in their psychological offensives and to launch a peace campaign in the West is in a sense to preach to the converted. To rearm the Eastern Germans—as the Russians have done—to give them back military formations, uniforms, weapons, slogans and interminable parades is to give back their daily bread. There will be no resistances there, least of all among the young. But in the West, rearmament is a troubling moral issue, approached with discomfort and accepted with foreboding.

There are, however, a number of points which we in the West can remember with profit as we face the distasteful task of looking to our defenses. The first is still highly theoretical and technical, but who knows how soon it may become fact? In the last war, the attacker broke through the static lines of earlier warfare and the bomber and the tank dominated a struggle on the whole of intense mobility—the kind of struggle which today, unless it moved only eastward, would be the ruin of Europe. There is, however, some evidence to show that the defense is once more catching up on the attack. Proximity fuses, radar-guided missiles, and irresistible armor-piercing anti-tank weapons may not be in production yet but there seems no doubt of the trend of scientific research toward ever more effective defense. This news is bad news indeed for any potential aggressor since it threatens him with a war of immobility. But for those whose sole interest is defense the possibility of weapons which create increasing invulnerability—even if it be invulnerability for *both* sides—is the best news the scientists can give. It slightly counteracts the uniformly gloomy reports they give of the increased powers of destruction inherent in modern weapons. Clearly less danger lies in science producing the super-hydrogen bomb if it can guarantee at the same time that no one will be able to deliver it.

Defensive weapons apart, it is not always true that to

prepare for defense is to prepare for war. Frontier defense—and this is in essence what the Western Powers have to be prepared to undertake—was the shield of the Roman Empire and if critics point out that in the end the shield was broken in part by the sheer expense of keeping it in being, we may justifiably say that some 400 years of relative peace was secured nonetheless. It is true that the conditions are not comparable. The disparity between Roman and barbarian armaments was no doubt greater than that which exists between the evenly matched equipment of the modern adversaries. But the Roman experience is a valuable reminder that civilizations can survive and flourish even though their garrisons and their outposts are always manned. On a smaller scale and in easier conditions, the combination of a mobile, well-armed, professional army and a powerful navy permitted Britain in the nineteenth century to provide the world with an elementary kind of police force. Again, the conditions are not comparable, but the effectiveness of the *Pax Britannica* shows that peace, not war, can be the consequence of judicious armament.

Perhaps the best reassurance that can be given is, however, the aim of any policy of containment. It cannot be repeated too often that the aim of containment is not war but peace. It is not to drive the enemy to defeat but to secure a settlement with him. The Western Powers have no claims upon Soviet Russia. It is not their aim—even though it might legitimately be so—to drive Russia out of Europe. It is no part of their plan to intervene further in the unhappy strife in China. Their aim is simply to create "positions of strength," on the basis of which firm bargains can be struck with the Soviet Union. They believe with considerable supporting evidence that the Soviet leaders are capable of reacting peaceably once the uselessness of alternative policies has been demonstrated. This is the underlying hope of containment—a completely unaggressive hope, one firmly based upon belief in the possibility of a settlement.

In any case, consider the alternative. Within this generation, the Western world has learned the disasters to which appeasement can lead. Each capitulation before the Nazis simply strengthened them for their next demand. The force which might have been checked without war in 1936 needed a world-wide coalition to defeat it after 1939. It is true that the Communist and the Nazi policies are not identical. Stalin has shown in the past a moderation and flexibility of tactics unknown to Hitler. Yet it does not follow that the Communist reaction to Western appeasement would be any different. If their means and methods have shown an element of caution, their ends and objectives show none. They aim at complete control whether their scene of action is a trade union, a conference, a political party, a government, a continent, or the world itself. There are no self-imposed limits to their ambition. They do not say as the British have said, "We cannot impose our control on nations that reject it." They do not believe, as the Americans believe, that there must be no interference in other nations' internal politics. The aim is always total intervention and total control. If, therefore, all external restraints upon this drive for power are removed, it will simply surge ahead, down every open channel and through every open door.

The Western Powers, however, never could remove all restraints to Soviet expansion. There would always come a point at which they would wish to call a halt. Some absolutely vital issue—such as national independence itself—would be seen to be at stake and then, belatedly, they would begin that resistance to Soviet pressure which is the essence of containment. But by then the change in policy would have come too late. The earlier appeasement would already have weakened, perhaps fatally and decisively, their efforts to make resistance effective. If there were halfway houses between containment and surrender, the men and women of Eastern Europe would already have found them. There would be genuine coalitions between the parties. The churches would survive with a measure of autonomy. Some universities would have preserved their independence. Some economies would have kept a balance between public and private enterprise. What in fact do we find? A Soviet *Gleichschaltung*, a totally imposed pattern of Communist uniformity from one end of Eastern Europe to the other. But no—there are two exceptions—Finland which has fought the Russians with astonishing effectiveness, and Jugoslavia which would do so in its turn. But these exceptions prove the rule. The Finns and the Jugoslavs alone in Eastern Europe are practicing "containment." Elsewhere the fatal consequences of appeasement are visible on every hand. Given these alternatives, can there be any doubt that the creation of "positions of strength" is a surer policy than to rely upon some hoped-for moderation in Communist ambition to which, on every evidence we have, no limits can be set?

Effective military defenses are, however, only one part of any effective program of containment. As we have seen, the Communists themselves place great reliance upon the chances of internal collapse among the free nations and nothing so tempts them to military activity as the belief that dissension and social strife have weakened the other side. The ideal outcome for the Kremlin would be to see a ring of civil wars break out along the whole frontier of the free world which could then be judiciously supported from without until the Communist faction gained the victory. Any intervention by other Western Powers could then be denounced as "intervention" while Soviet support would be camouflaged under local Communist cover and blandly denied in the world at large. The prevention of civil war and the maintenance of a good measure of social unity must therefore be aims of Western policy no less urgent than the building up of strong military defenses.

It is here that communism offers a unique challenge to the West. The free nations have faced before with success the threat of a totalitarian power, but their experience with the Nazis is little help to them in their new struggle against totalitarianism in its Communist guise. The Nazis said in effect to Western society, "We reject your principles. We reject your aims. We denounce and despise your ideals. Instead of democracy, we offer you the leadership principle, instead of solidarity and brotherhood, we proclaim the supremacy of Aryan blood. We abandon reason, we embrace instinct. We reject peace, we idolize war." Then they proceeded to put these principles into practice by breaking every working-class institution, destroying every independent political party, muzzling the universities, curbing the churches and plunging the world into Armageddon. In 1939 there was virtually no group in Western society that had not been flouted and outraged by the Nazis' tenets and tactics. The whole horrible episode was a profound betrayal of the deepest traditions of the West. Only men driven to extremes by fear or corrupted by their own ambitions could listen to the claptrap of blood and soil. The only allies the Nazis could find were the Lavals, the Degrelles, or the Quislings, men with twisted minds who already had the lie in the soul.

The challenge of communism is more effective and therefore far more dangerous. The Communists do not denounce and despise the tradition of Western liberal culture. On the contrary, they claim to be its only true exponents. They do not scorn "democracy." They claim to have the only genuine variety. They do not abandon the belief in human brotherhood. They merely deny that it can exist anywhere outside the Communist system. They speak the language of the Western states they attack. They extol the same ideals and claim to pursue the same ends. But they denounce their adversaries for producing sham democracy, sham liberty, sham political equality, sham justice and sham opportunity. They taunt the West for talking of liberty but confining it to a small minority, for speaking of "fair shares" and leaving the masses in poverty, for believing in justice and practicing the grossest economic inequality, for claiming to be a democracy but representing in fact the rule of the propertied few—"the financiers, the bankers and the monopolists"—over the unpropertied many. In a word, the Communists take the deepest aspirations of Western liberalism and turn them against our present version of Western society. They appeal, in the name of ideals which the West cannot but acknowledge, to the underprivileged who, they claim, get no advantage from those ideals. Their fundamental denunciation of Western society is that it is a mockery and a fake.

Let us, therefore, take our eyes for one moment off the evils and terrors of the Soviet system and look with undivided, and if possible unbiased, attention at our own society. When a good commander knows that he must withstand a long siege, he looks carefully at his defenses. He tries to discover the weak points, the hinges in his defense at which enemy armor may strike, the stretches where his men are thin on the ground, the lay of the land that favors his opponents. Our society is in just such a state of siege from an enemy without and from snipers and spies within. We shall not defend it better for doing so blindfolded in the conviction that all is well and there is no work for us to do. There are grave weaknesses and inconsistencies in Western society and these, more than anything else, give the Communists their opportunity.

# 4

## *Challenge to the West*

THE contradictions in our society are up to a point the result of the very strength and attraction of Western culture. If it claimed and offered less, men would expect less from it. But the Western idea is a dynamic force based upon the belief in the godlike destiny of man, the supreme value of the human personality, the perfectability of the social order and the vision of a society based on justice, brotherhood and peace. This is the tremendous heritage of our Christian and classical tradition, and if we claim less for our culture, we deny the very sources of its vitality and abandon the struggle for the soul of man into the willing hands of the Communists who do not care how much they claim. It is because the pretensions of Western society are so great, that its failures give rise to such frustration and danger.

There are excuses, of course. The ordinary recalcitrance of human nature and human institutions has always frustrated the activity of the West's reforming energy. But in the last two hundred years, the task has been made infinitely more complicated. Western society has itself been responsible for unleashing on the world the most violent and uncontrollable social forces mankind has ever experienced. Nationalism at the service of the nation-state, science dedicated to experiment and discovery, industry multiplying wealth and disrupting all pre-industrial economic and social relations—these are the three simultaneous floods pouring over Western society. It is not surprising that the torrents are still to a very great extent pursuing their own violent course and eluding man's efforts to dam them and canalize them and harness them to rational purposes.

It is significant that all three are emanations of the restless energy and dynamism of Western society. Non-Western societies and civilizations could not produce them. On the contrary, they have tended to be simply overwhelmed by them. In the last hundred and fifty years, few non-Western institutions have been able to withstand the furious incursion of the West in the shape of soldiers, merchants, industrialists, and the even more pervasive and infiltrating force of their ideas. On the threshold of our own day, Western man established for the first time in human history a single world—not admittedly a coherent or unified world, for it was linked by not much more than the world-wide commercial interests of the new industrial communities on the shores of the Atlantic—yet one world, nonetheless, in which news could be sent in a matter of seconds across oceans and continents and the concerns and upheavals of distant lands and peoples began to impinge on the lives of everybody else.

Yet the speedy extension of Western habits and ideas, made possible by science and thrust onward by the double energy of industrialism and nationalism, did not mean that these forces had been mastered in their native West. In the first place, industrialism came to societies in which the distribution of wealth and power was already irrational—so irrational indeed that the invention of Arkwright's spinning jenny and Crompton's mule almost coincided with the violent social explosion of the French Revolution.

The new force of industrialism did not simply of itself modify the old injustices and rigidities. In countries where the traditions of political freedom were strong and rooted in the centuries, it had the effect of breaking down some of the old barriers to opportunity and social change. For instance, in Britain, it helped to create a new and liberal middle class. In America, it laid the economic foundations of a nation devoted from its origins to political democracy. But in other parts of the West, the development was ominously different. In the crucial instance of Germany, for example, the feudal stamp on the old society was so strong that, in the new dispensation as under the old, great concentrations of wealth and irresponsible political power marked German society. Three times within a generation, the new feudal empires of industry allied themselves politically with the old Junker estates of the East and sought to solve their problems by the typical expedient of feudal society—the military conquest of new land and new resources. Much the same development followed Japan's superficial adoption of Western ideas. These are the extreme instances, but even in societies where political and economic advance continued unchecked—as in the United States or the Commonwealth—certain tensions and failures inherited from earlier days remained, modified perhaps, but not overcome while a number of new and unexpected problems were revealed by the unfolding of the industrial system.

One of the haunting instabilities of modern industrial society has been the recurrence of the trade cycle. Other evils—lack of property, bad working conditions, industrial slums—might have weighed less heavily on the mass of the people if the West's economic history had been one of steady and unflagging advance. Unhappily, the underlying hints of irrationality in Western industrialism have become from time to time very carnivals of unreason. To the ordinary man in the street, it cannot make sense. He wants work. He loses it. He needs goods. They are not produced, or, worse, they are destroyed to maintain prices. He sees around him the machines and the furnaces, the capital equipment designed for one purpose only—to produce wealth that he may consume. And they are idle while he goes in want. Before any more elaborate explanations are considered of how or why or when trade cycles happen, it is vital to remember that their chief characteristic in the eyes of the great majority of mankind is that they do not make sense. And it is when men are involved in this larger lunacy that they turn their restless eyes to other irrational features of industrialism—to irresponsible power, to great disproportions in wealth, to the lack of economic opportunity, to the exclusion of the rank and file from responsibility—which in normal times do not excite the attention of more than a minority.

These unsolved tensions in the economic life of the West have had unsettling political consequences. Nationalism is nothing new in the Western world. The nationhood of such peoples as the French or the British has a thousand years of separate political consciousness behind it. Nor is it new that states should claim absolute sovereignty and refuse to modify their interests for the sake of any wider community. The modern world in fact inherited a system of nation-states just as it inherited most of its social structure. In pre-industrial society, however, the contacts between states were more limited, each tended to be based upon a self-sufficient local economy supplemented only to a limited extent by foreign trade. The mass of the people were not concerned with events beyond their town and valley. The direct impact of government upon their lives was relatively small. In the last hundred years, however, as a result of the development of industrial society, the nation-state has undergone a double and almost completely contradictory development.

On the one hand, in all economies, even those least addicted to planning, the government has taken a steadily larger part in the economic and social ordering of society. The nation-state has become a complex mechanism of political adjustment, economic intervention and social initiative. There are few aspects of the life of the citizen which at some time or another are not the concern of government. On the other hand, the nation-state as such has become less and less able to meet the absolutely primary needs of its citizens—security and rising living standards. Industrialism applied to the waging of war has made all but the greatest states virtually defenseless. Industrialism applied to commerce has created a world-wide economy in which national barriers and obstructions have tended to become the greatest obstacle to economic expansion. In other words, the Western world is struggling with an irrational and intractable contradiction at the very center of its political system, between the pretensions of the nation-state and its inability to meet the reasonable claims made upon it.

If these are the inconsistencies and weaknesses apparent in the very core of Western society, what are we to say of its impact on other lands and other traditions? The great forces of nationalism and industrialism loosed on the world by the West have surged onward and in their tidal advance have usually had a shattering effect upon non-Western peoples and civilizations. They have broken down the old traditional social order and overlaid the peasant economies of Asia and Africa. But what came in their place was not always explicable or even justifiable. If the European worker sometimes frets at his sense of basic irresponsibility, of having neither say nor interest in the enterprise that absorbs his energies and his day, what must be said of the Rhodesian copper miner or the Indonesian oil operative or the unskilled laborer in the rubber plantations of Malaya? Only a tiny proportion acquired European skills. An even smaller number could enter the managerial grades. Not only social obstacles, but the great barriers of race, culture and speech separated the lower ranks of the economy from their leaders.

Unfortunately, the Western economic system has carried into colonial territories an instability of demand for primary products and violent fluctuations in their price. In the world-wide depression of the early thirties, the bottom fell out of most prices for foodstuffs and raw materials. Then, indeed, the forces governing the local colonial economy seemed remote and incomprehensible, and as such ceased to command much loyalty or support.

The Western version of nationalism has had equally unsettling and contradictory effects. The men who came out to Asia and Africa to trade and develop and administer believed in the primacy of their own nation and consciously or unconsciously accepted the final subordination of all interests to the nation-state. The more liberal among them looked forward to the day when the territory in which they worked would be equally sovereign, independent and absorbedly nationalist. The best of the local peoples, when they were sent to Europe to complete their education, learned the same lesson. The essence of nationalism is, however, its exclusiveness. Thy nation cannot be my nation. The effect of Western nationalism in non-Western lands was therefore to produce other versions of its own exclusive self, and once they had arisen, the days of its own dominion were numbered. If nationalism is the chief, almost the sole, basis of government—and the West recognized no other—then nations have no justification in seeking to govern beyond the confines of their own nationhood. The more speedily the Western Powers developed the consciousness and the capacity of their subject peoples, the more overwhelming became the native desire to be rid of Western rule.

These traces of economic instability and national conflict in the very heart of the Western system cannot be dismissed as minor blemishes which time itself can be relied upon to remove. Even if they were not the most effective entry points for Communist propaganda—and who can doubt on the evidence of the last thirty years that they are?—they have the capacity of producing within Western society itself deadlocks of such political and social violence that the temptation is strong to use violence to break them.

Whether we like it or not, we in the West must look steadfastly at the mystery of iniquity which has existed in our midst and not shrug it off or cover it up and try to forget it. Nazism is so staggering a phenomenon that it exhausts our powers of explanation. Here in a nation which had participated more or less fully in the unfolding of Western history, which was part of our culture, bound to us by ties of art and music and philosphy, sharing our great religious traditions and filling the very heartland of Europe, here, in short, in a nation which must be called "Western" if the word is to have any cultural or historical meaning, burst forth the most evil, the most violent, the most anti-social political force that the world has ever seen. It would be consoling to dismiss the whole thing as "non-Western" and "non-European." If we are honest, we cannot do so. There were, no doubt, special reasons for the German upheaval but the tragic fact remains that a Western nation has contrived to conduct itself in a more evil fashion than almost any other nation in human history—and that some of the chief reasons for this terrible aberration can be traced to contradictions which have existed and do exist in the West at large.

It is true that Germany was never fully part of the Roman Empire. It had no natural frontiers and lay in the way of almost any invasion from north or east. It came to be more sharply divided religiously than most other European communities and suffered more tragically in the religious wars of the seventeenth century. As a result, its political evolution was uncertain and its national unification delayed. Yet when all these allowances are made, the fact remains that the chief reasons for the collapse of German democracy and the rise of Hitler's nightmare empire have been common to all Western society and in Germany reached an extreme and uncontrollable form.

Industrialism developed there in a still largely feudal society. To the great agricultural baronies of the East were added the coal and steel baronies of the West, each industrial concern interlocked with the next in cartels and associations as close as the ties of family which bound together the Junker class. The mass of industrial workers were passively or actively alienated from the system, the middle class remained weak. Politically and economically, the base of the pyramid was not broad enough for the concentrations of power and wealth at its apex.

The workings of nationalism increased the instability of the economic system. German industrialism built up in the Ruhr a heavy industry capable of supplying and developing a continent, but by the time this vast machine had come into action, Europe's array of separate national economies was already set in a more or less protectionist pattern. The irrational barriers of national sovereignty impeded the flow and exchange of goods. Britain had had the start of the whole world, America could expand on a continental scale. German industry, on the contrary, outgrew its own frontiers. Behind the Kaiser's plan for *Mittel Europa* and Hitler's demands for *Lebensraum* lay one small element of fact—that tariff barriers based on national sovereignty were an anachronism under modern industrial conditions.

Even so, had the development of economic life in the West between the wars followed a reasonably regular course, Germany might, in spite of the manifest contradictions in its industrial and national life, have avoided the final explosion. Unhappily, the world's economy took a downward plunge in 1929 and out of the extreme of misery and bewilderment into which the onslaught of crisis threw the German people grew the Nazis' power, their numbers rocketing up as more and more men and women of all walks of life found themselves without work and without hope.

Nazism represents a nation's abandonment of the attempt to solve its problems by rational means. Once the fatal admission was made that the methods of legality and justice and co-operation could be abandoned, it was not only parliamentary democracy, the independent judicial system, and a legal and responsible police power that vanished. The Nazi upheaval involved the total abandonment of every Western standard. Truth vanished in the cult of Hitler's "great lie"—the lie of propaganda, the lie of mass-conditioning. Science gave way to the charlatanism of racial biology or was prostituted to the "research" which produced the Nazis' methods of mass extermination. From the darkest depths of man's divided nature, the Nazis dredged up submerged horrors—the racial superman, the scapegoat, the blood sacrifice, the exaltation of killing, the glorification of death. Beneath the once civilized surface of German life, behind the well-kept fields and tidy villages, behind the power of modern industrial cities, behind the monuments of a great culture and a long history, there opened an abyss of utter brutality and utter negation. We have hardly courage to approach its brink. Yet it opened *within* our own culture. The West has produced not only its own incomparable spirit but also that spirit's total rejection.

National Socialism, it is true, owes much to Communism.

Many of the methods Hitler used had been perfected beforehand in the Russian Revolution. The party itself borrowed some of its techniques from the powerful German Communist party and in the ten years before Hitler's coup, they first incited each other into a rising spiral of violence and counter-violence and, at a crucial period in 1932, joined hands to destroy legitimate government. Yet if we are considering dispassionately the weaknesses in our own society, we cannot dismiss the evidence of Nazism—or for that matter, of Fascism in Italy. The forces of unreason and confusion which grew into such a bitter harvest in the thirties are not yet entirely banished from among us and now, as then, they give the totalitarian—of right or left—his point of entry. Where-ever the Western peoples can themselves recognize cracks and fissures in their own social structure, there they will find Communists at work widening the gaps with every tool of propaganda and pressure upon which they can lay their hands. To rely upon military containment alone when social containment is so important would be the equivalent of defending a town whose gates are all but open to the enemy. As the fatal development of China's civil war has shown, weapons are useless in the hands of men who have lost the will to fight. The weakness, the divisions, the corruption, the inefficiency and the archaic outlook of the Nationalist regime made it certain that once a certain stage had been reached in the fighting, their armies would simply fade away. The Chinese people ceased to support a regime which, they felt, no longer supported them. The sweeping Communist advances were made possible because all effective support for the other side had come to an end.

The example of the Nationalist collapse in China is cited—as was the eruption of Nazism in Germany—simply in order to remind the Western Powers of the scale of the challenge they face. It is certainly not given to suggest that the issue is already decided and that the Communists have only to blow their trumpets louder for the walls of Jericho to fall. Communism may batten upon the strains and inconsistencies in Western society, but it is itself one of the most tremendous fakes ever perpetrated on bewildered humanity. Let us admit frankly that in our own society we have not fully mastered the forces of nationalism and industrialism and that they still produce results incompatible with the Western promise of freedom, personality, justice and equality. But can any one claim that Soviet Communism has produced an acceptable alternative? On the contrary, the last thirty years have shown with increasing violence and squalor that the cure it offers is worse than the disease. Nationalism has not been transcended in the Soviet system. All that has happened is that the nationalism of other nations has been sacrificed to the single overwhelmingly pretentious nationalism of Soviet Russia. While inside the Soviet Union, ludicrous and tragic extremes of nationalism are encouraged (for instance, the Russians now lay claim to every invention made by modern man, from nuclear physics to the umbrella), everywhere else nationalism is the unpardonable treason of "Titoism"—the crime of preferring one's own country and its interests to the "fatherland of the workers," the Soviet Union. This is not the transcendence of nationalism. It is nationalism running wild in a mood of imperialism which was banished in the West some twenty years ago and in the United States, at least, has hardly ever existed.

Nor can the Russians claim to have provided an acceptable alternative to the instabilities and injustices of Western industrialism. A planned economy which has total power over the allocation of labor, over wage rates, over prices, over the minutest detail of economic life is not an alternative to the Western system but a complete denial of it. No doubt full employment can be maintained in a prison where free choice is abolished, but the price the West is ready to pay for stability cannot include servitude, forced labor and penal settlements. The Soviet experiment may have economic lessons for the West, but it is virtually impossible to disentangle them from the economics of total control. Western society has, after all, already shown that it can achieve full production and stability under the complete planning of a war effort—the nearest approach in the West to the Soviet system—but a war economy is not one in which the vast majority of the Western world wish to live.

This is not the whole of the Soviet story. In estimating the strength of our adversary, we need to recognize the zeal for modernization and industrialization that has transformed the face of Russia. We need to accept the immense effort of popular education which has made millions upon millions accessible not only to the propaganda of the government, but also to wider horizons of literature and thought. We need above all to recognize that in its first impact upon Asiatic lands, communism can be a progressive force. But in the long run—and we are preparing for a long trial of strength—the rigid, inflexible, strictly controlled and perpetually regimented system should be no match for the vitalities of the free spirit of man. The Western world goes into the struggle with one priceless asset intact—the ability to learn from mistakes, to admit failure, to experiment and to draw upon the great reserves of spontaneous faith and hope which exist untapped in free society. Time, in the military sense, will not be on the side of the Western Powers unless they fulfill speedily and surely the implications of military containment. But in the wider social sphere, time is not with the totalitarians. Leviathan may seem an irresistible monster, but he can be at the mercy of an agile man with a spear. Far from fighting a losing fight, the Western Powers are engaged—if they will see it so—in an absorbing contest of spiritual vitality, one in which they can triumph and one in which already, in the last five years, some notable and encouraging successes have been secured.

# 5

# *Atlantic Pact and Marshall Plan*

IT WAS not until a year or two after 1945 that the Western Powers began seriously to look for a way of countering Soviet hostility. At first, they based all their hopes on the possibility of co-operation. The year of victory saw two conferences—Yalta and Potsdam—at which it was possible for the Allies to reach agreed policies. In 1946, although the prospects of cordial co-operation were growing steadily more dim, peace treaties were drawn up for Germany's satellites in Europe. UNRRA was still in operation. A framework of four-power control held shakily together in Europe. Problems from every quarter of the globe came under joint scrutiny in the many organs of the United Nations. The solutions were not very brilliant but at least there was no open breach between countries.

There were danger signals, however. Russian troops refused for a time to withdraw from northern Persia and the attempt was made—a technique with which the West was later to become more familiar—to incite a local left wing party, the Tudeh, to set up an independent regime in Persian Azerbaijan. Only when the local rising collapsed and the whole matter had been aired in the Security Council, did Russia withdraw. During the same period, the original Communist uprising in Greece had developed into an international war, the Communist states in the Balkans backing the Greek insurgents and offering them the hospitality of their frontiers as the fighting surged backward and forward across the mountains of Northern Greece. A United Nations Commission dispatched to the front, though unable to stop the fighting, at least established the complicity of Greece's Communist neighbors. One of the most disturbing accompaniments to this open aggression in Greece was the war of nerves inflicted by Soviet Russia on near-by Turkey. Throughout 1946, the Turkish army remained mobilized while the Moscow radio poured out ridicule and attack and actual territorial claims on two of Turkey's eastern provinces.

It was in fact in this corner of the Mediterranean that the idea of military containment first became the declared policy of the West. During 1945 and 1946, a small British Military Mission had given what support it could to the Greek Government. But in the winter of 1946–47, Communist pressure increased just as the effects of the economic crisis brought on by Europe's appalling winter of extreme cold and snow began to make themselves felt in Western Europe. Early in 1947, the British announced that they could no longer support the expense of a Mission in Greece. Then it was that President Truman proposed his first essay in containment—the so-called Truman Doctrine. He offered military assistance to nations menaced by communism and asked Congress for $250 million to be spent upon reinforcing the defenses of the Greeks and the Turks. Thus began a program of limited military containment which completely fulfilled its purpose. There can be no doubt that if the Greek state had been left unaided to stave off attacks from without and revolt from within, it must have succumbed, not necessarily because of the overwhelming strength of its opponents but because of its own economic exhaustion and war weariness, after nearly a decade of war and occupation. The military stiffening and assistance provided by the United States gave the Greek soldiers and the Greek people the means to continue and triumph in a merciless struggle which on several occasions came very near to disaster. Without that assistance, Stalin would undoubtedly have gathered in another satellite—with incalculable consequences for the security of the Mediterranean.

When the Greek commitment was undertaken, it was thought of as a specific act to meet a specific danger. The idea of a general policy of containment had not been evolved. Indeed, there was still little feeling that it was necessary. The Western Powers were very slow to accept the idea that in Soviet Russia they faced a force of general and undeviating hostility. They turned a blind eye to the very great disparity between their degree of disarmament and that of the Soviet Union. They observed with concern the gradual elimination of all non-Communists from positions of authority in Eastern Europe, but did not on that account feel less secure themselves. Even in the one sphere in which a cautious attitude toward the Soviet Union prevailed from the very beginning—the making of the atom bomb—the Americans put forward a plan for the international production and control of atomic energy which every member of the United Nations save Russia and its satellites was prepared to accept. It must be said, however, that the Russian refusal to co-operate coupled with the American decision not to bring the manufacture of atomic bombs to an end, gave the West—almost by chance—their only instrument of containment when a year or two later the true facts both of Soviet hostility and Soviet armament began to impinge fully upon the Western mind. But this awakening to reality did not in fact begin until the Communist coup in Prague in the spring of 1948. Then at last the Western Powers began to consider with some seriousness the problem of their own defenses.

The Communists' seizure of the Czech Government was a naked demonstration of their determination to keep the country under the total domination of Moscow. If there was any country in Europe in which a *modus vivendi* between East and West and communism and democracy might have been possible, it was in Czechoslovakia. The people as a whole combined a tradition of Western politics and Western trade with a genuine devotion to Russia. The general fear of a German revival made it absolutely certain that nothing would be allowed to disturb Czechoslovakia's close military ties with Russia. Not one of the Czech parties from right to left advocated anything but close diplomatic and strategic relations with the Soviet Union. In the elections held after liberation, the Czechs alone of any state in Eastern Europe returned the Communists as the largest party to power with something over 40 per cent of the votes.

Yet the Czechs had known political freedom and had their links and interests with the West. They would have joined, if they could, in the discussion of the Marshall Plan, had not Russia peremptorily forbidden them to do so. Discontent with Communist influence was growing in the workshops and trade unions, and in elections for local factory officials held in the winter of 1947 support for communism was obviously declining. Elections were to be held in 1948. Might not they show a decisive setback for Communist influence? True, the emergence of other parties in the lead would not have altered Czechoslovakia's devotion to the Russian alliance. Fear of Germany ensured that loyalty. But would the Communists in fact tolerate the democratic risk of ebbing and flowing periods of political power and influence? Apparently they would not, for during those winter months, Communists and Communist sympathizers were brought increasingly into the police forces and into the whole administrative structure of the Ministry of the Interior. The likelihood that any future election would be rigged increased. When a number of non-Communist ministers resigned to mark their protest against the process of Communist infiltration, the Communists seized their chance, took over the government and by a series of moves clearly planned carefully in advance transformed Czechoslovakia into a Communist police state in a matter of weeks.

It was this act more than any other that set the alarm bells ringing and the red lights winking all through the Atlantic world. It speeded up in Europe the creation of a close military alliance—the Brussels Pact of Western Union

—between Britain, France and the Low Countries. But there had been military arrangements before then in Europe in times of peace. The really unprecedented consequence of the Prague coup was to draw the United States into a positive general policy of military containment. It is so easy as history rushes by us like a torrent to forget that what we take for granted today was one of the world's wonders only yesterday. Would anyone, looking at the mood of the United States in 1939, have prophesied that only ten years later in 1949 it would be proposing the Atlantic Pact and leading a coalition of nations in a program of effective defense? The decision of the United States to enter into close and binding military relations with its Atlantic neighbors was and is the pre-condition and foundation of any genuine policy of containment.

During the course of the negotiations for the Atlantic Pact, the Russians intensified the impetus their seizure of Prague had already given to closer allied association. They attempted to blockade Berlin. There were many possible reasons for the move. The last two Foreign Ministers conferences on the unification of Germany had broken down since there seemed no way—except on the Communists' terms—of uniting sovietized East Germany with the Western Zones. The Russians may have hoped by cornering the Western Powers in their vulnerable outpost in Western Berlin to extort concessions from them on the wider issue of German unity. They may more simply have wished to inflict on them a damaging loss of prestige. They may even more simply have desired to close a chink in the Iron Curtain through which the West continued to pick up some direct knowledge of Soviet affairs and the men and women on the Communist side could still catch a glimpse of another world than theirs. Whatever the reason, the attempt at a complete blockade was made.

The arrangements for Berlin made in such confidence after victory were now turned against the Western Powers and not a car, not a train, not a barge was allowed to pass from Western Germany to the beleaguered city. The Western reply, the airlift, succeeded, however, in vindicating completely the underlying philosophy of containment—which is that pressure must be met not by appeasement but by resolute counter-pressure. After a contest of strength that lasted nine months, the Russians gave in and raised the blockade.

This sustained heightening of tension in Europe undoubtedly speeded up the negotiations of the Atlantic Pact which was finally signed by twelve countries [1] on April 4, 1949. It must be admitted, however, that thereafter the sense of urgency began to slacken. It was a year of relative quiet in Europe, the Greek Civil War came to an end, there were renewed direct negotiations with Russia on the question of Germany and Austria, the Western Powers were absorbedly feeling their own economic pulses on the eve of devaluation. It had been clearly laid down, when the Pact was signed and when President Truman first proposed his military aid program of a billion dollars to improve the defenses of Western Europe, that economic recovery should have priority. The Western partners were only too glad to observe the condition. They still found it very difficult to believe in any genuine risk of conflict with Russia. They listened to the men who told them of Russia's 175 divisions, one-third of them mechanized, its close on 3 million men under arms, a figure which could be doubled on mobilization, the 19,000 aircraft, the 25,000 tanks. But somehow this frightening array of military strength remained of almost academic interest. Fundamentally, people were unwilling to believe that there was any real danger. It is not surprising, therefore, that the year 1949 did not see the growth of any very important military superstructure on the twin foundations of Western Union and Atlantic Pact. The stones had been laid, but the builders did not seem to have their minds on the work. Throughout the year and on into the early days of 1950, the problems of economic recovery, not national survival, still gripped the attention of the Western world.

Such was the West's record of military containment on

[1] Belgium, Canada, Denmark, France, Iceland, Italy, Luxemburg, Netherlands, Norway, Portugal, United Kingdom, and the United States of America.

the eve of Korea. It is far from discouraging. In two specific instances—Greece and the Berlin airlift—the judicious use of Western force secured an end of Communist trouble-making and the restoration of peace. In the wider context of world strategy, while the scale of Russian armament was allowed to go for too long unnoticed, no era which includes the solemn pledging of the Atlantic Powers to each other's defense can be called a time of failure. On the contrary, a front of the free nations was created which, if it had existed in the thirties, might have spared the world the agony of war. If the period ends on a note of uncertainty, the story is not finished and the Western Powers have entered the new phase with foundations securely laid and the preliminaries all duly concluded.

Military containment is, however, only one side of the coin of effective defense. Particularly after a devastating war, it may be much more difficult to achieve success in the other vital field of containment—the restoration and maintenance of social unity and cohesion, the building up of sound economies and firmer governments, the recovery of hope and faith among men. But here, too, the Western record has to its credit a phenomenal achievement—the planning and execution of the Marshall Plan.

The Plan can be taken as a supreme example of successful, positive and creative containment. In 1947, Europe came within a hairsbreadth of total economic collapse. The external evidence was, of course, the dollar crisis. In the two years after victory, Europe had been almost completely dependent upon the United States for the materials of relief and recovery. All other sources of supply had passed under the harrow of war. Only in the United States had a tremendous and merciful expansion of production taken place. The goods—the foodstuffs, the raw materials, the capital equipment—could either be bought there or virtually not bought at all. But how was war-devastated Europe to pay for them? Some countries had been battlefields, Germany was at the point of starvation, even countries such as Britain, which had escaped direct invasion, had enormous wartime losses to make good. The inevitable result was this phenomenal dependence upon

American supplies. In 1946 and 1947, Europe bought in America goods worth nine billion dollars more than the exports that were sent there. For a time, this deficit was masked by American assistance in the shape of reconstruction loans—of which the British loan of three and a half billion dollars was the largest—by American contributions to UNRRA and by using up the European nations' own reserves of gold and dollars. But by 1947, all the countries of Western Europe were coming within sight of the end of their resources.

The position was aggravated by one of the worst winters in living memory, and in the summer of 1947 the plight of the nations was illustrated with dramatic force by the British attempt to restore convertibility to the pound sterling. In the belief in quick world recovery that had been so prevalent on the morrow of victory, a rider had been attached to the British Loan, laying it down that the pound sterling should become convertible into all other currencies—including dollars—within two years. No one foresaw that when the two years had run their course, the United States would still be the main source of supplies—particularly of food—most urgently needed by the rest of the world. Under these conditions, to make sterling freely convertible was virtually the equivalent of inviting Britain's trading partners to convert all available sterling into precious dollars. Between July 15 and August 20, Britain lost over a billion dollars from its reserves. Exchange control had to be re-established. The nakedness of the British position had been exposed.

During these crucial months, however, the United States determined to act. On June 4, the American Secretary of State, General Marshall, made his historic address at Harvard, asking the nations of Europe to come together to assess jointly what they could do for their own reconstruction and how much additional assistance they would need from the United States. Thus the European Recovery Program was born. The next stages can be quickly recalled. Mr. Bevin, the British Secretary of State for Foreign Affairs, instantly proposed joint consultations with the French. The Russians were then invited to participate. After a fruitless week end in Paris, however, Mr. Molotov withdrew and his withdrawal entailed that of Poland and Czechoslovakia whose governments had already sent eager acceptances. In the event, only the nations of Western Europe joined in the Program and their representatives spent the summer of 1947 working out the policies upon which, in modified form, the later Marshall Plan was based. The first project went to Washington in October. The first discussions in Congress began early in 1948 and—its pace somewhat accelerated by the Communist capture of Czechoslovakia—Congress agreed to an appropriation of 6 billion dollars for the first year, on April 3, 1948.

Thus began the most momentous act of statesmanship in the modern world. As an instrument of effective containment it was unsurpassed. In 1947, the possibility of civil war was a desperate reality in Western Europe. The Communists had only just left the government in France and Italy and commanded a formidable following among the people. Elections were due in Italy in the spring of 1948. Moreover, aid to Italy under the program of UNRRA was due to end at about the same time. What would have happened if, during that crucial winter, supplies of food had ceased, raw materials had no longer arrived in the factories and thousands of workless starving men and women had been left with no hope but the violent leadership offered them by the Communists? It is not difficult to imagine the disasters which would have followed, had it not been for the supremely imaginative intervention of the Marshall Plan.

The significance of the Plan was not confined to Europe. It shed a wholly new light on the quality of American statesmanship and on the growth of America to a position of responsible leadership in the world. It would after all have been easy to leave the European crisis to solve itself. The United States came out of the war with great hopes that a "normal" world would soon be restored and that, at the very worst, the new international agencies such as the World Bank or the International Monetary Fund would have sufficient scope and power to tide nations over their temporary troubles. But the whole point about the crisis which descended upon Europe in

1947 was that none of the old economic mechanisms nor any of the new international agencies could be relied upon to put it right. The self-balancing workings of the free international economy would, left to themselves, have produced a "solution"—but only in the sense that death is a solution. In terms of the free market, the tremendous dollar deficit of 1947 and the omniverous appetite of all Europeans for dollars would have been "solved" by the pricing of the dollar out of the market. The dollar would have risen to a dollar to the pound sterling or even more. Dollar goods would have reached fantastically high prices and the deficit would have "disappeared" when the last dollar had been spent. Free Europe would have disappeared about the same time.

The new agencies were equally powerless. The United Nations could have done nothing against the Russian veto. The World Bank was cautiously acquiring a sound reputation in order to attract American funds. The International Monetary Fund had funds enough to deal only with marginal disequilibrium in the movement of currencies and although it had the power to declare the dollar "scarce," such a move would only have given Europe the right to "discriminate" against American goods, in other words, to buy more expensive non-American supplies. But the whole point of the crisis was the absence of non-American supplies—and Europe's consequent dependence upon the United States.

There was thus no easy or automatic way out of the crisis. At the same time, the United States was under no direct compulsion to do anything about it. The pressures of its own economy were, on the whole, working against massive external aid in 1947. American businessmen who could sell everything they wished in a safe market at home were certainly not clamoring, as the Communists wished the world to believe, for markets outside. On the contrary, in the preliminary discussions of the Plan they showed little enthusiasm and some of the keenest support came from those rather peculiar allies of "imperialism," the trade unions. It could be argued that, politically, Europe was less in danger from Russia than it had been from Hitler in the late thirties, yet in those days—only a decade before—the American attitude to Europe's plight had been to pass the Neutrality Act. Not even fear of communism could have compelled the Americans to take a great and creative decision. Their response to the Communist *coup d'état* in Prague might have been a return to isolationism, not a deliberate abandonment of it.

As it turned out, President and Congress alike acted with great courage and enlightenment. There were no panic fears, no witch hunts, no ideological crusades for home consumption, no attempts to give first priority to removing Communists or suspected Communists from their jobs in the Western countries that were to receive aid. Instead, the cool calculation was made that communism's purposes would best be served by starvation, misery and despair in Europe and that the most effective way to frustrate the Communists was therefore to make European recovery possible. As a result, before the first dollar of Marshall aid had reached Europe's shores, the promise of it alone was enough to revive courage and confidence and to make possible such major defeats for Communist strategy as the splitting of the French trade unions in the winter of 1947 and the emergence of the anti-Communist *Force Ouvrière*.

The material success of the Marshall Plan should not be underestimated. By the end of 1949, prewar standards of production had been surpassed—in some areas by as much as 25 per cent—throughout Western Europe. Germany was the chief exception, for obvious reasons. The country was now divided between East and West and until 1948 was hamstrung by the restrictions on its industrial revival imposed as a result of the Potsdam agreements and by the uncontrollable inflation inherited from the war. Yet even here, after the introduction of a drastic currency reform in the summer of 1948, production began to rise phenomenally fast and by the end of 1949, the West German economy was at least within sight of its old levels of activity. The restoration of production—in Germany and throughout Western Europe—had thus taken only four years. After the First World War, when the dislocations and disturbances and destruction were infinitely less—

the Ruhr, for instance, emerged intact from the struggle—the standards of 1914 had taken seven years to reach. The primary purpose of the Marshall Plan—to wipe out the effects of war and to restore prewar levels of production—was thus achieved triumphantly not after the four years' forecast at the beginning of the Marshall Plan, but within not much more than eighteen months of its beginning.

Yet in spite of this remarkable material achievement, the greatest significance of the Marshall Plan lies in the sphere of social containment. The beginning of the Plan found a continent shattered by war, divided between warring parties, fearful, uncertain, lacking the thread of hope and faith that all men need to guide them out of the labyrinth. Within two years, there had been created, if not a continent without problems, at least a community with a sense of promise and purpose. It would, however, be misleading to suggest that with the successful development of the Marshall Plan, all Europe's problems of social containment have been solved. In fact, the picture of Western co-operation for social and economic ends resembled, in the middle of 1950, the West's important but uncompleted plans for military co-operation. A fine start had been made and some revolutionary changes had been introduced, but, as the crisis in Korea approached, there was a note of uncertainty, even a slackening of impetus in the program of economic and social co-operation.

These are difficulties to which it will be necessary to return. At this point, two factors should be mentioned. The first is the realization, which has grown steadily stronger through the two years of the Plan, that a mere restoration of European production is not enough to solve the problem of Western Europe's economic place in the postwar world. The collapse of old patterns of trade, the emergence of the Far East as a consumer of capital, the inescapable dominance of the dollar—all these difficulties, which create new problems for Britain and Europe cannot be solved within the framework of the Marshall Plan. It has cleared the ground and given a breathing space. But the problems have to be tackled by new expedients if economic crisis is not once more to shake the political and social foundations of Europe.

The other factor is the jolt given to world confidence by the slight American recession in 1949. It represented only a 5 per cent fall in American industrial activity. But this was translated into a 30 per cent fall in America's purchases from the outside world. In a few months, the amount of dollars made available by American trade to other countries fell by $500,000 and the mood of confidence in Europe which had been growing stronger throughout the winter of 1948–49 was followed by a period of intense uncertainty and disturbance, culminating in the general devaluation of non-American currencies in September, 1949. The upswing of the American economy that coincided with devaluation has since drawn up the world in its wake, but the episode was a sharp reminder of the economic problems of securing internal equilibrium and an external balance of trade which still remain, outside the orbit of the Marshall Plan, for the free nations to solve. In economic co-operation, as in joint defense, they had taken by 1950 a number of revolutionary first steps along a road full of hope and promise. But they were not by any means within sight of the goal of a stable and peaceful world.

# 6

## *East of Suez*

IN 1945, in spite of the war and the destruction, in spite of the impact of communism, in spite of the millions of refugees on the march, in spite of the risk of starvation and collapse on every side, Europe was a stable structure compared with the volcano of Asia. In Europe, at least, there was widely diffused administrative competence and training, the distances were relatively short, the industrial machine could be quickly set to work, the peasants had passed, on the whole, a comfortable and well-fed war. On these foundations, social order could be restored with relative speed.

In Asia, everything seemed in doubt. The Japanese had shattered the framework of Western rule in Southeast Asia. During the war the old rulers—British, French and Dutch—had been driven out, and even if the "independence" offered by the Japanese within their Co-prosperity sphere had been totally illusory, it sharpened the appetite for national independence which, among the tiny group of Asian intellectuals and leaders, had been growing steadily for the last forty years. In each country, too, a small core of Communists were already at work. Usually they were of Chinese origin, linked with the party of Mao Tse-tung. Some—such as Ho Chi-minh in Indo-China—were Moscow trained. They had had a hand in resistance to the Japanese and were now a fanatical spearhead of the campaign against the maintenance of links with the West.

The economic outlook was no less threatening. War had disrupted the production of Asia's staple food—rice. Only Siam had contrived to avoid the dislocations of fighting, bombing and the mass movements of refugees. The old sources of supply—Burma, Indo-China—had gone under the harrow. Starvation threatened to add itself to the political evils of insurrection and terrorism. In a word, the whole of Asia might have dissolved in a welter of banditry, civil war and economic collapse from which one power and one only would have drawn any final benefit—the Soviet Union.

If we feel inclined today to take a discouraged and hopeless view of the chances of containment in Asia, it is as well to consider how much has been done since 1945 and how infinitely less favorable the developments there might have been. Today at least—in spite of debacle in China, war in Korea and Indo-China, civil struggle in Burma and terrorism in Malaya—there is something to contain. There might easily have been nothing but anarchy and revolt. Three Western moves appear above all responsible for whatever degree of stability has been maintained. The first has been the American occupation of Japan and the vast economic assistance given to the Japanese people by the American taxpayer. It is too soon to judge of the permanent consequences of this occupation but one has only to compare Japan's present state with the situation in Germany to realize how much disturbance and friction has been avoided. It seems likely, too, that one or two of the decisions of General MacArthur will have a lasting effect. Throughout the Far East, the revolt of the peasant against the tyranny of landlord and moneylender has been one of the most frequent entry points for effective Communist propaganda. In Japan, a land reform carried through in 1946 has spared the authorities this particular difficulty. Communist activity among the trade unions and in the cities has not been backed by revolt and agitation in the countryside.

A second factor in ensuring stability has been the extent of Western economic assistance to the whole area. The supplies of food financed by the West have been on such a scale that, against all the predictions of 1945 and 1946, there has been no severe shortage of food. (The only famine since the war in this vulnerable area occurred in North China after the Communists had taken over control.) Massive imports of grain from America and Australia made good the catastrophic decline in the production and trading of rice, and these imports of food have been almost entirely financed from Western sources—from the funds of the American occupation authorities, from the funds made available first under UNRRA and then under the Marshall Plan, from the loans of the Import Export Bank, and from the sum of about £700 million, which the British have pumped into the area since the end of the war.

In a sense, much of this financing has been a joint Anglo-American venture although it was never formally planned in that way. If Britain had not received direct economic assistance in the shape of the American loan and the allocations to Britain under Marshall aid, the scale of its assistance to Asia would have been infinitely smaller. In 1945, India had claims on Britain amounting to some £1,108 million. This debt had been incurred as a result of the services provided by India to the allied war effort in the campaigns in the Far East, and it accounted for a sizable share of the "sterling balances"—which were in essence war debts—with which Britain found itself saddled at the end of the war. There will be more to say later about the effect of these sterling balances upon Britain's position in world trade. Here it is only necessary to point out that since India was able to use these claims on sterling to secure vital imports and services, they cannot be discounted as a factor making for economic stability in Asia. The method has been somewhat roundabout. The United States provided aid to Britain. Britain passed on much of that aid to Asia. But, in the event, the effect—the maintenance of a functioning economy in Britain and the preservation of a measure of stability in Asia—has not been altogether unfavorable. The procedure may indeed raise some delicate political issues. But the economic effects are there for all to see.

This flood of Western assistance would, however, have been ineffective had it not been for a crucial political decision which, more than anything else, has given the West some hope of developing an effective partnership with Asia. That decision was the British withdrawal from India and Burma and the setting up in the place of the old imperial connection of four independent states, three of which, India, Pakistan, and Ceylon, have freely decided to remain as independent Dominions within the fellowship of the Commonwealth. When after much greater hesitation, Holland followed the same course in Indonesia, there emerged a group of states each able to draw upon the political strength of independent Asiatic nationalism and each anxious to ensure its own survival against the pressure of local communism. The overwhelming danger of 1945—that the Communists would be able to place themselves at the head of the revolt of all Asia against Western rule—has been decisively defeated. This more than anything else must be counted containment's greatest achievement in Asia since the war.

It is perhaps premature to look further into the future and ask whether in time the peoples of Asia will come to compare the Western imperialisms that are withdrawing with Soviet imperialism now in the ascendant. It is surely significant that whereas the Western reaction after 1945 has been almost wholly one of withdrawal from Asia, the Soviet Union in its treaty with the Chinese Nationalists in 1945—a treaty, incidentally, drawn up while it was preparing to arm the Chinese Communists—demanded and received from China the old Czarist concession at Port Arthur and control of the Chinese Eastern Railway across Manchuria.[1] Russia's contribution to the Japanese war was to occupy and strip Manchuria of its considerable industrial wealth and then to ensure a

[1] Even when a Communist government took control in Nanking, Stalin insisted that the concession should be maintained for some years.

Communist victory there. Since that time, it has been difficult to establish whether Moscow or Peking is in effective control in Manchuria.

Yet, in spite of these more distant possibilities and in spite, too, of the present measure of recovery and stability created in such improbable and unfavorable circumstances, the picture in Asia remains dark indeed. There are two problems above all others. The first is that Asian nationalism is not a universal solution. It cannot be made the basis of independence in countries such as Malaya where three separate races—Malays, Chinese and Indians—live in almost equal numbers. The creation of an independent Malay state is a thing of the future. Meanwhile a small group of Communist terrorists, backed by the passive assistance of the large Chinese community who fear the extension of Chinese Communist power, contrives to create conditions of such uncertainty and danger that the existence of the colony is in jeopardy. In Burma, the granting of independence to a country of mixed racial groups has led to a prolonged civil war whose settlement is not yet in sight. Even on the Indian continent itself, where the creation of independent Asian nations has the best chances of success, the division between the Hindu and Moslem communities has already produced hideous communal disasters and, in Kashmir, provides a center of potential war which involves both Dominions in ruinous military preparation and prevents them from exercising the influence that could be theirs throughout Asia. Finally, in Indo-China, the French face a nationalist movement which has already been captured by the Communists and it is an open question whether the rival French-supported nationalism of Bao Dai can secure legitimacy in the eyes of the Indo-Chinese people.

Thus the sense of Asian nationalism, although it offers the chief emotional resistance to the pretensions of communism, cannot exercise a universal appeal. Nor can it, unhappily, provide more than a small part of the political and social answers necessary to hold Communist revolution in check. In the first place, the leaders of Asian nationalism do not necessarily possess the administrative capacity to hold together their community and give it the minimum of good government necessary to check growing discontent among the masses. The record of the new leaders in Indonesia is not encouraging. With every sort of urgent work of economic and social reconstruction on their hands, they have preferred to devote their energies to crushing the federal aspirations of the different states in the new union. In Burma, civil war may have increased the general administrative disorder of the new state, but the disorder would probably have occurred without it, especially since the new government has added to its other responsibilities that of nationalizing a large part of Burma's industries.

This lack of administrative grip complicates the problem of external economic assistance. Burma has received considerable financial assistance from the British Government and from foreign business interests in Burma. So far, there is little to show for it. The speed with which an incompetent government can swallow up assistance can also be illustrated from American experience in the Philippines where some $2 billion of external assistance vanished almost without trace in a couple of years.

The disappointing results of much of the aid that has been given must also be put down to the confusions in social and economic policy prevailing in the new states in Asia. The primary occupation of nearly all these communities is still the land. Where the peasant owns his own land and there is some possibility for the building of co-operative organization for processing and marketing his product, a reasonably stable social order can be maintained in the countryside. Where, however, as in the Philippines, in parts of India, Indo-China, and Malaya, the landlord-tenant relationship persists, diversified in some places by the holding of large plantations by foreign interests, communism can take root among the peasants and grow, as it has done with the Philippine bands of the Hukbalahaps, into a perpetual source of local terrorism and agrarian unrest. In parts of the Philippines, the disturbances are so regular that landlords have removed themselves and their families to the safety of the towns, leaving their estates to be exploited by managers. In this way, absentee landlordism plays all the more steadily into the hands of the Communists.

The difficulties are not confined to the peasant and the land. Industrialism is either an established force or on its way in many of the countries, but it would take a bold man to say that Chinese traders and bankers or local Asiatic businessmen yet provide a class of responsible political and social leadership. There are problems enough in the way of securing social unity in the old industrial communities of the Atlantic where strong political traditions and a well-developed civic spirit encourage leaders on both sides of industry to consider the welfare of the community as a whole. There are no such traditions in the new states of Asia. On the contrary, a combination of commercial instinct and the notorious corruption of pre-Western government survives. Certainly, one reason why, beyond Suez, so much external aid can be spent so quickly on so little is that it finds its way to many private pockets in the process.

The picture is naturally not uniform. In the new Dominions, in particular, a tradition of public service undoubtedly exists. But even there the lack of social cohesion is widespread enough to give communism its opportunity. To be misgoverned is no new thing in Asia. A fatalistic acceptance of the combined tyranny of landlord, moneylender, merchant or government official has long been the background of Asian politics. The Communists promise to burst these bonds and to replace them with the puritan administration of incorruptible commissars, and such promises cannot fail to have their appeal to the small group of politically conscious men and women who decide public opinion in Eastern lands. Compared with the confused and in part corrupt and unstable rule which Western ideas grafted on to Asian nationalism seem to provide, the supposed and untried benefits of communism have the double attraction of clarity and social force.

Nowhere has the insufficiency of Asian nationalism as a bulwark against the spread of communism appeared more clearly than in China. If nationalism had been enough, no regime could have been safer than that of Generalissimo Chiang Kai-shek. He had led from the very outset the Chinese people's ten-year struggle against the Japanese and for years during the war, his capital at Chungking was the very symbol of China's determination to maintain its national independence. It was under his rule, too, that China was welcomed into the community of Great Powers, was associated with their victory and took its permanent seat in the Security Council. Nor was economic assistance lacking. Throughout the war financial aid was given and, after the war, massive sums were dispatched to the Nationalist regime first to rebuild the Chinese economy and then to strengthen it in the growing struggle with the Communists.

China's Communists started with none of these apparent advantages. A tiny fragment of China's millions, shattered after their attempted rising in Shanghai in 1927, they were harried first to the south, then into the mountains before they made their forced march through the interior to establish their rule in remote Shensi. But it was during the ten years in the wilderness that they abandoned the aim of being primarily an urban party of the proletariat and learned to use the key that was to unlock China for them—peasant discontent and agrarian reform.

After 1936, they joined Chiang in his struggle against the Japanese and developed their unsensational but effective program of lowering rents, remitting debt and associating peasants with local government in the rural areas which, even under Japanese occupation of cities, roads and railways, they effectively controlled. It was this pervasive occupation of parts of North China and Manchuria that made it possible for them to receive their first external asset in the struggle against Chiang—which broke out again once the Japanese faced defeat. This was the transfer to them by the Russians of the armaments captured in Manchuria. Thereafter, however, it was as much the weakness and disintegration of the Nationalist front as their own military force that made possible their total victory in 1948 and early 1949—a sweeping tide of victory that took them from the Great Wall to Canton in a year.

Those who wish to study in detail the disintegration of the Nationalist regime cannot do better than read the dispassionate account General Marshall wrote of his attempt in 1947 to end the civil war by mediation. The backbone of the Nationalist cause remained an alliance of landlords, warlords and the bankers and merchants of the coast. In the provinces, the local warlord could no doubt rely upon old feudal loyalties, but no new ideas or purposes or popular ideals inspired support for the Nationalist government and administration in the country at large. On the contrary, corruption, extortion, incompetence and a rigid opposition to all forms of social change fettered the system and drove the few men of enlightened views to despair or opposition. It was of little avail to give money or arms to a movement so governed and so led. The arms were sold to the Communists by defaulting commanders or by hungry soldiers whose pay was six months in arrears. Money vanished into private holdings and even found its way back to be invested in the United States. The final debacle of the Nationalists was not so much defeat in the battlefield as collapse everywhere else. The support of the people simply faded away and as often as not a Communist victory consisted simply in the entire Nationalist army changing sides. The end of Chiang Kai-shek's rule in continental China was a social rather than a military phenomenon.

No clearer or more pregnant warning could be given that, in Asia, nationalism is no longer enough. The fact of social change, the hope of economic progress and the cry for elementary human rights are now fundamental facts of the Asian scene. If the Western Powers desire—as they must desire—to contain effectively the flooding of communism through the Far East and Southeast Asia, they cannot rely simply upon the support of local nationalism and the giving of economic aid. Both policies have paid them some dividends in the last five years and both are the starting points for any future policy, but they are not enough. No other conclusion can be drawn from the Chinese debacle.

The transfer to the Communist side of the world of one of the most ancient and most populous civilizations in the history of man is an historical event of shattering importance. It has consequences and repercussions far beyond the confines of China. Throughout Southeast Asia live vast Chinese communities—in Siam, in Malaya, in Indonesia. They were once the faithful supporters of Chiang Kai-shek's Kuomintang. The transfer of that loyalty to Mao Tse-tung is virtually certain and who knows how soon they may not be the effective spearheads of a new imperialism in which—as in Soviet Russia—old national instincts and a new political crusade are fused? Moreover, throughout the Orient—and is it confined to the Orient?—respect for success is immense. Communism, the beaten child of China, hiding away in a mountain province and going about the consolidation of its power by stealth, had little appeal to the masses beyond the frontiers. But what must be said of a political force which commands the backing of the two greatest states of Asia? And which is guided by men who are utterly ruthless in their pursuit and maintenance of power? If success succeeds, communism can count on further victories in Asia.

But perhaps so far the most signal consequence of the Communist victory in China has been the disarray and confusion into which it has thrown the Western camp. Discouraged by the successful emergence of a hostile power in China, many Americans have spoken of the Far East as a liability in the event of war. A year ago, Japan was shaken to the core by the rumors that the Americans considered it "expendable" in wartime and might withdraw their occupation forces. In South Korea, the evacuation of American troops did in fact take place.

Another dangerous development was the split between British and American policy over the question of recognizing the new Communist regime in Peking and supporting or blocking its claim to take over the Nationalists' place in the Security Council. The British, with large commercial interests at stake, agreed that the basis of recognition was not legitimacy but the fact of effective control, and it could not be denied that the Communists did in fact control the Chinese mainland. Accordingly, the British Government took the decision, late in 1949, to recognize the Peking regime. The United States Government, more completely committed to Generalissimo Chiang Kai-shek and harassed at home by a very powerful group of Chiang's supporters—the China lobby—inside and outside Congress, preferred to bide its time. The Administration was aware of the disadvantages of leaving Communist China in lonely *tête-à-tête* with the Soviet Union. Equally, they could argue that the new regime should show a greater readiness to pursue normal international relations before the advantages of membership in the United Nations should be conferred upon it.

There remained, too, the troublesome problem of Formosa, whither the Generalissimo had retired after his total defeat in China. Formerly a possession of Japan, it had been promised to China at the Cairo talks in 1943. Legally, no doubt, it belonged formally to Japan until a peace treaty could be signed. It was claimed by the Communists who began to mount an invasion fleet to conquer it. It was actually in the possession of the Nationalists. It would be difficult to invent a problem more likely to divide policies and confuse minds. Certainly it had the effect of increasing the divergence between British and American policies—a consequence little short of disastrous in any effective Western policy for Asia.

The Chinese disaster handed the apple of discord not only to America and its allies but to the American political parties as well. Throughout the first two years of the Marshall Plan, the level of American political leadership was a constant source of encouragement to the West. Under the unequaled authority of General Marshall and the wise guidance of Senator Vandenberg, the Administration and the Republican opposition presented to the world a picture of political responsibility which was an inspiration and comfort to the friends of free government everywhere. Unhappily, the bipartisan approach had never been so clearly applied in the sphere of Far Eastern policies and the collapse in China gave the extremer members of the Republican Party an opportunity to break from a unity with the Administration on foreign policy which many of them had found irksome and probably thought disadvantageous to their electoral chances.

The attack upon the Administration was concentrated upon the accusation that aid to Chiang Kai-shek had been sabotaged by Communists inside the State Department and there followed, under the guidance of Senator MacCarthy, a witch hunt of suspects in all walks of American public life that created among America's allies abroad a bewildering sense of having totally lost touch with the leadership and the moral authority which they had become accustomed to find in Washington. For some months it seemed as though the effectiveness of the whole governmental machine in Washington and even the influence of American foreign policy itself would be brought to a full stop by the activities of a single senator.

We cannot gauge the minds of dictators. We do not know how the timing of their actions is determined, who precisely takes the decisions and how, today, in the vast empire controlled from Moscow, local plans are put into effect. But if for a moment we try to put ourselves in the place of Stalin in May and June of 1950, is it not possible that we should say to ourselves: "The Americans have cleared out of Korea and are speaking of leaving Japan. They are at loggerheads with the British over the recognition of the Peking Government. They are also in a fair state of indecision and concern over their hunt for Communists in the State Department and quite a number of influential Americans have been suggesting that it is more important to keep Communists out of America than to fight them abroad. All in all, it seems to me that my Western friends are very muddled over their Far Eastern policy. They do not know how to react and certainly they show no sign of wishing to act together. Shall I risk another little straightening of my line? Another little demonstration of my local power and superiority? Yes, I think I will."

On June 25 at dawn, North Korean forces crossed the South Korean frontier and opened the attack.

# 7

# *After Korea*

IT SEEMS certain that the Soviet Union, in sponsoring the North Korean aggression, expected no greater reaction from the Western Powers than a wringing of hands, a passing of helpless resolutions and a general flurry of passive condemnation lasting long enough to permit the unopposed annexation of South Korea. The Communists, however, reckoned without three things. The first was the lesson that had been branded upon the minds of the free peoples between 1936 and 1939—the lesson that aggression cannot be checked by submission. On the contrary, it simply whets the appetite of the aggressor and undermines still further the defenders' will to resist. The attacker's strength and the victim's weakness increase in a geometrical progression once the process of appeasement sets in.

The second factor was the capacity of the ordinary, honest citizen, represented to a supreme degree by President Truman, to rise to an extraordinary situation. Speedy reactions and quick decisions have been all too often assumed to be the dictator's prerogative. The dictator in the Kremlin appears to have thought so. This time, he was wrong.

The third factor was Russia's self-imposed banishment from the Security Council. When the question of China's representation on the Security Council went in favor of the Nationalist regime in January, 1950, the Russians marched out, announcing that they would return only when the Peking government had ousted the Nationalists. When the North Korean invasion began they were still absent, not foreseeing how effectively the United Nations would be able to function without them.

Events after June 25 moved with great speed. The American Government summoned the Security Council which on the twenty-seventh ordered a cease fire and a North Korean withdrawal to the 38th parallel. It had before it a report of its own United Nations Commission on the spot in South Korea and this independent source left it in no doubt that the North Koreans were responsible for the invasion and were not, as the Communists later claimed, repulsing a South Korean attack. Needless to say, the North Koreans took no notice of the Security Council's decision. The American Government, therefore, acting under Article 51 of the United Nations Charter, which lays down a state's right to defend itself and to receive assistance from other member states when exposed to aggression, announced that it was placing American naval and air forces at the disposal of the South Korean Government. On the following day, the Security Council met again and called upon all member nations to render aid to the South Koreans. The resolution was passed with one vote against it (Jugoslavia) and two abstentions (India and Egypt), but the Indian Government associated itself fully with the resolution on the following day. Thus, freed by Russia's own choice from the crippling effect of the Russian veto, the United Nations moved into action to bring the aggression in Korea to an end. Britain and the Commonwealth joined the Americans immediately in the dispatch of air and sea forces to the battlefront. Within a week, however, it was clear that the North Koreans had mobilized a full-scale army—probably drawn in part from the Korean divisions that had taken part in the civil war in China—and greatly outclassed, both in numbers and fire power, the lightly armed South Korean gendarmerie. The American Government accepted the implications of this disparity and sent American ground forces into action.

The North Korean invasion, which might otherwise have been crowned with success within a very few days, was slowed down by delaying actions fought by inexperienced American troops against a much more numerous enemy. The aggressors' advance continued and as the campaign developed, the crucial needs for allied manpower became daily more obvious. Mr. Trygve Lie sent telegrams to all the member nations urging them to send ground troops to fight under the United Nations commander, General MacArthur. By the end of the fourth week of fighting, Britain, Australia, New Zealand, Turkey and Siam had promised contingents to back the main effort made by the United States. A genuinely international force thus began to assemble at precisely the moment at which General MacArthur announced for the first time his belief that a bridgehead could be held in Korea and used as the basis of an effective counteroffensive.

That counteroffensive came more speedily than even the most sanguine supporters of the United Nations action could have hoped. The climax came in the last weeks of August. The North Koreans had fixed August 15 as their day of triumph and for an anxious fortnight, it seemed that blow after blow from the North would break through the United Nations thinly held line along the Naktong river. But General MacArthur used his fresh reinforcements in a masterly thrust behind the North Korean lines and on September 15, American, Commonwealth and South Korean forces landed at Inchon and within a week, Seoul, the capital, had been liberated and the main body of the Communist forces trapped between the two United Nations armies.

Thus ended the first phase of the campaign. After a delay for regrouping which enabled the General Assembly of the United Nations to vote by 45 to 5—with 7 abstentions—for the advance into North Korea, the United Nations forces surged over the 38th parallel, advanced to the North Korean capital, Pyongyang, and pursued the scattered remnants of the Communist armies to the borders of Manchuria.

At the time of writing, it cannot be said whether the

intervention of Chinese troops on the side of the North Koreans will lead to a dangerous extension of the conflict and to the frustration of the United Nations' attempt to make their police action entirely local, but, even allowing for this uncertainty, two problems can already be seen looming beyond the Korean campaign. The first is a local one—in Korea itself to secure a really generous far-sighted and inspiring policy of reconstruction. The second, in the general field of international relations, is to draw the correct conclusions from the achievement of the Korean campaign, for, horrible as it has been in the damage and loss of life that it has brought with it, it may yet prove a timely and essential turning point in the history of Western containment. Containment depends for its efficacy upon two things—the potential aggressor's knowledge that, if necessary, force will be used to check aggression and an equal realization that the force available is sufficient to beat aggression back. The American reaction in North Korea, backed and supported by the rest of the free world, has given half the answer. Notice has been served upon the Soviet Union that force will be met by force. The very remoteness of Korea, the fact that its defense involves no vital Western interests, even the earlier American decision to withdraw its occupation forces, all underline the fact that the West is resisting only one thing in Korea—the naked reality of aggression.

On the other hand, the Korean war has shown that the Western Powers have been living in a cloud cuckoo-land of totally inadequate defenses. When the North Koreans launched their attack, only American predominance in the production of atom bombs offered the West any effective shield against a general war. In every other field of defense, the Allies were almost ludicrously weak. Moreover, if it is true that the North Korean aggression was partly inspired by the evidence of disharmony between the free nations, it must also be admitted that their psychological defenses were also well below the level needed for successful containment. Korea has put an end to the illusions and the dreams. In the first weeks of the campaign, the Western Powers were shown to lack the force to stop even the smallest Russian puppet dead in its tracks. Even when the tide turned and the United Nations could advance, the campaign could be felt to be absorbing an undue proportion of the West's available manpower and armaments. This in turn underlined the fact that Western Europe was wide open to a Soviet invasion. Defense Ministers have hardly dared to disclose the thinness of Western forces on the ground. These are the bare bleak facts. As a result of Korea, they are being looked at with realism and in public—for the first time.

There is therefore the chance—it is not yet a certainty—that the shock and the impetus provided by Korea will lead the Western Powers to make containment at last a reality. For over a year, they have talked of it as their policy. Their diplomacy has been based upon it. The decision to defend South Korea was a direct outcome of it. But the diplomacy was a "deficit diplomacy" because it lacked the arms and the plans to make it effective. The reason is only too obvious. A foreign policy had been based upon the speeches of a few statesmen. Defense policy makes claims on the pockets of the taxpayer. The truth is that throughout 1949 and early 1950, the Western Powers were affording themselves the luxury of a foreign policy for which they were not prepared to pay. Korea showed them that a foreign policy based on containment was correct. It also showed them how far they were from meeting its cost. The incident can therefore mark the beginnings of an effective effort to make foreign policy and a defense policy march in step, provided the Western Powers are now prepared to meet the political, economic and moral costs inescapably involved in effective containment.

This book attempts, in a tentative fashion, to outline some of these costs. Since the West has no fixed, dogmatic view of the future, the policies that should be pursued cannot be predicted with absolute certainty. We ought to know the direction and to measure the risks. But a free society cannot survive without the greatest flexibility in the methods it employs. But it is permissible to be dogmatic about one thing—and that is the general spirit in which the new phase of containment must be undertaken. We shall certainly fail unless our effort is at once sustained, calm and supremely positive.

This may sound like a truism. So it may be—in theory. In practice these three qualities are probably the most testing that can be demanded from the Western world. "Sustained"—a policy which envisages not short bursts and quick achievements but long patience, a long effort, a dedicated purpose stretching over the decades and the generations. Will such a policy prove easy to the Western Powers? Let us be perfectly frank. The whole conception is alien to the experience and effort of the Western world in the hundred and fifty years that have passed since the Industrial Revolution ushered in the modern age. The outlook of every government and every people is likely to be more influenced by past history—by what has happened—than by any estimate, however clear and compelling, of what is likely to happen next. And in the recent past of the West, the years during which it seemed that peace and prosperity could be had for the asking have tended to outweigh the briefer periods of fearful realization that there are forces of destruction loose in the world which must be positively, actively and lengthily contained if Western society is to survive.

For many people, the nineteenth and early twentieth centuries must still seem a golden age. The political order of the world was underpinned by two apparently automatic devices—the balance of power in Europe and the world-wide supremacy of the British Navy. The new world economy created by the Industrial Revolution also appeared to be regulated by self-functioning rules and devices. Early industrialism had grown up and flourished by throwing off the stifling controls of incompetent bureaucracies. The production of capital for internal and international development seemed no problem in days without income tax and without the modern multiplication of charges for social and colonial welfare. Above all, the workings of the economy as a whole was eased and simplified by Britain's unique position. A small island, needing to import food and raw materials in return for the manufactures and capital it began to export all over the world, it acted as a kind of natural regulator of world trade and world finance. Only when, some fifty years later, the United States in all its self-sufficiency became the most powerful economy in history did people begin to realize how much of the supposedly "free" workings of international trade had been due to Britain's almost unconscious creation of commercial and financial equilibrium.

A second world war within a generation might, it is true, be supposed to have dealt a death blow to all surviving beliefs in an automatically secure, self-regulating world. But is it certain that the lesson was finally learned by 1945? Was there not some striking evidence to suggest that in parts of the West, particularly in America, the idea of war as a German-caused interlude to an otherwise normal and peaceful international order still had some adherents? The United States, it is true, made haste to repair what seemed to be the errors of 1919. It agreed to share in the policing of Germany, it joined the new League—the United Nations—and accepted partnership in a renewed scheme for collective security. Yet behind this new spirit of internationalism lurked the old mood of optimism about the world's capacity to run itself. What better index could there be of this mood than the hurried disarmament of the West or the ending of Lend-Lease from one day to the next, as though the vast dislocations of war could be relied upon to vanish with a formal signing of an armistice? Even the most striking sign of a new and active internationalism—support for the United Nations and its agencies—was made possible to some extent because people felt that international institutions would deal with external difficulties and frictions "automatically." The concern of every nation in 1945 and 1946 was to an overwhelming extent with its own particular problems of readjustment, and, in America at least, the belief in a quick recovery and the return of "normal" conditions was particularly buoyant. Admittedly, the reaction was infinitely more moderate and responsible than the sloughing off of all commitments that had occurred twenty-five years before. But neither in the United States nor in Western Europe did people fully believe that an immense effort of effective international co-operation lasting over a generation would be necessary to re-create—by active adjustment and constant vigilance—the peaceful conditions achieved so painlessly only fifty years earlier. The dream of the Victorian golden age still stirred the slumbers of the Western world.

This is the heavy weight of historical experience against which the Western Powers must now react if their containment is to be not another spurt, not another local and temporary effort, but a genuine campaign, sustained over the years, to rebuild a secure and peaceful world. The temptation will be strong to shirk the issue. For instance, the last sign of Russian withdrawal from its present extreme attitude of hostility may well cause us all to throw our caps in the air, sing hosannas and go back to the pursuit of separate, unregulated, nationalist politics and economics which before long will offer the Communists a renewed spectacle of Western confusion and weakness and tempt them once again to renew their attack.

Equally, however, unwillingness to face a sustained effort may lead the Western Powers into the opposite danger if Russian hostility remains unchanged and if it is expressed in further acts of local pressure and aggression. There would then be some temptation to say: "We shall never have peace while this brutal and hostile dictatorship is forever probing and undermining and attacking. Let us get the issue over once and for all. Let us put an end to this miserable half-life between war and peace—drop the atom bomb on the Kremlin now." This is not the mood of responsible leaders but it could become a ground swell of popular opinion, and there can be no doubt about its dangerous appeal. If there were a short cut to total world peace, who would not be tempted to take it? But there are no short cuts. An atomic war remains almost the worst evil mankind can envisage. Little would be left of the highly civilized, liberal, temperate society of the West once Europe and even parts of America had been blasted to ruin and sterility. Communism might not perhaps triumph in the ruins, but anarchy would. If by any legitimate means such a war can be avoided, the West must make that effort. There can be no "trigger happiness" in the Western approach to the bomb, for it offers no quick way to peace. It only makes general war certain and can be used, therefore, only when war has been inescapably thrust upon the Western Powers by Soviet Russia. And since this is the situation which it is the whole aim of containment to avoid, it cannot be precipitated in containment's name.

A sustained effort, therefore, and a calm effort—these are two preconditions of success in the West. But there is a third and this perhaps is the most testing of all. If containment is to be fully effective, the notion of containment must at last be left behind. It is, after all, a negative concept. We check Soviet advances, we mend the dykes and repair the dams, but all the time, the initiative is left to the Communist world and we fall almost into the posture of finding out what Stalin is doing and telling him not to. In the short run, negative containment is excellent and essential. In the military field, it will always remain to a large extent predominant since the Western Powers are concerned essentially with defense, not with devising ways of carrying the war into the Soviet camp. But in the vital and finally decisive sphere of social containment, the West must capture the initiative or risk defeat.

We have seen already that the forces which the West has let loose upon the world by its own decision and invention in the last two hundred years—industrialism, nationalism, the transforming power of science—have created a society which is dynamic and changing and full of latent capacity but at the same time, a prey to irrationalities, confusions and injustices which threaten, even without Communist pressure, to bring it down. The period during which we could rely upon automatic and self-regulating forces to produce a tolerable social and economic order has passed. Nazism is a detestable reminder of what our own Western form of society can produce in the way of ugliness, violence and degeneration if the forces of unreason and maladjustment are not controlled and checked. Today, therefore, there is no solution for the West either in leaving things to take their course or in snatching at violent and negative totalitarian solutions. If the Western Powers are not to become the passive victims of Communist pressure or of their own inner contradictions—or, of a combination of the two—then the only shield lies in positive and creative action, in building in the West a social order in which the great promises of Western culture—"freedom, brotherhood and an equal law"—are recognizably achieved. In place of the warring nationalisms that have torn us apart and the social barriers and class conflicts that break our inner cohesion, we must create an effective unity. In place of an uncontrolled industrialism which plunges us from prosperity to depression and back again and creates in the minds of the masses a sense equally compounded of irrationality and irresponsibility, we need economic expansion, economic stability and economic citizenship. Above all we need to recover the sense of the great ideals and affirmations of Western civilization which a century of cynical rationalism, popular Marxism, cheapened science and practical materialism have almost lost to our sight. A formidable program? Perhaps, but not less formidable than the challenge presented by our adversaries. They at least have no illusions. They at least do not expect to conquer the world without struggle, without patience and without arms. They do not hope to build their own version of society without the driving force of faith. And there, above all, they show greater wisdom than the Western peoples, for if one thing is certain from the long history of man, it is that a crusading faith cannot be defeated save by a faith equal to its own.

# PART II · *Strength*

# 8

# *Strength for Strength*

IT IS not difficult to show that dollar for dollar and ton for ton, the advantage in the present trial of strength lies with the Western world. Whether one compares national incomes or industrial power or availability of resources, the Soviet Union and its satellites lag behind. Only in manpower is the situation more doubtful. A glance at the accompanying table shows that the national incomes of the effective members of the Western world vastly exceed that of the Soviet Union, while their ability to secure the economic resources necessary for a strong military and industrial machine are in every case larger—decisively so in that key to military mobility, oil. The reason why the manpower figures are less certain is that there is no way of judging a number of unknown factors. What are the Soviet Union's reserves likely to be in view of the fact that its losses were greater than any other combatant, save Germany, in the last war? How many of the victorious Communist armies in China may be available for adventures beyond their frontiers? The disposal in a backward community of large numbers of soldiers after prolonged fighting has always been a problem. There is no reason to suppose that Mao Tse-tung will find it any less so.

And what of Europe? In France and Italy the active and passive supporters of communism may still number some mil-

## Relative Strength in 1949

| Country | Population | National Incomes, Million U. S. dollars: At pre-devaluation rates of exchange | National Incomes, Million U. S. dollars: At April 1950 rate of exchange | Steel | Hard Coal | Crude Oil | Electricity[a] |
|---|---|---|---|---|---|---|---|
| | *Thousands* | | | *'000 metric tons* | *'000 metric tons* | *'000 metric tons* | *million kw-hr* |
| United States | 149,215 | 216,831 | 216,831 | 70,635 | 433,332 | 252,996 | 344,500 |
| United Kingdom | 50,363 | 41,210 | 28,633 | 15,816 | 218,580[b] | 46 | 49,115[b] |
| France | 41,180 | 25,418 | 19,803 | 9,111 | 51,200 | 58 | 28,560 |
| W. Germany | 47,585 | 25,450[d] | 20,000[d] | 9,157 | 103,236 | 842 | 38,170 |
| Canada | 13,549 | 12,977 | 11,797 | 2,892 | 15,649 | 2,829 | 46,672 |
| Australia | 7,912 | 6,335 | 4,400 | 1,149 | 14,332 | ... | 9,017 |
| U.S.S.R. | 193,000[c] | 101,900[d] | 135,000[d] | 22,000 | 220,000 | 33,200 | 70,000 |

[a] Electricity generated by public utilities for Great Britain and Canada; figures for other countries include production of establishments generating electricity for their own use.

[b] Excluding N. Ireland.

[c] *1946.*

[d] Rough estimates.

Estimates for Russia are unofficial; figures for French production exclude Saar.

lions. Togliatti has announced that his party will fight any "American invaders" to the death. The French Communist Party have tightened their discipline and reinforced their militant groups in order to be ready for sabotage and Fifth Column work. The French Minister of Defense has announced the formation of a loyal "Home Guard" to defend the rear of the armies. All this sounds ominous enough. It should, however, be remembered that in spite of a triumphant blowing of Communist fanfares in the spring of 1950, no serious interference has occurred in the landing of American-manufactured war equipment in French and Italian ports. It is easier to threaten sabotage than to persuade men to carry it out under the shadow of heavy penalties. Nor should the likelihood of a Fifth Column in Eastern Europe be underestimated. Many of the dispossessed and disinherited openly look to war as their only hope. The reports of disillusion in all classes in Czechoslovakia are too circumstantial to be only wish fulfillment and sporadic resistance still flares up along the mountainous frontiers of Poland and Rumania. Throughout the area, the peasants would probably be as passively hostile to a Soviet war effort as sections of the industrial workers in the West might be to the campaigns of the Allies. All in all, calculations of manpower must remain rather imprecise. There is, however, no doubt about the general verdict—that the balance of economic strength lies with the West.

It is or should be impossible for anyone to read such words without recalling in dismay similar estimates made in 1939 and early 1940. Pamphlet after pamphlet appeared, article after article was written to point out that the free world was bound to win because its resources were infinitely greater than those of Nazi Germany. Lists of raw materials, charts and maps colored to show the concentration of allied resources were the chief instruments of propaganda in the first months of the "phony war" when the Allies seemed to hope more from blockading the enemy by means of economic warfare than from meeting him in the field. When at last they did so in the grim days of May and June, 1940, they found that one tank now is more than a match for millions of tons of steel available at Pittsburgh and that not the scale of a nation's resources but the extent to which it has mobilized them is the key to victory.

Once again, the free world has come to the brink of making the same mistake. Its vast reserves and riches should give it the courage to face a long defense and a long containment, but the only effective factor in the next year or so is the amount of those reserves that can be made immediately available for combat. Since the war, the Soviet Union with its smaller reserves, has nevertheless outstripped the free world simply by turning those reserves into a greater flow of armaments. In one field only have the Western Powers retained their superiority—the atom bomb—and that weapon remains, as Mr. Churchill never ceases to point out, the only shield of Western Europe. For the rest, we know—the facts cannot be repeated too often—that Russia has 175 divisions ready, one-third of them mechanized, and the whole force supported by 25,000 tanks and 19,000 aircraft, that these numbers are being expanded and that mobilization could double the 3 million men under arms. We know, from the lessons of Korea, that arms and training have been supplied lavishly to a ring of satellites and that the arms are in some cases better than the weapons used at present by American troops. We also know what, in the autumn of 1950, was available to counter them—12 understrength divisions in Western Europe with not more than four to six thousand aircraft, a British division dispersed through the Middle East and further forces concentrated in Malaya and Hong Kong, 120,000 of France's regular army of some 200,000 men pinned down in Indo-China, 10 understrength divisions in the United States for reinforcement not only in Europe but—as the Korean campaign has shown—all along the Soviet perimeter as well. The plain truth is that in front line strength the disparity between Russia and the free world when the North Koreans' adventure at last shocked the Allies to their senses, was greater than Europe's weakness before Hitler in 1939.

The need to re-create an effective defensive position has been the basis of Western policy ever since the Korean campaign forced them to face the implications of their weakness. Nor has there been much disagreement about the general strategy—to permit no further expansion of Russian-backed Communism. This means in effect to remove all possibility of a speedy overrunning of Europe by Soviet forces and to stiffen local resistance to Communist pressure wherever else it may begin to probe. The European aspect of this strategy is difficult, no doubt, but appears relatively straightforward—a question of estimating the likely strength of the attack and providing sufficient forces sufficiently equipped to act, one may hope, as a deterrent, but in the event of war, to hold a line while general Western mobilization occurs and the atomic attack is carried into Russia. In other words, the chief task is to hold any possible offensive as the German offensive was held in 1914 and to avoid the disastrous collapse of 1940. This presumably is the first datum upon which the expansion and the priorities of the Western defense forces have been based.

The second responsibility—the reinforcement of threatened points along the whole Soviet periphery—appears far less straightforward and has, indeed, given rise to a great deal of gloomy comment in the West. Since the Nationalist defeat in China, many Western observers have come more and more to believe that "the wave of the future" is flowing too strongly in Russia's favor for local defense against Communist forces to be really effective. The corruption and ineffectiveness of the Chiang regime are quoted as proof that Western support will always come to people unworthy to receive it and certain to abuse it. The Russians, on the other hand, having on their side "the forces of history," will not need to engage their own strength. They will simply spur on their satellites whereas the Western Powers will have to use their own troops—as the Americans are doing in Korea or the French in Indo-China and the British in Malaya. The result of such a one-sided conflict will be that more and more Western strength will be dissipated in local struggles in Asia while the Soviet Union will preserve its own strength intact. Then, should a general struggle occur, the full weight of Soviet military might could be unleashed on the critical

European front while Western forces would be pinned down from Suez to Korea.

No one will deny that the Asian fronts offer a problem to the free world of a most intractable kind. But it is important to keep difficulties as well as assets in perspective and it certainly is far from the truth to represent the Soviet Union as a vast impassive giant surrounded by pigmies so weak that a prod of its Buddha-like toe is enough to send them spinning unless they are propped up and supported at enormous cost in manpower and materials by the Western Powers. The North Korean technique has after all been tried once before—in Greece—and it cannot be said that the cost of resisting the Communist attack was crippling to the West. Greece is only one example. If a dispassionate survey of the Soviet perimeter is made, the perpetration of further Koreas, though possible, is not bound by ineluctable fate to lead to Communist victories.

Two free elections have established the fact that the great majority of the Japanese people are not Communist and that the problem of controlling a local revolt is not by any means insoluble. The danger, therefore, would come from external attack. It is true that the Japanese Government may not be anxious to enter peace negotiations that will leave it committed to accepting American bases on Japanese territory, but this reluctance is not due to pacifism or defeatism but to the desire of the Japanese to recover the means of defending themselves. The Russians are playing upon this desire and have promised to end their demilitarization once they are in the Soviet camp. Meanwhile a number of Japanese ex-prisoners of war—officers and men—have been added to the heterogeneous general staff of Far Eastern Communist imperialism—one or two are reported to be acting as military advisers in Korea, a country they know well from their thirty-year occupation. As in the case of Germany, where Russian policy is actively to press forward with the process of rearmament and to play upon old militarist sentiment, the Western Powers find themselves acting to some extent against a strong stream of local opinion.

So far, the idea of any rearmament of Japan has been resisted, but clearly a measure of local defense is necessary unless the Americans intend to provide complete cover themselves. In the circumstances, it would seem wiser to give the Japanese adequate forces for defense but no opportunities for renewed aggression. Since their power is island-based, strict limitations upon any revival of their navy should be sufficient to ensure the purely defensive character of their military effort. Naval security in the area could remain an Anglo-American responsibility, as it is today. The decisive point, however, is that the internal verdict of Japan, a highly evolved industrial state, has been given against communism while the provision of the means of local defense against external attack present no striking strategic problems. In the longer run, the economic future of the country must be assured in such a way that the verdict against communism is not revised later on by growing discontent and misery. But in the short run, and from a primarily military point of view, Japan is not a likely scene for a new Korea.

Moving to the south, we come upon Formosa and the Philippines. More must be said later about the difficult and challenging situation presented by the clash of rival claims in Formosa. Here it should be noted that the strategic factor dominating the Philippines is that it is separated from the Communist-dominated land mass of China by hundreds of miles of water and must involve any would-be invader in difficult amphibious operations. It is true that the Russians have concentrated much effort upon the development of the submarine and profited much from the technique and experience of Germans taken to Russia since the end of the war. Operations in the China seas would no doubt offer a searching test to the British and American navies. But they could not be effortlessly pursued by Russia's satellites and would certainly involve direct Soviet intervention. Thus they would not conform to the picture of an inactive Soviet Union directing its satellites in a wasting war in which the Western Powers only would be directly involved.

Indo-China, lying along China's frontiers, and open to

every kind of infiltration from the Communist North, has already conformed to the chosen pattern of Communist expansion and has become an ever greater direct drain on the West as Chinese Communist aid increases. Here the pessimists have cause enough for their tone of gloom, although there are some signs of a growing rally of opinion and support round Bao Dai. One reason is that help from China has, throughout Southeast Asia, an element of the Trojan Horse. When Western imperialism penetrated to this part of Asia, not much more than a hundred years ago, it only repeated with sudden violence a tale of imperialist pressure carried on over the centuries by the Chinese. Western imperialism is fading. The memory of the older incursions is therefore coming to the surface again. The Chinese, even bringing the gifts of Communist revolt and military assistance, are feared. It is significant that whereas until this year, the Communist (Viet Minh) radio in Indo-China always referred to the struggle as the Viet Nam war against the French invader, it now complains petulantly that the adherence of more and more people to Bao Dai is turning it into "a civil war." There is therefore perhaps a slender hope that a local Asian nationalism opposed to Communist domination may arise in an area in which, so far, the stiffening and the fighting have been done by France. Its growth depends upon French readiness to concede the substance not the shadow of independence to Bao Dai, but the pressure of Western opinion in this direction is probably too strong to be resisted.

The vulnerability of Indo-China threatens, nonetheless, its neighbors in Burma, Siam and Malaya. But of the first two, it cannot be said that they would cede power without resistance to Communist pressure from without. Siam is a well-knit, independent, largely peasant state. There is little local communism, the large Chinese community is strongly distrusted, the Government itself has sided more openly than any other with the West. Marshal Pipul has recognized Bao Dai and offered to send troops to Korea. If a general Communist victory in the whole area became certain, the Siamese Government might repeat the tactics of 1942 and give in as gracefully as it did before the Japanese advance. But its leaders are shrewdly aware that no gentlemanly truce would be their lot under Communist control.

The Burmese Government, socialist in philosophy, has already shown its reaction to communism by fighting two local brands of it in a prolonged civil war out of which it is emerging shakily victorious. A Communist thrust, backed by China, across its frontiers would almost certainly be resisted and the difficulties of the mountainous terrain would give the defenders the advantage of guerrilla warfare. There is no love for China among the frontier peoples of Burma—the Kachins and the Karens—and possibly the threat of an invasion from without would settle more quickly than any other the government's dispute with the large racial minority of the Karens, which it has carried on simultaneously with its anti-Communist campaigns. The Karens are no friends to Communists or Chinese and a threat across the frontiers might rally the country to the unity it so desperately needs. Moreover the Burmese Government, representing a genuinely and completely independent Asian country, might be able to count on military assistance from India and Pakistan. Similarly Indonesia, however chaotic the conditions and uncertain the government's hold, can for the time being control its local Communists, and invasion from without would have to come by sea, a formidable undertaking unless the Soviet Union lent naval aid.

It is necessary to point out these facts not to lull the West into the idea that Southeast Asia can be easily held and presents no major challenge to their strategy, their policy and their resources. Southeast Asia is in mortal danger and the amount of social, economic and political dynamite stored there can lead to a major explosion. The facts are rehearsed only in the hope of countering the opposite danger—the belief that "the rice bowl of Asia is lost," that there is nothing in the whole of Southeast Asia solid enough to withstand one determined Communist offensive, that the Western Powers are so tainted with imperialism that any intervention by them will do more harm than good, above all, that each country in Asia is a ripe plum which Stalin can shake easily from the tree. The ring of states round the Soviet center present a far more complex picture than these fears suggest.

India and Pakistan are hardly threatened by invasion from without. In any case, only Russia could do the invading and the pattern therefore of "aggression by proxy" would not hold good. In Persia, the country is exposed enough and its internal situation sufficiently abject and unstable. Once again, however, aggression could only be undertaken by Soviet troops. The Persian Azerbaijani are not, at least according to the experience of 1946, such stuff as Mao Tse-tungs are made of. The attempt at a local civil war was a complete failure, and since that time, the Persian instrument of that attempted revolt, the Tudeh party, has been in very low water. No one can deny that Persia may well stand high on the list of areas ready for "Soviet liberation," but the process could not be carried through by a local satellite—there are none—and once Russia commits its own forces, it must squarely face the risk of general war.

The neighboring state of Iraq is weak enough and the Kurds on the northern frontier could and do provide a suitable center of "civil war" but again the only reinforcements would be Soviet reinforcements, and since the frontiers of Iraq and the Soviet Union are not contiguous, Russian infiltration would be almost impossible. The readiness of the Turks to fight is obvious, and, unless Bulgaria were used—surely an ineffectual instrument—the only possible attack from without would, once again, have to be launched from Soviet soil.

On the fringe of Europe, the Korean technique has been tried and has failed in Greece. Bulgaria, Rumania and Hungary might be let loose on the unrepentant Tito, but no one doubts that the Jugoslavs would give a good account of themselves. Russia cannot be certain that its own intervention would not be required. There remains the ominous problem of Germany. Of all the irresponsible and indefensible policies pursued by the Soviet Union since the war, the rearming of the Germans is the one which it is the most impossible to condone or even to explain. Has not Europe suffered enough from the scourge of German militarism? Have not the Russians themselves been sufficiently massacred and martyred? Would not demilitarization and permanent neutrality of Germany have created a common interest between East and West—and a buffer state as well? Yet the Soviet Government possessed by we know not what mad Marxist interpretation of the European situation, believing presumably in the "inevitable hostility of capitalist America" and seeing in the scattered garrisons of reluctant doughboys the vanguards of an imperialist attack, have perpetrated the crowning crime and folly of putting arms back into the hands of the Germans, Germans whose new-found Communism is a mask for yesterday's Nazism, Germans who find in the mass marching, the slogans, the organized hatred and the party discipline of the new East German *Bereitschaften* an exact resurrection of their former tyranny. The Western Powers must now, however reluctantly, include in their military calculations the fact of a small mobile army in Eastern Germany, not yet heavily armed but receiving the preliminary training necessary for the handling of larger weapons.

The situation is all the more disturbing in that it almost exactly resembles the development of the crisis in Korea. In Korea as in Germany, the Russians frustrated the attempts to achieve unification between the different zones of occupation. In Korea—as in Germany—the first aim of Russian policy has been to create a military machine. In Korea—as in Germany—the Western half remained virtually disarmed. The Western Powers have, therefore, at least to take into account the possibility that the resemblance will be carried further. The Communists in Eastern Germany already claim to speak for the whole community and denounce the authority of the Federal Government at Bonn. Is it so difficult to take the next step and decide to put an end to that authority by force? Local sabotage and unrest have already been decreed. May not the East German *Bereitschaften* at some convenient stage cross the zonal frontier on the pretext of "unifying the country and ending civil war"?

Here, apparently, is the situation in which the Korean debacle might be most exactly repeated. Many people draw from it the conclusion that the Western Powers should instantly respond by arming the Western Germans. Otherwise, they claim, Western Germany will either be overrun or the Allies themselves will have to do the fighting while Soviet Russia looks on, quietly reinforcing the Eastern side. The problem of a German army will be discussed later, but, in the short run, it is not decisive. The supply of arms to any Western force will be scarce in the next year or so. It would be foolish to give weapons to Germans while French and British and American soldiers go without, and since the garrisons maintained by the Western Powers in Western Germany should in any case be strong enough to meet a possible Soviet offensive, they should be able to make short work of any attack made by the still lightly armed East German forces, and, indeed, to clear Eastern Germany of them before the fighting ceased. To say so much is enough to show that Soviet Russia could only with great difficulty stay aloof from such a conflict. Once the East Germans were defeated, it would have the choice of seeing Germany united under a free government or of sending in its own troops. It should therefore be clear to Russia from the start that any attempt to foster civil war in Germany would lead almost inevitably to general conflict.

With Eastern Germany, we reach the end of the list of potential areas of "aggression by proxy." Once the Far East is left behind, there is almost no place where a Communist attack can be launched in the certainty that the Soviet Union will not be directly involved. The area of danger lies in Southeast Asia and even there, the outlook, though desperate, is not hopeless. The extent, therefore, to which Russia can wear down the West by engaging them in exhausting struggles with its satellites while it retains its own strength unimpaired, should not be exaggerated. It is a tiresome rather than a fatal fact. Certainly it is not one which the Western Powers, with their marked superiority of mobilizable resources, cannot face. Defeatism, not defeat, may be their real danger here.

The dual responsibility of Western defense—the building of a line in Europe and the containment of the Soviet periphery—is a possible one. It does not demand of the Western Powers efforts beyond their physical capacity or their ability to plan and produce. The question remains on what scale their effort should be undertaken. It is clearly not a matter of total mobilization. At the height of the struggle with Hitler, 50 to 60 per cent of the resources of the United States and of Britain were devoted to the waging of war and in some ways, such a position presented fewer problems to the military and political planners than the more delicate task of catering for both effective defense and for normal civilian life within the same economy. In the war effort, the minimum with which civil life could be carried on had to be established. Over and above that, everything could then be devoted to the war effort. No such simple scale of priorities exists now. Soviet Russia is not fully mobilized. Its satellites are not mobilized. Between them they have achieved a very great predominance of military strength, but the Soviet Union's expenditure on armaments does not apparently amount to much more than 13 per cent of its national income. Would a corresponding percentage in the Western world put it in an effective posture of defense?

Before the Korean war sounded the alarm, the percentages spent by the Atlantic powers were considerably less.[1] Since then, however, both the United States and the United Kingdom have announced programs that bring their annual expenditure on armaments up to well above 10 per cent of their national income.[2] Given the differences in national in-

[1] *Percentages of national income spent on defense 1949–50*

| | | | |
|---|---|---|---|
| United Kingdom | 7.4 | Sweden | 3.6 |
| Netherlands | 6.1 | Canada | 3.0 |
| United States | 5.9 | Switzerland | 2.7 |
| Turkey | 5.8 | Belgium | 2.5 |
| France | 5.0 | Norway | 2.5 |
| Italy | 3.8 | Denmark | 1.9 |

*Source:* Bank of International Settlements

[2] The British are to spend at an annual rate of about £1,133 million for the next three years. The American expenditure for 1950–51 has risen from $13 billion to $23 billion with an additional $5 billion for allies overseas. President Truman has forecast the figure of $30 billion for 1951–52 and in later years as well.

come between Russia and the West, it must presumably be assumed that the United States and its allies can produce very much more in the way of weapons and supplies from any given percentage of their national income than can the Russians. On this basis, it would seem that the new level would permit the West to establish an effective defense *vis-à-vis* the Soviet Union fairly speedily. The Western Powers are not preparing for an attack. They do not need the superiority of three to one which, for safety, a potential aggressor must command. For this reason, if the Soviet Union chooses to turn the West's restoration of minimal defenses into a challenge to an arms race, the strain upon the Russian economy would be infinitely greater than upon the West and might well be one which sane leaders would hesitate to undertake.

These are points upon which a layman cannot write with any certainty. The percentage which has been chosen as the proper basis for Western rearmament has, one may hope, been calculated in the light of a clear assessment of what is needed to hold Russian ambitions in check. There is a disturbing hint in British plans that the rate has been fixed not on the basis of what is necessary but of what is the most that can be done without upsetting anything else. The increased spending of some £300 million a year will not apparently interfere with any present plans. It is supposed—with possibly undue optimism—merely to absorb the expected rate of improvement in productivity and output. If an effective position of defense can be built up by this means, the British people—and their allies—have no grounds for uneasiness. Yet it would be a poor service to a community to give it the instruments of better living—the schools, the hospitals, the industrial investment—but leave it without the means of defending these good things. It may be difficult to determine what is "enough" to hold back aggression. But no other calculation should be used as the basis of plans for rearmament.

This consideration is all the more urgent in that our adversaries at least do not make any such mistake. The Soviet Union, incomparably a poorer state than many in the West, has consistently devoted a higher proportion of its resources to defense. More of its precious wealth, which might have gone into raising living standards and expanding consumption, have been poured into tanks and guns and aircraft. Moreover, a higher part of the expenditure devoted to military purposes finds its way into the actual munitions of war. The canteens, the book rooms, the USO, the ice-cream landing craft, the general maintenance of near-civilian standards of pay and comfort which absorb so large a share of defense expenditure in the West have little or no counterpart in the Soviet Union. That this is so is due in part to the more primitive conditions prevailing in Russia, in part to the greater discipline which an absolute dictatorship can impose, in part to the idealistic disregard for comfort a crusading army sometimes achieves. But it may also be due to a shrewd military calculation that once an infantryman is in the field, he would prefer a good anti-tank gun by his hand to the certainty of finding the works of William Shakespeare at his base.

If, therefore, the Soviet Union is prepared to devote a higher percentage of its national product to armament and also continues to spend more of its military budget directly upon the weapons of war, can the Western Powers be absolutely certain that a smaller percentage spent in the West really meets their urgent needs? This is a calculation which no layman can make. On the one hand is the fact that the Western Powers enjoy a larger national income and that their arming is essentially defensive. In theory, they can therefore afford less. On the other hand is the greater proportion of national income allotted to arms in Russia and the Soviet Government's ability to devote more of that percentage to actual armament. The answer cannot be given dogmatically without full information, but it can be said dogmatically that it would be folly to err on the modest side.

# 9

## *Defense Is Not Enough*

THE problem of the proper scale of defense expenditure cannot, however, be solved by plunging in the other direction and devoting such a share of the nation's resources to armaments that the civilian economy is threatened with collapse. The West is not practicing total war. It is practicing containment and this policy demands staying power as well as strength. It is a policy the Western Powers must be able to imagine still in operation, if necessary, twenty and thirty years hence. Clearly, therefore, the expenditure on defense must be one that can be reasonably carried year after year without threatening economic breakdown. If there is a lower limit fixed by the scale of Russia's preparations, there is an upper one fixed by the need to maintain, over a long period, social and economic stability in the West.

With communism as the adversary, the need is far more urgent than it would be in other less ideological struggles. In theory, at least, the Soviet Government hopes to achieve far more by the decay and collapse of the non-Communist world than by frontal attacks upon it. If only this doctrine of capitalist decline did not include the refinement that Communists may attempt to accelerate disaster by well-judged interventions, one might hold that the Kremlin would in any circumstances wait for disaster to occur in the West and not risk any struggle before Western collapse was an accomplished fact. Unluckily, belief in the effectiveness of giving history a helping hand has taken deep root in Moscow. Signs of weakness in the non-communist half, signs of economic instability and contradiction are the signals not for confident non-intervention but for hopeful little shoves such as North Korea administered to its neighbor. If a policy of defense in the West went hand in hand with economic instability and social confusion, the one would cancel out the other. It is the essence of the Soviet challenge to proceed on two fronts—on the military and the social—and to hope that the two will interact to the Communists' advantage.

Since the war, the Communists appear to have pinned their chief faith upon three developments—the first has been mentioned already, a resounding slump in the United States, spreading alarm and despondency through every market in the free world. The second has been the discontent and resentment of sections of the European working class at their want of status, their low standards and their general lack of a constructive future under the weary and unenterprising capitalism of such countries as Italy and France. The third, and, since the victory of Mao Tse-tung, perhaps the chief, has been the deep revolt of Asia against subordinate status and abysmal poverty in a world still partly dominated by the great nations of the West.

Of the reality both of unrest in Asia and of discouragement among sections of the European working class there can be no doubt at all. The Chinese Communist victory or the three-year struggle of the Indonesians against the Dutch are evidence enough of the one; the numbers voting for the Communist Party in Italy and France—a figure amounting to about 25 per cent of the electorate—confirms the other. It may seem that the hope of a slump in the Western world has seemed fairly wide of the mark but even here, for a short time in 1949, it seemed that this Communist prediction was to be realized as well. The decline in American business activity was small, its repercussions on the world economy disproportionally large. The nations' suddenly intensified hunger for dollars started a new run on sterling—the one currency which was in supply and oversupply throughout the world—and this in turn precipitated the crisis of general devaluation in the autumn of 1949. Had the decline in the American economy continued, there is no doubt at all that the rest of the free world would have joined in the same downward spiral with falling production, falling standards and rising unemployment. In 1949, for the first time in Europe, there was a significant increase in unemployment not only in Western Germany and Italy with their special problems of overpopulation, but in normal economies such as Belgium. Fortunately, as we know, the American recession proved to be the merest wobble in the ascending line of American progress, and before the winter had passed, a renewed wave of prosperity carried the United States to new records of national wealth and swept the world upward on its flowing tide. In the second quarter of 1950, the British trading system—the sterling area—which covers about 50 per cent of world trade, achieved for the first time since the war a credit in its trade with the dollar area on current account.

This, then, was the position in the free world when the Korean War came to shatter the illusion of "normal times." The vital question now is the extent to which the decision to rearm and make containment a reality decreases or increases the chances of social and economic stability in the West. The Communist hope after all must still be that steadily worsening economic difficulties in the West will finally produce a state of such unsteady balance that a well-directed Communist lunge will bring the whole structure to the ground. What basis have they for their hopes? Have the West's social and economic prospects deteriorated as a result of their new and realistic approach to defense? Or has realism given them better ballast and a better chance?

In the first place, it can be said with absolute certainty that the Communists have contrived to compel the West to avoid the crisis to which, in Communist theory and perhaps in actual fact as well, they are most prone—the slump brought on by a slackening of demand in the economy. Marx's classical depression was brought about in capitalist communities by the overproduction of goods. In such societies, he argued, the workers never received enough purchasing power to catch up with the growing productivity of the machines. Their needs were never matched with enough effective demand, in the shape of high wages. Periodically, a glut of unsalable merchandise would appear in the midst of a community hungering for all manner of goods, but too poor to purchase them. Nor can we hold that history has altogether nullified Marx's analysis, first made as far back as 1848. Even if the recurrent crises of the Western world have hardly conformed to his simplified explanations and simple patterns, "overproduction" has nevertheless appeared in the past and goods have been destroyed in the midst of want. It was, moreover, one of the achievements of economic thinking in the thirties, under the guidance of Lord Keynes, to discover that it was in fact possible for capitalist society to settle down at a level of consumption much less than its ability to produce goods would warrant, since no natural forces of equilibrium compelled a free economy to produce as much as it could.

An armaments program is, however, the most potent and the most straightforward creator of demand. It is also a curious kind of demand. It is usually insatiable and yet no glut follows on the ordinary market. The process which normally checks expanding production—the outstripping of demand by supply—hardly holds good when the market is the demands of war. Either the goods are expended in combat or grow obsolete and are replaced or they rot, without anyone caring, in ammunition dumps and tank parks. The nations could, of course, maintain demand by throwing an equivalent amount of metal and machinery into the sea. The point here is that the appetite of an arms program for the products of industry is such that slumps springing from a slackening in demand do not normally accompany or follow a policy of rearmament. Now that the free world has been compelled to the decision to look to its defenses, it is likely to avoid the evil to which in the past it has seemed most prone. The North Koreans and their Soviet masters, by shaking the West out of its lethargy and complacency, have banished, in the short run at least, the prospect to which they pinned most hope—the general Western slump.

The reaction of rearmament policy upon the other two sources of Western weakness—working-class discontent in Europe and Asian claims and aspirations—is not so reassuring. In the three largest states in Western Europe (France, Italy and Western Germany) it is only in the last year that prewar standards of production have been reached. In all three, the population has grown in the last ten years and in none of them has the war had the effect that is observable in the United States and Britain—that of increasing the share of the national income going to the workers. On the contrary, a recent survey of comparative incomes in France suggests that while the peasants and the commercial classes have gained a larger part of the country's national output, the share going to the workers has fallen markedly and would have fallen even further had not a lavish system of family allowances been introduced after the war.

Compared with the thirties, the average working-class family in these three key countries, France, Italy and Western Germany, tends to find conditions more difficult—one factor which helps to explain the remarkable hold the Communist Party retains on the loyalty of the workers and would no doubt command in Western Germany as well, did not so many workers know at firsthand of the infinitely worse conditions prevailing in the Soviet Zone. It is only in the last eighteen months that prospects have begun to improve in France and Germany while in Italy a policy of continuous deflation has swelled the ranks of the unemployed and the underemployed ever since it was introduced in 1947.

An armament program could have the effect of taking up some of the slack of unemployment in Germany and Italy, and, incidentally, in Belgium. But in France there is almost full employment and to produce armaments means diverting men and machines from the production of other things. And in all these countries, where civilian needs are so urgent and the conditions of so many workers still unsatisfactory, the diversion of industry from civilian goods to armaments can mean an end to the improvements of the last year and a new fall in standards. The margin of available goods and raw materials is too narrow for any great transfer from the civilian to the military sector to be absorbed unnoticed in the economy at large. More guns must mean less butter in countries where many people only see butter once a week as it is.

This is not the only difficulty. The degree of recovery achieved so far in Western Europe has been made possible by American vision and generosity in the shape of the Marshall Plan. None of the countries within the Plan is self-sufficient. All depend for the steady functioning of their economies upon their capacity to export and to buy abroad. In 1947, as we have seen, their ability to buy essential raw materials in the United States had almost come to an end. Had not the American people come to their aid with free grants of dollars their whole economic system would have been brought almost to a standstill by lack of grain and coal and vital machinery. Since those dangerous months, the Marshall Plan has done two things—it has enabled Western Europe to continue its essential purchases in the United States and it has revived in Europe an industrial system capable of exporting goods all over the world. As Europe's ability to sell everywhere has increased, its direct dependence upon the United States has declined in the same measure. Marshall aid has been reduced from nearly 6 billion in 1948 to just under 4 billion in 1949 and to 3 billion in 1950. During the same period the value of Western European exports has risen in spite of devaluation from $7,700 million in the first half of 1948 to $8,850 million in the first half of 1950.

This process of restoring to Europe the capacity to pay its way in the world and to secure from the United States and elsewhere the goods it needs to maintain its economic life is not, however, complete. Even the original planning of Marshall aid did not expect the purposes of the Plan to be achieved before the end of 1951. Moreover, in spite of Europe's phenomenally quick recovery of production in the last two years, it is now generally recognized that some of its deeper problems of economic adjustment can hardly be solved within the Plan's proposed time limit. In particular, Europe's future relations with the dollar area are still uncertain, and in 1950 even the most optimistic surveys spoke of a "dollar gap" after 1951, of between one and two billion dollars a year. When the Korean war began, the Marshall Plan constituted highly successful but nevertheless unfinished business.

Western rearmament cuts across the orderly procedures of the Plan. One can dismiss for the time being the risk of a "dollar shortage." Congress has already voted 5 billion dollars for its allies' defense and not all this allocation will necessarily arrive in the shape of finished arms. Some of the equipment will be manufactured in Western Europe and may be paid for in dollars. Dollars are also being made available for extra purchases in the United States since the raw materials and the machinery which are essential to any rapid expansion of Western defense can only be secured in America. Where the arms effort does complicate Western Europe's international position is in cutting down its ability to maintain vital exports to other countries. The engineering industries which are most immediately affected by plans for rearmament are also the backbone of Europe's export drive. When so great an effort has been made to rebuild trading connections broken during the five years of war, it is bitter indeed to lose them again within a year or so of their re-establishment. The dilemma is particularly painful in Britain whose dependence upon exports for the very food the people eat is absolute. Nor is it simply a question of inconvenience and disappointment. If Germany and Italy are to put men back to work on armaments, these workers must receive adequate wages. They will therefore begin to consume more than they did before when they were unemployed and their demand will increase the need for more imports at a time when ability to export is being diminished. There is thus a double risk to be met in Europe. The first is the reduction of standards which must follow from the direct diversion of civilian production to military purposes. The second is the indirect reduction that can follow upon a decline in the country's capacity to export. If either consequence were to bear down too heavily upon the poorer sections of the community—those who by definition are least able to bear the strain—communism might find a new entry point of frustration and misery.

However, it is in Asia that the Communists must surely believe their best hopes to lie. There is no question here of the need for rearmament cutting across and complicating a constructive policy upon which the Western world has already embarked. The cost of rearmament may have a much more tragic effect. It may provide one more reason for not having a policy at all. The Western Powers have not yet faced the realities of the Asian scene with anything like the courage and open-mindedness that has made the European Recovery Program an outstanding act of international co-operation. So far there has been little more than sporadic talk and sporadic interest. At the beginning of 1949, President Truman excited the world with his announcement of a "bold, new program" of technical assistance to backward areas—his Point IV—but eighteen months of deliberation have persuaded a reluctant Congress to do no more than vote some $35 million to meet Asia's infinitude of need. Individual Americans have spoken more boldly. Senator McMahon appealed for a global plan of aid extending over the years and putting behind economic development the sums which would otherwise be spent on suicidal preparations for war. Mr. Walter Reuther, the American labor leader, has appealed for a development program which could pledge some $13 billion a year to raising the standards and the productivity of the masses living beyond the privileged Atlantic ring. The United Nations has launched —with unanimous support—its own $85 million program of technical assistance. Britain has spent some $400 million upon colonial welfare and development, and, as we have seen, made large sums available to the new Dominions in Asia. Australia has taken the initiative in proposing a Commonwealth scheme of mutual economic assistance and at the first conference held to discuss the scheme—at Sydney—a sum of £8 million was set aside to be spent at once upon urgent technical needs and to provide a symbol of the greater aid that would follow. Finally, the Labour Party has proposed, in its 1950 program, the introduction of a World Plan for Mutual Aid.

Yet if these tentative moves and proposals have been made, equally strong forces move in the opposite direction. The appalling waste of American money in the hands of Nationalists in China, the swallowing up of aid with nothing to show for it in the Philippines, the rebukes the ECA authorities had to deliver to the South Korean Government on its handling of Marshall aid have helped to build up a school of thought that is completely disillusioned over the effectiveness of large-scale assistance provided by governments. This mood has reinforced a belief already held in the United States as a result of various disastrous experiences in the 1920's—the belief that it is unsafe and unwise to lend to governments. A large part of American business opinion holds that foreign lending should be the responsibility of private enterprise—as it has been in the past—and that the investment should be made in good commercial ventures whose profitability can be reasonably assessed. It is largely in deference to this belief that the International Bank for Reconstruction and Development, which depends in part on the confidence of American leaders in its soundness and solvency, has tended to confine its investment to single operations which offer "good risks" and has been unwilling to lend to governments for general purposes of development.

One fundamental misapprehension underlies this whole cautious Western approach. It is that in dealing with the Asian situation today, economics and "business as usual" are enough. To say so much does not mean, naturally, that measures and controls to ensure the proper use of funds are unnecessary. On the contrary, the misuse of economic aid, by individuals and by governments, is one of the greatest obstacles any program for Asia has to surmount, and we shall have to return later to the problem of the proper methods of oversight and guidance. The reason why the purely economic approach is insufficient lies in the first place in a profound change in world conditions in this century. The days in which the opening up of new resources and the adjustment of old economies to new circumstances could be made by private movements of capital alone have to a large extent vanished. No one will deny that private investment, which was responsible for the opening up of the United States, of much of the British Commonwealth and South America and of parts of Asia itself, achieved remarkable results and created for many long years an expanding world economy. But that expansion belongs to that fortunate century during which the natural forces of uncontrolled and unguided economic interest did really appear to be achieving not only the individual but the common good. The background was one of world-wide peace, of low taxation, of infinitesimal social responsibilities to workers or colonial peoples, to a general tradition of governmental nonintervention. In this open world through which the tides of wealth could ebb and flow almost unimpeded, private initiative could successfully bear the main responsibility for opening up backward areas.

Yet there was another side to the nineteenth century's coin of expansion and prosperity—the fact of exploitation at home and abroad, the neglect of the masses, the irrationality of slump and boom, the despair bred of unemployment—in a word, the bitter underside of the prosperous Victorian world which Marx described, analyzed and synthesized in the theory of Communist revolution that has exploded and expanded through the world ever since. The reaction of the West to the darker aspects of the capitalist achievement has been the growth of taxation, the greater distribution of profits through social and colonial welfare, the intervention by governments to safeguard—by tariffs and quotas and controls—firms against bankruptcy and workers against unemployment and farmers and peasants against low prices. The reaction on the Marxist side has been to preach revolt to the workers at home and the colonial peoples abroad and to offer them liberation and bread if they will cast off their own masters or the colonial rulers from the West. These two reactions—Western and Marxist—have come together to make the old economic approach to the development of backward areas impracticable in our modern world. Too many controls and barriers and imposts introduced by Western governments impede the free search for profit. Too many claims and hopes and rights demanded by the Asian peoples stand in the way of development by Western private enterprise. If no other driving power were harnessed to the economic expansion of the East, some investments—for instance, in oil—would no doubt continue on a wide scale, producing genuinely commercial products. But the first needs of Asia—seed and fertilizer for the peasant, electricity for the land, roads, transport and public utilities (all of which, in earlier years, Western capital was ready to provide) would go by default. In a word, the old nineteenth-century identification of economic and public interest has been disastrously weakened in the last 30 years. The yardstick of profitability alone no longer measures Asia's needs or its potential growth.

From all this follows another reason why economics are not enough. The Western Powers do not face in Asia a normal peaceful scene waiting for orderly development. They face a battlefield in which a vast ideological struggle is being fought out—a war which is a war indeed even if it is still localized and may remain so. No one, however, fights a war by economic rule of thumb. We do not ask ourselves how many tanks or aircraft we can afford. We ask how many are needed to contain the enemy. Equally, in the mortally threatened continent of Asia, the only criteria to apply today are those of political warfare. What sort of assurances of aid will keep Pandit Nehru of India, Mr. Liaquat Ali Khan of Pakistan, Mr. Sennanyake of Ceylon, Mr. Hatta of Indonesia, President Quirino of the Philippines upright on their feet against the ceaseless pressure of Asian discontent and Communist propaganda? If these men knew that in framing their plans for economic development and social welfare they could count on an annual Western fund of assistance of a few billion dollars, is it not certain that their plans would be bolder, their assurance more steady, their confidence more serene? But what is the prospect before them now? Simply that Western aid is highly problematical and that even the hope of it may be swallowed up either in a Western arms program or else in a Western slump. It is almost impossible for men in the West to realize what unstable partners they appear to the new independent rulers of Asia. Equally it is almost impossible for them to realize what an immense political consolidation could follow from a Western decision to announce and implement a fifty-year development program for the free nations of Asia.

There will be many to say at this point, "But we cannot afford it." Leaving on one side, however, the question whether or not "afford" is the right yardstick to apply to what is essentially a situation of warfare, one may say with certainty that the cost of an effective development plan is not exorbitant. Will any Western statesman really declare that political peace in Asia is not worth—what? One per cent of the West's combined national incomes? Such a sum—perhaps five billion dollars—is already larger than any to which the free peoples of Asia have so far dared to aspire. It is not much more than the investment which, before the First World War, the industrial nations of Europe used to pump out into the outside world. Are our systems so much less productive today? Is our confidence so much more dim? A sum for Asian development far exceeding anything else that has been planned so far absorbs only a small part of the West's capacity to produce wealth. The economics of aid are almost derisory compared with the burdens the West has easily borne over and over again in the past.

Unhappily this economic issue may fail even to be discussed at this stage. The whole issue is likely to go by default simply because no general acceptance of the need for expansion in Asia has yet made its way into current Western thought. The vision has not been kindled. The idea makes little claim on the imagination of the West. The result is all too likely to be the flat statement: "We cannot afford it" and the need for an armaments program makes such a reaction all the more probable. We have not yet the statesmanship to see that the two programs are simply different facets of the same Western need—the need for strength.

Let us suppose, however, that the Western Powers do determine to flank their armament program with bold policies for maintaining social stability in Europe and for building up the economic potential of Asia. Politically such a decision would exorcise the worst dangers that face them now. Economically it would banish, for the time being at least, the Communists' continuing hope of a general Western depression. But the Western Powers would face a new economic risk. Indeed, they face it simply by embarking on an armament program, quite apart from any further commitments. The risk is the opposite risk to that of a slump, the risk that too many demands may be made upon the West's power to produce goods and that their combined economies will be unable to withstand the strain. The risk is, in short, the risk of inflation.

# 10

## *The Risk of Inflation*

ALL economies still have to take as their starting point the fact that there is not enough to go round. Not all the advances of modern science and modern technology have yet contrived to change the fact that in any modern community there are more wants than there are means to satisfy them. At any one time, an economy—a vast economy like that of the United States or a small economy such as Denmark—has only a certain amount of raw materials and manpower and machine power at its disposal in the form either of domestic production or of the imports it can obtain from abroad. These resources, which combine to make up the whole supply of goods and services available in an economy, can be increased, of course, but not all at once. In the past, a normal rate of expansion in industrial economies has not been much above 3 per cent a year. At any given moment, therefore, there are definite limits to what an economy can supply in response to all the demands that are likely to be made upon it.

Effective demand—need backed by purchasing power—takes many forms in a modern economy. There is the immediate day to day consumption of goods by the ordinary citizen. There is also, and increasingly, the consumption of goods indulged in by governments. Both private and public bodies also invest resources in permanent buildings, in plant and machinery, in stocks and inventories, all designed to expand future consumption at the cost of diverting some resources from immediate use. The economy almost invariably must provide exports as well. These are the main headings of demand and an economy is balanced and stable if the supplies available from domestic production and imports are roughly equal to the claims coming on them for immediate use, for investment and for the export market.

The whole history of modern industrialism has shown how difficult it is to keep this balance. The failure may come on either side. Sometimes it is demand that slackens, goods become unsalable, profits vanish, firms reduce their output or close down, men are thrown out of work. This is the typical crisis of deflation. Equally it may be supply that proves too small and the phenomenon of "too much money chasing too few goods" sends prices soaring, starts wages off in a vain chase to catch up with them and creates the "wage-price spiral" which, more quickly than anything else, can disrupt all normal economic transactions by undermining people's confidence in their own currency. This is the typical crisis of inflation. In its one hundred and fifty years of development, industrial society has known both crises and known them with a certain monotonous regularity—that of boom and slump—but the fact that the two phenomena are frequent and well known and possibly more studied than any other characteristic piece of economic behavior does not mean that there is anything like agreement on how they are caused or how to control them or how stability can be maintained in an economy.

Since the war, for instance, particularly in Europe, a dispute has arisen between the supporters and opponents of controls and planning which turns, in essence, upon the twin issues of inflation and deflation. The supporters of a measure of planning maintain that government action is necessary to keep demand both for consumption and for investment high and stable. Only thus can all the resources of the community be fully employed and men kept at work. If in the process of maintaining demand some slight inflation takes place—in other words, if demand begins to outstrip available supplies—then controls can be used to keep it in check. Licenses and permits can prevent the draining off of raw materials to inessential industries, limitations on wages and dividends will hold back the wage-price spiral and price controls, coupled if necessary by rationing, can keep the prices of essential goods from racing upward.

These views are strenuously attacked by the opponents of control. They argue that "artificial stimulants" to demand such as government encouragement of private consumption or public sponsoring of expanded investment must always lead to inflation and the cure is thus worse than the disease. Inflation moreover removes all incentive, they say, to hard work and competitive management. If everything can be sold, why bother to produce it well and cheaply? Meanwhile, the community foots the bill in the shape of expensive and shoddy work. Inflation also reduces the incentive to sell abroad and, by lowering quality, the ability to do so. At the same time, it increases a nation's tendency to import goods to satisfy abundant internal demand. The process of selling less and buying more abroad has very definite limits—the reserves of foreign currency held by the Central Bank. A "run on the reserves" is usually a signal of internal inflation and can bring a trading nation to bankruptcy. All this, the opponents of control claim, is a high price to pay for overstimulating demand. Better a little deflation with falling prices, stable money, competitive conditions and rising foreign reserves, even if the cost is some unemployment.

This is not an academic argument. It has run fiercely through every phase of the Marshall Plan, and Europe itself is divided between those who have sought to maintain demand even at some risk of inflation (Great Britain, the Scandinavian countries and Holland) and those who have tended to consider deflation the lesser of the two evils (Western Germany, Italy and Belgium and to a more limited extent, France). But there is one point at least upon which both can agree—that the debate over the rival risks of inflation and deflation belongs essentially to the settled days of peace.

Once the first and overwhelming duty of every state is to look to its defenses and to divert a quite considerable part of its resources into armaments, one danger alone is to be feared, the danger of inflation. No form of production is better calculated to force demand far beyond the limits of supply. Weapons do not satisfy any civilian demand. They are abstracted from the economy the moment they are made. But wages and salaries are paid to those who produce them and this money is *not* abstracted from the economy. On the contrary, it circulates in the shape of active demand. Since long hours are often worked during periods of rearmament, the wages earned in time and overtime may be exceptionally high. The appetite of the arms factories for metals and machines and capital equipment of all sorts must also mean that for the time being there are less of these available for other forms of production and the output of goods destined to civilian consumption and investment is likely to fall. Ordinary supply thus falls still further at a time when there has been no slackening of demand. On the contrary, it may well have increased. Thus the classical definition of inflation—of monetary demand outstripping available supplies—is almost unavoidable in times of rearmament.

These are the general difficulties. They can be increased in particular countries by local circumstances. For instance, in 1939, in both Britain and the United States there was a considerable slack in the economy which could be taken up in the early stages of rearming. Both economies were "deflated," both had a considerable pool of unemployed workers, capital lying idle and relatively low tax rates. It was the fact that some ten million men were out of work in the United States in 1939 that goes some way to explain the economy's ability to increase both civilian and military consumption in the fantastic expansion achieved by 1944. But where an economy is already using all its resources to the full, a defense effort can be achieved only by transferring plant and workers from civilian goods to the making of weapons, and this transfer of men from productive work to output that is "sterilized" as far as civilian use is concerned must increase the risk of inflation.

Another difficulty is raised in countries which may have a slack in both manpower and in plant—men unemployed and machines standing idle—but do not produce locally the raw materials needed in the making of weapons and have not the foreign currency to buy the materials abroad. Germany and Italy today have millions unemployed and in both countries there is spare capacity. But they cannot embark unaided on the production of weapons. They cannot afford to import all the necessary materials nor have they the foreign exchange necessary to buy further civilian imports to satisfy the fresh demand of unemployed men once they are put to work and earn good wages. Another variant of this difficulty occurs throughout Western Europe. Civilian consumption depends precariously on the remarkable recovery of exports that has occurred since 1945. But if the engineering trades are in part to be switched to making weapons, exports will fall and with them the earnings necessary to buy goods overseas. Civilian supplies will fall and once again the risk of inflation will increase.

To what extent is the Atlantic community, on whom the chief strain of defense now falls, open to these various risks? Are they near full employment? Are there inflationary tendencies already at work in their economy? Have they any slack? Do they depend to a very great extent on imports? These are the questions that have to be answered before the capacity of the West to defend itself can be fairly assessed. The pivot of it all is, naturally, the economy of the United States. Its performance determines not only its own economic climate but that of the entire free world. The degree of American employment, the scale of America's foreign trade, the American price level have now become the dominant factors in every other economy. Like smaller ships following a great liner, they move up and down in its mighty wake. This has become true of the workings of the various economies in peacetime. It is infinitely more so of any joint effort of defense. The speed of much rearmament outside the United States depends upon the speed with which vital raw materials and machinery only procurable in the dollar area are released for use among America's allies. But this in turn depends upon the speed with which the United States is prepared to release materials, plant and manpower from civilian work.

That it is a question of "release" is proved by the fact that there is very little "slack" in the American economy. In June, 1950, when the blow fell in Korea, every economic index in the United States pointed to an exceptionally full employment of American resources. The gross national product (the total output of goods and services) was at a level of $267 billion, $100 billion higher than in 1939 and $3 billion higher than the previous peacetime record of 1948. The index of industrial production which had stood at 110 in 1939 was now 199. Employment, with 61,500,000 men and women at work, was higher than ever before and unemployment, which had risen a little in 1949—to the unconcealed delight of the Communist propagandists—fell to under 4 million. The production of a number of vital industrial products told the same tale. Steel, the crucial material of the modern economy in peace or war, was being produced at the rate of 100 million tons a year in June, 1950—the figure for 1939 had been 53 million—and this level represented the use of every steel-making plant to capacity and beyond it. Oil, the other sinew of war and peace, reached the annual rate of nearly 2 billion barrels a year. At the peak of the war effort in 1944, the figure had only been 1,600 million.

These tremendous figures of production and supply were being maintained by phenomenally high levels of investment and consumption. Investment was absorbing a large share of the national income because a variety of causes—the need to restore stocks depleted during the last war, to make good postponed maintenance and replacement, to keep abreast with new machines in the competitive drive and to make use of the new discoveries made in every field of science and technology—had kept investment well above the levels necessary in the eyes of the economists to maintain "high and stable employment." In the last year, largely to offset the slight recession which made itself felt in 1949, the government has reinforced the high level of demand by sponsoring and aiding an immense program of housing which spreads demand through every section of industry from the steel of the contractors down to the doormats and the frying pans. High wages and high profits have looked after personal consumption and government expenditure has competed with private spending to the tune of over $40 billion.

One thing, therefore, is obvious. There is not a great deal of slack in the economy. The claims of a new armaments program must be met to a great extent by diverting manpower and materials from present civilian production. Thus, while monetary demand will remain unchanged or increase, the amount of goods available to satisfy it must fall. The wages and the profits of the armament makers will compete with the purchasing power of the men in the civilian economy for cars and television sets and refrigerators and every sort of consumer goods. But such goods use the same materials and the same skills as tanks and trucks and radar equipment and as the materials are diverted to the defense effort, the price of the reduced supply of consumer goods will be forced up and the producers of these goods will compete all the more fiercely for the smaller supplies of steel and components and manpower available to make them. A sharp rise in prices, a sharp fall in the value of money, an increased cost of living—these would be classic danger signals of inflation, the inevitable consequences of maintaining demand and reducing supply in the American economy, if no steps were taken to offset them.

The risk is all the greater in that in 1950 there were already some signs that demand was getting the upper hand. In certain circumstances, for instance, an unbalanced budget can be a sign that too much demand is being created. If an economy is working at full stretch and, in the short run, no more supplies will come on the market if extra demand is created, to pump more purchasing power into the community simply increases the pressure of demand on existing supplies and forces prices upwards. A budget deficit at such times does create extra purchasing power because it means that the government is not cancelling out private purchasing power by taxation or by non-negotiable loans before it issues its own orders to industry. It is simply creating new money on its own.

In 1950, as we have seen, the American economy was producing more than ever before in its peacetime history. Yet there was a budget deficit of nearly $5 billion which threatened to increase to $15 billion as soon as the larger defense effort was approved. The sum of $15 billion may seem small in a national product of nearly $270 billion, but when an economy is at full stretch, it is the marginal effect, the last straw of demand on the camel's overloaded back of supply, that can set really dangerous inflationary movements into motion. The verdict on the American economy in 1950 must therefore be that the immensity of its productive achievement is no certain guarantee against the risk of inflation.

Admittedly there are some dangers that it does not run. No shortages of raw materials, only obtainable from abroad in return for precious foreign currency, will check its expansion. The dollar can buy anything, from one end of the world to the other. The only risk here is the level to which the prices of vital raw materials are being forced up in the world market by the pressure of buying for strategic needs. Nor, strictly, should a shortage of manpower hold America back. Quite apart from the 3 million unemployed and the annual entry of about a million new workers into employment, there is hardly a worker in the world who would not live under canvas and on army rations in return for the chance of working in the United States.

The picture is very different in the other central economy of the Western effort—that of Britain. Even if there were no external obstacles to financial stability, the dependence of the country upon external trade presents it with some frankly insoluble dilemmas. During World War II, all Britain's export markets were dislocated and its overseas investments lost. From 1945, a grim and sustained effort was necessary to divert goods from the hungry market at home and to send them overseas. In 1949, for instance, two-thirds of the passenger cars and half the commercial vehicles produced went to export. Two-fifths of all agricultural machinery, three-fifths of the internal combustion engines and a third of the machine tools went the same way. By 1950, this long effort, coupled with generous American aid, seemed to be on the verge of success. Britain's balance of payments on current account had been stabilized. Even with the dollar area, a small surplus had been earned. Unhappily for future national stability, the contribution made to this success by the key industries of a defense effort was crucial. The engineering trades, producing cars, tractors, engines and machine tools, are precisely those which are first called upon to switch their production to armaments. If the British Government decides to provide the necessary capacity for rearmament by cutting exports, the problem of the country's balance of payments will return to the center of the national stage, just as the approach to a solution was in sight. If the government cuts still further the supplies going to the home market, the risk of inflationary pressure will instantly increase.

It will do so all the more rapidly in that the British economy has lived on the verge of open inflation ever since 1945. The chief hallmark of British economic policy since the war has been to attempt almost every possible and desirable policy simultaneously. The national income has had to provide the resources to supply a rate of exports rising to 50 per cent above the prewar level, to maintain a level of investment amounting to about 19 per cent of the country's total resources, to supply complete social security—including a free health scheme—to build a million new homes, to provide the school buildings made necessary both by a higher school-leaving age and higher minimum standards, to provide over £400 million in food subsidies each year to keep down the price of the basic foods, to maintain larger armed forces than has ever been done before in peacetime, and to finance, largely by the release of sterling balances, a considerable part of Asian reconstruction. These are the chief items in a formidable list of demands upon the nation's resources. Not one of the expenditures has been undesirable in itself. In fact, so little are most of them a matter of dispute that they appear on the electoral programs of both great parties. But added all together they have created a steadily inflationary demand in the community which can be measured by phenomenally full employment—not more than 1.5 per cent of the insured population is out of work—and by a steady fall in the value of money. The devaluation of 1949 which reduced the pound sterling from $4 to $2.80 was in part the result of the war and all its losses and disorders. But it was also due to the steady pressure of inflation in the postwar years.

This pressure of inflation has been held in check in part by the assistance offered by the United States and in part by a system of very widespread domestic controls. The chief check has been a budget surplus achieved by a rate of taxation which in 1950 handed over 40 per cent of the private citizen's earnings to the government to be spent for him. Controls are maintained over new capital issues and a system of licenses regulates the consumption of vital raw materials and has been used vigorously to encourage the drive for exports. Exchange control has been carried over from the war and movements of capital abroad are regulated. This general picture has been completed by a series of voluntary agreements between government and both sides of industry "freezing" wages and limiting dividends and thus cutting down the amount of income available for private spending. By all these means, severe inflation has been checked and the economy has been kept in some degree of balance.

This is the economy which must support defense expenditure of at least another £300 to £400 million a year. Far from a slack existing, the general state of the economy is one of extreme extension. The pressure of demand on available supplies is already intense, the risk of inflation already present. A defense effort which maintains or even expands demand but depletes available supplies cannot fail to increase the danger. Moreover, in the case of Britain, the risk is not only an internal risk. If the defense efforts drastically reduce the country's capacity to export, the old haunting problem of the balance of payments will return with new urgency.

So much for the two pivotal economies of the Western world. In Europe itself, the problems presented by an overextended economy are still acute in Norway and to a lesser extent in Holland. France has not completely conquered the inflation that has undermined its economy since the war—in spite of a startling recovery of stability in 1949—and its proposed defense expenditure of some 2,000 billion francs (about £2 billion) spread over the next three years must be found from a budget which is already in deficit and from a country whose dislike of taxation is proverbial.

A genuine slack can be said to exist only in the economies of Western Germany, Italy and Belgium. In all three countries, there are men out of work and factories standing idle. In both Germany and Italy, it is true, the degree of unemployment is due in part to special causes—to a very high birth rate in Italy, to the stream of refugees arriving from the east in Germany, but in all three countries, the governments have also practiced policies of quite severe deflation, cutting down governmental expenditure, discouraging private investment and attempting by these means to lower prices and stabilize their currencies. But these are the exception, not the rule. Generally throughout the Atlantic world, the first phase of rearmament must increase the risk of inflation.

The problem should not, however, be allowed to become a bogy. Too often, particularly in Europe, public opinion conjures up a terrifying picture of millions of paper notes paid out to buy half a pound of butter, of a currency that has become completely valueless and has swept away into the abyss the savings and the fixed incomes of the great mass of the people. Such an inflation did, indeed, occur in Germany and in Central Europe after the First World War and many of the worst evils in the interwar years, including even the rise of Hitler, must be attributed to the horrific shock which inflation dealt to normally a stable and responsible group—the middle class. But since 1924 there has been another great war even more appalling in its destructiveness and in the dislocations it has brought about. One has only to compare the Ruhr of 1919 with the bombed, ruined, flattened Ruhr of 1945 to see to what extent the second disaster exceeded the first. Yet the financial consequences of the second conflict have been much more amenable to orderly control. Compared with the ruin and collapse accompanying the first German inflation, the dislocations of Western Germany to which the currency reform of 1948 put an efficient end seems almost mild. And Germany was the extreme example. Elsewhere, in spite of strong inflationary pressure, monetary stability has on the whole been restored, the vertiginous rise in prices checked and confidence revived in the currency.

The reason is quite simply that government, financial advisers and economists know considerably more about the techniques of financial policy and behavior of inflating and deflating economies than was the case twenty and thirty years ago. Although anyone looking back on the years since the war may find them full of misunderstandings, disputes, acrimonious accusations and apparently unbridgeable gulfs of economic policy, the fact remains that by the time that the Communists struck their blow in Korea, the immediate consequences of the last war had been largely banished from the Western world as a result of intelligent local action and a high degree of international co-operation. The risk of inflation had been very much lessened and, by one means or another, the governments had found their way back to a reasonable level of stability. Having done it once, they need not fear any lack of ability to do it again.

Nor is the problem of the same order of magnitude. If containment is the effective and sufficient answer to the Soviet's restless probing ambition, the Western Powers are not required to face the disaster of a general war. The degree of mobilization they require probably lies at a level of about 15 per cent of their national incomes. At the height of the last war, the United States was devoting 50 per cent of its resources to the war effort, Britain 60 per cent. Such a diversion of supply from the civilian economy was bound to create the strongest possible inflationary pressure and one which could only be held in check by the most drastic means. The risk which the Western world runs now is on a much smaller scale and more moderate controls should be sufficient.

There is no secret about the fundamental aim of all regulations and restraints introduced to check inflation and the more exactly they fulfill their aim, the smoother is the development of the economy. The aim is balance—balance between the purchasing power in the hands of the community and the amount of civilian supplies available once priority has been given to armaments. Since it is the essence of a defense effort to destroy this balance, the government, backed by the co-operation and good sense of the community, has to take steps to restore it. Once the scale of rearmament has been judged and powers taken to ensure that all the needed materials and manpower are available for the defense effort, the government has a reasonable idea of the manpower and materials that have been locked up in the defense effort and therefore of the amount of surplus demand for civilian goods the program is likely to create. If there is a large "slack" in the economy, the disturbance may not be large, but, as we have seen, only in Belgium is there much slack that can be taken in. Everywhere else, the defense effort impinges immediately upon civilian production and civilian demand.

The first step is therefore to cut down other less necessary expenditure. Wherever an economy is operating at full stretch—and this is, in general, the case in the West—there are inevitably a number of desirable but postponable projects upon which the public would like to embark. Their priority has to fall. Given the fact that throughout Europe about 20 per cent of the nations' resources are being devoted to capital goods—a very high percentage compared with the prewar level—a part of this investment can be diverted to defense. Housing, school building, road building, the re-equipment of factories and transport, can be re-examined in the light of the overriding need for security. Such postponement is particularly needed in economies such as that of Britain, in which the level of taxation has remained virtually at its wartime height and there is not much "slack" to be taken up in the citizen's pocket. In the United States, one of President Truman's first moves was to restrict the credit available to those who were anxious to buy houses and other desirable goods on the installment plan. A housing program is clearly a keen competitor for many of the materials and skills needed on a defense effort and in both the United States and Britain, it is a part of the nation's expenditure that could reasonably be reduced. Indeed, in Britain, government spending has been so lavish that a general cut in most departments would seem an essential preliminary to the addition of a defense program to all the other claims on British resources.

These cuts in general expenditure will all help to reduce the pressure of demand on manpower and materials and will release both to the armaments industries. But it is quite possible that the cuts will be insufficient and that rising prices and hot competition for supplies will be warning signals that there is still too much effective demand for goods pressing in upon the economy. Governments would then be obliged to use direct means of reducing the purchasing power circulating among their people. In some parts of Europe, income taxes are relatively low, the contribution made by the wealthier groups disproportionately small and much revenue is raised indirectly. Ideally, higher direct taxation and even in some cases a capital tax would be both sufficient and equitable. It is unlikely, however, that new efforts would be any more successful than the old in persuading taxpayers to meet their obligations fully. Both France and Italy have reshaped their system of taxation in the hopes of making it simpler and more effective. It will take longer to build up the social sense that accepts the "discipline of taxes." Some experts have suggested that a general European defense tax, levied by each government and given separate and special publicity would bring in a return that few administrations acting alone could achieve. The expedient is worth trying, but it possibly overrates the appeal of the European idea to those whom patriotism has never touched in the past.

In the two economies on which the chief burden of rearmament will fall—the United States in the very first place, and Britain behind—the government's ability to collect taxes is, however, great. Nor is there any doubt that the peoples, however despondently, will accept the need for high taxation if inflation is the alternative. An increase in corporate taxes was voted in the United States within two months of the Korean war. In Britain, however, increases in taxation would be tolerated only after less essential government spending had been reduced.

There are alternatives to taxation. The experiment of "postwar credits" employed in Britain might be used more extensively. The tax authorities could withdraw the money from current circulation but with the guarantee that it would be released later as inflationary pressure subsided. Such releases might be an effective method of maintaining demand at a time when insufficiency of demand, not of supply, threatened to be the enemy of stability. Loans could also be used to mop up excessive purchasing power. In World War II, rather more than half the war effort in the United States was financed by loans. The proportion in Britain was lower and more war finance was drawn directly from taxation. Much of this borrowing represented borrowing from banks and other credit institutions and cannot therefore be called a genuinely anti-inflationary measure. On the contrary, it sometimes meant that the government undertook to pay interest upon money which might otherwise have lain idle upon deposit. But the small Savings Campaign in Britain and the War Bonds in the United States were a genuinely anti-inflationary device. They took the money out of the pockets of people who might otherwise have spent it at once. In this way they reduced the immediate pressure of their public's spending power.

Some critics believe that every sort of borrowing is inflationary and that it is the duty of governments to finance the whole of the defense effort from taxation. They point to the size of the national debt in the United States which rose from about $60,000 million in 1940 to $259,100 million by 1947, or in Britain which was below £7,000 million at the beginning of the last war and ended it above £20,000 million. A national debt, however, is not necessarily inflationary. It does not involve a new burden on the community but a redistribution of wealth within it. One set of people are taxed to provide interest on the debt and the sinking fund, another set receives the interest. The purchasing power made available in this way has thus been absorbed elsewhere. The debt could become inflationary only if the rates paid were so high and the share of the budget necessary to cover them so large that they became a crucial factor in the inflation of public expenditure. In fact, borrowing for defense is normally at low rates and the cost is not prohibitive. In 1944, one of the economists assisting Lord Beveridge in his inquiry into full employment estimated that if only 2 per cent were paid in interest, the British national debt could be increased by £755 million a year for twenty-two years in succession without extra taxation being necessary to cover its cost. The recent experience of the United States tends to bear out the contention that the existence of a public debt is not in itself a factor in inflation. Between 1922 and 1940, the national debt grew steadily from some $35 billion to about $60 billion. The two decades saw the American economy pass through a violent boom, a violent depression and several minor ups and downs. It cannot be said that the national debt was responsible for any of them.

A national debt risks being inflationary only at the time at which the government is doing the borrowing. If it borrows and spends money which would otherwise not have been spent—much of the money in deposit in banks may be idle in this sense—it is clearly creating new purchasing power and adding to the pressure of demand at that time. Other means such as taxation, plans for deferred spending, restraints on wages and profits must then be used to counteract this immediate inflationary effect. But the existence of the debt itself is not an imminent danger.

The more effective the measures used for controlling purchasing power, the less the government needs to intervene on the side of controlling supply. If a falling off in domestic demand is releasing resources for the defense effort and men and materials are moving, say, from the production of refrigerators and television sets and automobiles to the building of armaments, detailed controls and interventions may not be needed. But the government's ability to reduce consuming power to that degree cannot be taken for granted. Indeed, in the United States, no less an expert than Mr. Bernard Baruch argued on the morrow of the North Korean attack that half-way measures to check inflation would be insufficient and that Congress should give the President the fullest powers to "freeze" wages and profits, increase taxation and introduce a system of controls over supply.

Mr. Baruch had in mind the full apparatus of wartime controls which were used not only to check demand but to give government full powers to direct and use the community's supplies of men and materials—licenses and controls over industrial raw materials to divert them to the defense effort, powers to direct factories and workers to undertake war work, rationing and price control over essential civilian goods such as basic foodstuffs, clothing and fuel. There is no need to elaborate here this full apparatus of control. The Western world is relatively familiar with it. Six and seven years ago, such controls were the general rule and in one or two countries—Britain among them—the rationing of food continues. The techniques are therefore familiar and hardly need to be described. But two things should be said. The first is that the West need presumably engage in a 15 per cent defense effort, not a 50 to 60 per cent all out drive for armaments. The degree of controls and restrictions should therefore be far less severe than those necessary during the war.

The second point is of crucial importance. In nothing so much as the combating of inflation do the moral qualities of a people appear. The shopper who goes in for panic buying and hoarding, the supplier who cynically exploits the panic, the industrialist who seeks the biggest profit he can get out of a scarce commodity, the worker who uses the shortage of his skill to force an exorbitant wage bargain—these are the germ carriers of the most violent forms of inflation. And such activities compel the government to introduce the most rigorous forms of control and regimentation. Particularly in a defense effort which is less than complete, which is in essence preventive and not offensive and which, of its nature, must be sustained over a long time, the response of the citizen to that effort will probably do more than anything else to determine the form of its impact upon the community. Every antisocial reaction, every manifestation of group selfishness, every indifferent neglect of the general interest will make the defense effort so much more onerous for everyone else. It will prove as true of rearming as of government itself—each people will get the defense effort they deserve.

# 11

## *More Wealth*

THERE is one point in common to all the anti-inflationary measures discussed so far. They are all negative. They are all designed to prevent something. They all start from the premise that if one thing has to be achieved, another must be sacrificed. In the short run, such an approach is inevitable. Neither democrats nor dictators have magic wands to wave to turn pumpkins into gun carriers or parrots into airplanes. But as the only policies for combating inflation, as the chief weapons in the Western armory for achieving both defense and stability, they are all frankly unsatisfactory and insufficient. The very last mood to overtake the free world should be that of defensiveness, careful accountancy and general national cheeseparing. In inflation as in everything else the best defense is attack. The primary aim of the West in anything more than the shortest run must be not to cut purchasing power so that the defense effort can be achieved without risk but to expand wealth and supply and capacity so that high civilian standards and a defense effort can be secured simultaneously.

Let us assume that we in the West accept in the fullest sense the new obligations of successful containment—of which the chief are the need for rearmament and the no less urgent need for an ambitious program of aid and development in Asia and other backward areas. Let us also assume that these new responsibilities demand between 15 and 20 per cent of the Western Powers' current national incomes. Such a percentage will be a drain upon them only so long as they are content to reckon their economies at their present level. But if they made it the first aim of their policy to add 20 per cent to their national resources in the next two years, the extra obligations of containment could then be managed with little risk of inflation, with no more controls and no greater inroads upon the private spending of the community than existed in June, 1950. The proportion of the West's resources devoted to containment would then be little larger than it is today. The difference would lie in its sufficiency and effectiveness.

But can it be done? The economies of the West are many of them working already near the limit of their capacity. How can they be boosted by nearly 20 per cent in the next three years? In fact, the percentage is not as sensational as it seems. Without any extra stimulus, without any force beyond its own momentum, an industrial economy can, given reasonable stability, add millions to its wealth year by year. It is essentially dynamic. The secret of its growth is the steadily increasing productivity of labor, and this in turn springs from the application of more and more elaborate and effective machine power to each pair of working hands. Professor Sumner Slichter has estimated that without any especial stimulus, with a rate of fresh capital investment taking only about 6 per cent of the nation's resources, and with the average working week falling to 30 hours, the total output of the American economy could rise at a conservative estimate to some $400 billion and more probably to $500 billion in the next thirty years. Thus on a reasonably conservative estimate, nearly half the desired increase of 20 per cent in two years could be provided by the normal dynamics of a healthy industrial system.

American experience since 1946 bears out these figures. Between 1946 and 1950, total output has risen from $248 billion to $267 billion (the figures are expressed in 1949 prices and are therefore strictly comparable). An annual rate of increase of about 5 per cent is already taking place and without any extra effort or program or plan, half the desired expansion of the American economy should have taken place in any case by 1953.

Even the far more vulnerable and unstable economies of Europe tell something of the same tale. The British economy increased its industrial production by 20 per cent between 1947 and 1949 and the increase in output per worker (the index of the country's productivity) has gone up by about 6 per cent a year. In continental Europe, postwar conditions have been so exceptional and levels of activity so low that the figure of industrial expansion—about 10 per cent a year—is not strictly comparable. But the speed of recovery is perhaps relevant. In Germany, for instance, in spite of the ruin, the disorganization, the truncating of the country and every other conceivable obstacle, an expansion in industrial production by about 40 per cent has occurred since the currency reform of 1948.

These are increases which have been produced on the whole without a special effort. The economy, left to itself, could be practically relied upon to produce nearly half the desired expansion. What of the rest? Can free economies be made to spurt as well as jog along? Can exceptional periods of expansion be achieved rather as the runner puts on an extra turn of speed to put himself in the lead, or a climber makes a special effort to lift himself from one level on the rock face up to a higher ledge, from which he can advance at a steadier pace?

Obviously such efforts are possible. We have only to look back to the recent history of the American economy to see that much of its present prosperity is due to just such a heaving up of the whole level of the economy which took place in the first years of the last war. In 1939, the total output of goods and services in America was at a level of some $160 billion a year. Within five years, it had risen by nearly $100 billion. The rate of increase had been of the order of $20 billion a year. Today the starting point of such a program would be not $160 billion but $267 billion. An annual increase of only 10 per cent would give more than the $20 billion achieved then. The effort proportionately is smaller. Can we really suppose that what was possible in the 1940's has become impossible in the 1950's? That the achievement cannot be repeated? That the accomplishment was simply a stroke of luck and not a consistent policy?

We underestimate our own capacity and our own understanding if we suppose any such thing. The techniques that were applicable in 1940 and 1941 are equally useful today. The answer, with some modifications, is the same. It is to finance the defense effort and the aid program on the same generous scale and to see that the necessary capital expansion takes place at once. President Truman has said that there is enough spare capacity and manpower in the community to provide an extra $10 billion of output within twelve months on the basis of existing industrial resources. The other $16 billion necessary to create a 10 per cent increase each year must go to new capital, new capacity, new machines, to a steel industry able to produce not 100 million but 110 and more million tons of steel a year, to oil companies ready to expand production by another 300 to 500 million barrels a year, to a higher output of electrical power, to more metals, more trucks and freight cars, more tools and equipment of every sort. What is needed is an upsurge of the economy not perhaps on the scale of 1941 and 1942—the danger is not so great—but on a scale which meets the present necessities of defense and economic aid and by 1953 or 1954 gives the United States a national output of $300 billion a year.

To such a project the immediate protest will be made: "But this is the midsummer folly of inflation itself! Into an economy which you admit to be on the verge of producing to capacity, you propose to pump in another $16 billion of demand. There can be only one result. The pressure of this new purchasing power upon the price level will force every price upward in an uncontrollable spiral with wages racing behind. Before we know where we are, the whole economy will be out of control." But this would be the result only if no anti-inflationary measures accompanied this heroic piece of capital expansion. In the short run, the creation of new factories and new capacity, the extension of steel plant and engineering works does withdraw resources from immediate consumption. In the short run, the steel that is going to build an extension to the steel works is not available for Mr. Jones's new car. But once the new capacity is functioning, the added supplies that flow out into the community may be enough to build the Jones's car and the government's tank as well. There is thus a period of shortage to be overcome but on the far side lies greater plenty than ever.

If the essence of any anti-inflationary policy is, as we have seen, to keep a balance between demand and supply, the financing of a containment program—of defense and aid—falls into two phases. In the first phase, stern measures are necessary to cut purchasing power back while available materials and man-hours are going into the new plants and machines and extensions of existing capacity. Then when all these new sources of wealth are swinging into production, the exceptional checks on spending can be relaxed. This, after all, in a rough and ready way, was the policy pursued during World War II and its aftermath. While 50 per cent of the country's production was going into armaments, a number of anti-inflationary devices (taxation and War Bonds and voluntary checks on wages and profits) kept purchasing power below the figure to which it would have sprung if all the money earned in the course of the war effort had been allowed to rush through the depleted economy. Once the war was over, the checks were removed (some say they were removed too speedily) and the immense flood of insatiable civilian demand swept through the factories and shops busily being reconverted from war to peace and launched them all on a tide of civilian production that has been flowing ever since.

Cannot such a policy be repeated now on a smaller and more efficient scale—although admittedly any such program will be a little ragged at the edges? The decision to spend, let us say, $30 billion more on defense and aid and to give the signal for the necessary industrial expansion could be accompanied by a special defense levy chargeable on all incomes and graduated to follow the income tax, a Defense Loan designed to absorb the balance of purchasing power which might still need to be withdrawn from circulation, an undertaking from management and labor that during the necessary period of, say, two years, neither wages nor profits would be increased and lastly, as the special contribution of organized labor, a guarantee to add a given number of hours to the working week for a specified period without increased payments for overtime. These measures, every one of them disinflationary, would prevent any flooding of the economy with excessive purchasing power during the critical phase of expansion, but would permit incomes and wages to increase once the new level of output and prosperity had been reached.

Such a program must, naturally, be able to stand up to a number of severe criticisms. Some will say that the materials and manpower are not available for such an ambitious expansion. But is this really so? The difficulty of extra manpower could be met in part by a lengthening of the working week, by the absorption of some of the three million American unemployed and in part, perhaps, by increasing immigration. Incidentally, nothing would so contribute to stability in Germany and Italy than the knowledge that opportunities for work in America might become available. As for raw materials, the American economy, alone among the free nations, knows no limitations on its supplies. Every country in the world is only too anxious to sell to the United States in return for dollars and one way of keeping a balance between the contribution to the Western effort made by America and by its allies could lie in using a high proportion of foreign supplies in the crucial two years of expansion. Imports tend to act as a deflationary force since the goods brought in have made no demands on the local market's productive capacity. True, such imports, being other nations' exports, might increase inflationary pressure elsewhere. The balance of sacrifice would need to be decided by way of joint consultation and agreement.

Other critics may say: "Once again it is Uncle Sam who

is to carry the burden. It is the American economy that is to commit itself to hazardous policies of expansion and to undertake the risk of violent inflation. Why, if the effort of containment is a joint effort, should all the emphasis be placed upon the American economy? Is the burden to be carried alone?" No such suggestion is intended here. It is the essence of the common effort upon which the Western Powers are engaged that they should put into the pool an equal effort and be prepared to devote a comparable share of their resources to the joint pursuit of defense and stability. If the proportion of its total output which the United States is prepared to devote to containment equals 15 to 20 per cent —15 per cent for defense, 2 or 3 per cent for programs of economic assistance—the other partners in the Western coalition should attempt the same percentage. In poorer countries, so high a figure may not be possible, but it should be the target for all. The Atlantic Pact powers are already considering the use of a common yardstick based upon national income per head of population.

The only reason why no detailed discussion of the policies of the other Western nations is given at this point is that they are not on the same footing as the United States. They cannot at will expand their economies because the physical impossibility of securing the necessary materials will limit them if they seek to advance beyond a certain point. The expansion of their economies should clearly be the final aim of Western policy, but the realization of this aim does not depend upon them alone. It depends upon the degree of co-operation they can achieve both with each other and with their mighty American partner. Already in the very first days after Korea, both the British and French Governments had to declare that the speed of their rearmament would depend upon the materials and the machines and the assistance they could secure from the United States and this limiting factor will continue to shape their policies. They are not completely free agents. To achieve their best results, they need unity and co-operation. A discussion of their effort therefore fits more appropriately into the following section, whose theme is unity in the West.

There is one more criticism that can be made of any plan for the rapid expansion of a nation's productive resources. It is a fundamental criticism and must be squarely faced. If, the critics argue, a tremendous increase takes place in a community's plant, machinery and general capacity to pour out wealth, how can anyone be sure that the economy will not become overcapitalized, overextended and overprovided with industrial equipment? The managers of the expanded factories and the newly built plant may find in four and five years' time that there is no market for the goods they can produce in such enormous quantities. There are physical limits to the number of houses, cars, refrigerators and television sets any one community can absorb. There are limits, too, to the amount of furnishings and fittings and trimmings an ordinary family can afford. Demand must surely slacken at some point and then the slump when it comes may be all the more devastating on account of the previous overexpansion—as it was in 1929.

The risk of overexpansion does not, however, seem very grave in the short run. For the next three years at least a sizable part of the new capacity would be devoted to rearmament and to the program of economic assistance. Neither would lead to a glut in the domestic market since in both cases the products would be absorbed elsewhere—arms into the armories and stockpiles, goods for the assistance programs in the markets of other states. The program of containment, by combining armament and aid, would carry within itself a certain check upon the risk of overproduction.

Other facts would also diminish the possibility of a glut—in the short run. Throughout most of the Western world a fairly steady growth of population is occurring and by 1953 or 1954, the mouths to be fed and the hands to work will have grown by many millions. They create fresh demand, they supply fresh sources of work and skill.

It is also probable that a new expansion of the West's

productive capacity would bring about a raising of incomes among the poorer groups and thus a rise in the general level of demand. In the United States, between 1936 and 1945, the number of people whose incomes were less than $1,000 a year fell from 46 per cent of the population to 20 per cent and the numbers enjoying incomes of between $2,000 and $3,000 increased from 11 per cent to 22 per cent. It was as though the ocean bed of the economy had been raised several feet and a new level of purchasing power established as a result. Something of the same development occurred in Britain. Here, however, it was accompanied by a decline in middle-class income which, in the United States had, on the contrary, contrived to expand. The result of this upheaval in America was an increase in general personal income from $72 billion in 1939 to $171 billion in 1945. The figures are a clear index of how much more the community could consume at the end of the economy's immense wartime expansion than before that expansion took place. These figures cannot, incidentally, be dismissed as mere monetary inflation. Real increases in consumption occurred. For instance, food consumption in America was eleven times larger in 1950 than in 1939.

Such were the effects of a total war effort. The much milder expansion of the economy that is needed in order to make containment effective would not have such sensational consequences. But some increase in consuming power would occur and if the program of capital expansion were accompanied—as it should be—by strict temporary checks on spending, there would be in 1953 and 1954, as there was in 1946, a tide of unsatisfied demand waiting to flow out into the economy. More people, higher incomes, deferred demand should contrive to keep the new factories and machines at work—at least in the short run.

Containment, however, is not a program to be considered only in the short run. It is based upon the assumption that a steady and vigilant opposition to Communist pressure must continue for a long time. Even if Western resources are speedily expanded to meet the new claims upon them, the expansion will not serve much purpose if some five years later, the whole level of production is allowed to fall again and both the physical and moral resistance of the West is fatally weakened by the recurrence of a serious slump. Once the Western economy has grown by the 20 per cent needed for containment, armament and aid will have been successfully absorbed into the community's running costs. But the West will not necessarily be any better able to evolve a policy for keeping its economy lastingly stable at that or at any other level. This—the problem of full employment, or rather, the problem of maintaining stable and expanding prosperity—remains the central economic problem of the free world. As has been noted the Communists make no secret of their confident belief that the West's present prosperity is a mere flash-in-the-pan, a postwar phenomenon that will, with all the majestic certainty of Marxist-Leninism, give way to slump and poverty and despair. The pitch to which this doctrine is central to Communist thinking has been illustrated—almost ludicrously—by the propaganda accompanying the Korean war. Week after week Moscow radio blared out to the world—to the world of Asia with special emphasis—the news that American imperialism had "attacked" in Korea because a shattering slump had shaken America, because unemployment and the anger of the people were rising and because war was the only means of securing fresh markets for American goods (in North Korea?) and of breaking the spirit of the unemployed by drafting them into the trenches.

Such nonsense would be comic if it did not portray such a terrifying picture of the ignorance and fanaticism of the men who guide Communism's war on the West. But even if such propaganda is idiotic and ludicrous, it is unsafe to dismiss its effect upon innocent minds or to minimize the explosive force it would acquire if, at any point, unemployment and depression did begin once again to sweep the free world. The campaign against Communism is not one that will conveniently fade after 1953. The Western Powers must be prepared for a containment not only of today and tomorrow but for decades to come. And the Communists have served notice on them that the center of their keenest hopes and the focus of their most insistent propaganda is the return of depression to the West. Even if we do not take full employment seriously, our enemies do. This in itself should be warning enough.

A candid examination of the problem of future stability can lead to only one conclusion—that the West is no more certain to avoid a devastating future slump now than it was, say, in the twenties. Present levels of prosperity are no guarantee against future collapse. The downward spiral, the acceleration of collapse can occur at any level of production and when the critics say that the problem of future demand is one of the crucial issues raised by the economics of containment, they put their finger on the real conundrum of the trade cycle—how, in the modern community, government and business and labor together can contrive to ensure stable demand for the goods which industry can pour out in such quantities. How can they make demand sufficient without lapsing into inflation? How can they make it stable without falling into rigidity? Even if the Western world has been dominated since the war with the problem of overdemand and inflation and even if the immediate risk of the containment program is renewed inflationary pressure, undersupply is not the typical predicament of modern industrial society. It is the insufficiency and the irregularity of demand.

Those who despair of finding a solution to the problem can take comfort in the fact that it is really only very recently that the problem could even be defined. One reason was the extent to which, until recent decades, the economic system as a whole ran blind. The amount of precise information available to governments or businessmen was small. The collection of statistics was only just beginning on a systematic scale. The facts needed for an understanding of the trade cycle were simply not available.

Possibly for the same reason, the economists' theories of why the alternation of boom and slump, of inflation and deflation, of full employment and unemployment came about were very various and often contradictory. In the classical economic thinking of the nineteenth century, the starting point had been the belief that demand and supply would automatically tend to find a balance in the economy. The economists argued that this would be the case because the cost of producing an article is equivalent to the incomes of the people who have been concerned in the processes of manufacture. In the economy as a whole, the argument ran, demand would always tend to be equal to supply since the process of supplying goods creates the income to buy them, as it were, en route. Why, then, did unemployment occur and why, from the very first period for which statistics are available (the end of the eighteenth century), did this unemployment in manufacturing countries tend to rise and fall in perfectly well-marked cycles of about ten years' duration? The economists agreed that unemployment could occur—temporarily—if the wrong things were reproduced, but the possible reasons for such maladjustments proved too numerous for a really consistent theory of unemployment to be based upon them. A full explanation of the trade cycle seemed even more elusive.

If the position today is completely revolutionized and if it has become possible to base both a theory of the trade cycle and a possible policy to combat it on the phenomenon of demand in industrial society, the credit must go largely to Lord Keynes whose *General Theory of Employment, Interest and Money*, published in 1936, created a new basis to men's thinking about unemployment. It is true that historical circumstances had molded his thought and made others ready to listen to him. The experience of full employment in the First World War could, by 1936, be sharply contrasted with the devastating depression of the early thirties. It was possible to reflect that whereas in wartime the nations' demand for the weapons of war could be completely satisfied and almost no limit set to it in an industrial economy, no such satisfaction was possible when the demand was a demand for the weapons of peace. Whatever influence these contrasts had upon Lord Keynes himself, they very greatly increased the speed with which his analysis was accepted by other people, especially since the Second World War followed so soon after to confirm his main thesis—that provided demand is high, unemployment can be banished from the community.

The essence of the Keynesian revolution was to break away from the nineteenth-century belief that supply and demand tend to find a natural balance in the community. He pointed out that such an equilibrium would come about only if all the money earned in the process of producing goods was actually spent, either on consumers' goods or on new capital equipment. If the money was put by and not spent at all, disequilibrium might be introduced and no automatic forces could be relied on to draw the money back into circulation. It would be quite possible for the monetary demand in the community to be permanently lower than the level needed to absorb all the goods the economy could produce.

This fact—that total demand may be insufficient to absorb total supply—is however only the starting point of the problems of the trade cycle. In modern industrial society, it is not only that demand may be insufficient to keep the whole economy employed. The difficulty is that the whole cycle of employment tends to move up and down. There has been a basic instability in the modern industrial system which seems to have grown worse in this century. All sorts of different reasons may set the cycle in motion—bad harvests, sudden inventions which upset old established enterprises, a sensational financial failure—but the significant factor is that, with interruptions caused by war, the cycles tend to follow roughly a ten-year course from boom through depression and back again to boom. This regularity suggests that explanations based upon this or that event—crop failure or technical change—are less important than some innate trend in the system itself. This at least is the argument that makes most converts to Marxism and is being drilled into the millions in Asia now coming under Communist control. There is no more constant theme in Communist propaganda than "the innate contradictions of capitalist society" and "the dialectical necessity" that produces slump and boom. Once again it must be said that anything that causes our enemies such passionate interest is not a factor that we ourselves can neglect.

But is there any agreed explanation of the rhythmical nature of the trade cycle? In the last decade, many economists have come to agree that here, too, the Western world faces a problem of demand. The difficulty again is a failure of demand, not of demand in general this time but of a particular demand—the demand for capital goods or for further investment. There is something potentially unsettling to the market in the life cycle of a machine. The food a man buys has to be replaced tomorrow and his demand is likely to be constant. But there is usually a decade of good work to be got out of a machine and since businessmen are extremely influenced by the decision of other businessmen and the general "feel" of the economic situation, the new investments in machinery and expansions in plant may very well tend to be made at about the same time. The expansion of output in the industries producing factory equipment and machines—in the capital goods industry—spreads through the whole economy. Confidence expands with expanding demand. New equipment is ordered, new extensions are made. But as the cycle swings upward, a number of checks to further demand begin to shadow the confident atmosphere. The consumers' demand is partly satisfied, the boom has brought new businesses into existence and their increased output lowers prices and profits. New machines add to the flood of goods and old machines no longer give such good returns. A growing shortage of labor sends up wages and these rises, too, reduce profits. Finally, there comes a point where further expansion seems unprofitable and once again the "feel" of the economy communicates itself from management to management, orders for more capital goods are cancelled, slack times begin in the heavy industries, the multiplier spreads the effects through consumer industries. The fall spirals downward as surely as the former expansion rose. Thus there seems an innate tendency for private investment to expand and contract in the regular rhythm of the trade cycle.

If therefore the Western Powers take seriously the problem of future stability—and it is assuredly the basis of containment or of any other successful policy for the defense of the West—they must consider two tendencies which in modern industrial society do not seem automatically to correct themselves. The first is the possibility that demand in the community as a whole may fall below what is necessary to consume all that the community produces. The second is the certainty that investment, left to itself, will cause the cycle of boom and depression. Investment needs to be stabilized. Demand needs to be held steady.

To some extent, these are simply different ways of saying the same thing, but this is not altogether the case. For instance, it would be possible for a government to concentrate all its attention upon keeping the purchasing power of the community high enough to absorb all that is produced—to increase purchasing power whenever more is likely to be produced. On the other hand, it might decide to concentrate upon keeping up a high and stable level of investment in industry and leave the prosperity of heavy industry to keep the whole community in balance—the man who makes machines buying from the man who makes food and the man who makes food buying more machines in return. Most governments would probably decide to pursue both policies, but there is room here for a difference of emphasis.

We do not know much about the origins of wealth. The beginning of our modern economy lies in the largely unchronicled eighteenth century and we have to rely on guess work to trace many of the original impulses and decisions which launched mankind on the vast and terrifying Industrial Revolution. But as the system has developed it is clear that in the West at least, wealth has grown in the measure to which machines have come in to supplement and supplant human labor. Output per man-hour primarily depends today upon the machine power that can be put behind each pair of hands. Wealth is greatest where mechanization is most complete. Wealth advances most rapidly in communities prepared to devote a sizable percentage of their national incomes to the introduction of the machines. Other factors play their part, but the chief reason why the United States is the wealthiest community in the world is that the machine power behind each American worker's effort is two or three times that of Britain and five or six times that of Europe.

On the other hand, the example of Russia has shown that there are or should be limits to the amount of the national income devoted to investment and the expansion of machine power. The development of industry and the mechanization of agriculture in Soviet Russia between the wars probably swallowed up a higher proportion of the national income in capital investment than in any other country in any other period. The people lived miserably while the factories and the powerhouses went up. It certainly cannot be said that Russia's rulers made the wrong decision. From some of those factories came the guns and tanks that defended Stalingrad. But it can be said that in a democratic community, a government must take more thought of its citizens' present wants and cannot impose too ruthless a sacrifice on one generation in the interests of others, as yet unborn.

Thus there may be a tug of war in government policy between a full employment policy which concentrates upon increasing and stabilizing the community's capital equipment and thus its power to produce more wealth and a policy which puts its emphasis on making more purchasing power available directly to the consumers so that they can lead better and fuller lives now. In practice, this possible collision of interest will probably be solved by different governments according to the degree of development already reached in their community. In a wealthy, highly developed, highly mechanized community, the right emphasis would lie upon maintaining generous levels of consumption so that the riches which pour from the factories and the machines can be absorbed by the public. In backward communities, more emphasis would be put upon investment, upon the expansion of the power to produce wealth once international measures of assistance and support had raised the economy above the absolute poverty line. Indeed, the fundamental justification for the drive to produce more wealth and to accept the risks of an expanding economy is the degree of grinding need and harsh poverty still prevailing in the world today.

# 12

## *The Expanding Economy*

THERE are many people in the Western world who, while sincerely believing that the economic life of the West must be strengthened and its capacity for meeting human needs greatly enlarged, hesitate to accept the idea of a controlled, planned and purposeful effort to achieve these ends. A planned effort, to secure full and expanding use of all a nation's resources must, they point out, involve government intervention. No other body has the information or the necessary authority. But government intervention and regulation are, in their view, positive evils which impede not only economic growth but potentially liberty as well. It is true that in most countries in Europe—and with particular emphasis on Britain and Scandinavia—the idea that government must exercise a decisive influence in the economy is very generally accepted. But there has been a strong reaction against this view since the war. The Belgian, Italian and German Governments have all attempted to reduce state action to a minimum. And in the United States, the opponents of most forms of government intervention are many and influential.

The question, therefore, is whether the opposition to any form of governmental intervention is so strong, particularly in the pivotal economy of the United States, as to nullify all attempts to achieve economic stability and expansion by planning and forethought. For the critics are right in supposing that given the present structure of the Western world, co-ordinated programs of expansion cannot be pursued *without* government. Only the central authority possesses, year by year, a picture of the economy as a whole. Only the central authority has sufficient monetary resources to create more demand if it becomes necessary. It alone has the power to check spending drastically if inflation begins to recur. Other factors are involved in a policy of full expansion and employment. But the rôle of the government remains crucial.

European radicals and socialists accept this point, and influential groups in the United States also agree to its necessity. But clearly the more widespread the acceptance of a policy in a democratic community, the more smoothly and efficiently it will run. This is particularly true of any economic policy which must be able to command sufficient support among business leaders and the labor unions for their co-operation to be assured. But it is in the business community that many of the strongest—and most honest—doubts and hesitations are to be found. There are, however, two considerations which could perhaps modify this attitude. The first is the degree to which state intervention is in fact a completely accepted phenomenon even in the most laisser-faire economies. It is not simply a question of tariffs, export subsidies, price supports, financial assistance to hard hit industries and all the other direct and indirect governmental aids to business interests that are almost as old as the industrial system itself. The crucial fact is that even the most passive governments have in the past intervened, willy-nilly, in the workings of the trade cycle. No one today is so wedded to laisser faire that they would wish to remove all governmental powers of taxation. The raising of taxes to cover unavoidable state expenditure is a universally accepted necessity. But this very instrument of taxation has in the past tended to aggravate the instabilities of the trade cycle. As the boom swung upward, prosperity increased and revenue from taxation grew as a result, the government tended to remit taxation and thus release a new flow of purchasing power into the inflating economy. But as the cycle swung downward again and revenue fell, there was a tendency both to cut government expenditure and to raise other taxes to make up for lost revenue, and thus more purchasing power was removed from the deflating economy. The net result was a form of government intervention calculated to accentuate both the upswings and the downswings of the trade cycle. The government's use of its powers of taxation alone tended to make the deflations worse and the booms more uncontrolled. If, now, as a result of greater knowledge and greater insight, the government decides to ensure that its interventions steady the economy rather than upset it further, this change does not imply a greater measure of intervention. It simply means the substitution of a potentially sound intervention for a certainly bad one.

This point suggests a second consideration—that in the modern world, nations reach the disaster of total governmental control and dictatorship more speedily by way of bad times and of prolonged deflation than by way of high levels of economic activity. Nothing for instance has so restored the prestige and confidence of business leaders in America as the brilliant war effort conducted by American industry—with the backing of not a few "inflationary" expedients in finance—and the ability of the American economy to meet all demands made on it in the years since the war. At the other end of the political scale, the first group of dictators, with Mussolini at their head, appeared in the deflations and depressions of the early twenties and the second and fatal batch, Nazism in Germany and militarism in Japan, sprang up in the Depression of the thirties. And apart from such sensational consequences, it is clear that when times are very bad, with mortgages being foreclosed, banks failing, businesses collapsing, the citizen—be he worker, or banker or farmer or manager—inevitably turns to the state for help. Where else should he turn? It is a fact that many of the extensions of state ownership into business in the last fifty years have taken place at the bottom of slumps because the state has not been content to sit by and see vital industries collapse. This generation hardly needs reminding that in the extremer interventions of Mussolini and Hitler, large sections of industry were handed over to public ownership. The Fascist-sponsored *Istituto di Ricostruzione Industriale* (the IRI) owned something like 60 per cent of the shares in Italian banking, heavy industry and transport by 1939.

In fact, if the record between the wars is taken as a guide, it is clear that the way of depression and stagnation leads to massive intervention by the state as certainly as grave disease calls for the far-reaching intervention of doctors and surgeons. It is true that the attempt to balance the economy at a high level cannot be made without a measure of governmental action but the more successful it is, the less, apparently, is it necessary for government to intervene in the details and the intimate organization of business and labor. A buoyant, expanding economy which is steadily creating and distributing more wealth can most securely dispense with day-to-day controls by the state.

The maximum degree of direct intervention in the American economy occurred under the New Deal during the thirties when the business world was stunned and disorganized by the catastrophe of 1929. Then followed the war effort which expanded demand to such a fantastic degree that it not only exhausted the possibilities of the existing economy but created another economy as big on top of the old to meet the insatiable hunger of the war effort. At the end of the struggle, the United States' economy had not only four years of pent-up civilian demand to satisfy, it had nearly twice as much capital equipment as in 1939 with which to meet this flood of demand. Since then, with one slight pause for breath in 1949, the vast economy has maintained the same momentum. As a result, the need for government intervention has grown less, the philosophy of free enterprise has regained confidence. Not least of the paradoxes of the postwar world is that the most massive state intervention in the history of America (or perhaps of the West)—the American war effort, guided, controlled and largely financed by the state—has led not to increased state intervention in peacetime but to a revival of confidence in private enterprise and to a new belief—not only among the supporters of laisser faire, but also among liberals and radicals—that a partnership between the guiding and directing powers of government and the dynamic efforts of private management is possible.

For the moment, therefore, let it be conceded that, even if government action is involved in the attempt to defeat the trade cycle and to make stability and expansion the long term goal of the Western economy, an even greater risk of governmental intervention may be involved in the opposite policy of allowing the alternation of boom and slump to return unchecked. Moreover, state intervention in the event of renewed instability would be a panic intervention, called for by millions of desperate men who might, in their bewilderment, be ready to sacrifice even their basic liberties in return for the promise of work. The dictatorships thrown up by depressions have always been the most ruthless and the most irrational, and their policies have reflected their desperate origins. But democratic governments deciding in advance the measure of control necessary to preserve equilibrium in society, need be neither ruthless nor irrational. On the contrary, any examination of the possible methods of control must reveal the fact that there is nothing in them to offend the common sense and the free choice of the responsible citizen.

Most of the methods of maintaining and expanding demand suggested in these pages have been put forward as possible expedients in the Report on Full Employment [1] published recently by the United Nations. The significance of the Report is underlined by the fact that it was a unanimous document and that it was the work of five economists, two American, two British and one French. These men, drawn from very different academic and political backgrounds, were nevertheless able to agree upon a diagnosis of the trade cycle and upon possible measures of countering it. Those who despair of common understanding and agreement in the West may take comfort from this fact.

In examining the great variety of policies for maintaining economic stability, one can distinguish between the methods which aim at a direct stimulation of the consumers' income, and those which look to the stabilization—or expansion—of investments. In practice, the methods may overlap

[1] *National and International Measures for Full Employment*, 1949.

and most states are likely to use both. A government can approach the problem of stimulating demand by a number of routes. For instance, at signs of slackening activity, the income tax can be reduced and more purchasing power released in this way. The contributions made by individual citizens to their social security schemes can be varied; in good times, the proportion contributed could be at one level but once there were signs of economic decline, the contribution could be reduced; it might even be waived altogether for a time. Veterans' bonuses could also be made to fluctuate in the same way if higher grants were made by the state when times promised to be bad. Some economists believe that, since in a modern industrial economy so many payments go on automatically, whatever the state of the economy, the government has already gone far toward stabilizing demand. These "built-in" factors in the economy are already achieving a degree of regularity in demand unheard-of twenty years ago. It should, however, be remembered that no major recession has occurred recently. If it threatened to do so, the lowering of social security contributions and the increasing of some allowances might be useful methods of maintaining demand. There are many countries, it is true, where neither the income tax nor the social security system are well enough organized for variations of this kind to be practicable. Some backward countries still depend very largely upon indirect taxation. Even here, however, alternations in the level of taxation might be a possible method of expanding demand. A general sales tax could, in theory at least, be moved up and down by government decree.

The use of fiscal measures to iron out variations in private demand is, however, less important—for the time being, at least—than the maintenance of high standards of investment and expansion. The world is still much too far from even minimum standards of well-being for the emphasis to be shifted yet from the means of creating more wealth—in other words from capital investment. A high rate of capital investment is an effective means, as we have seen, of maintaining demand right through the economy and it is the chief means whereby the economy expands its power to produce a greater flow of goods with less effort and at lower prices. For this reason, too, it is not enough to think of using increased investment—say, the expansion and contraction of a program of public works—simply to counter the possibility that private action may be insufficient. It is better to do that than to do nothing, but it is not enough. The need is rather to think of means of maintaining over a number of years a steadily high level of investment of all kinds—both private and public—and to frame official policy to that end. If this overriding need of stability and expansion is accepted, then there are a number of ways in which government, in consultation and co-operation with business and labor, can act.

On the one hand, it can proceed to stimulate private investment by reducing taxation on profits plowed back into industry, by increasing the scale on which claims can be made for amortization, by giving generous tax relief to new enterprises and subsidies to group research in industry, even perhaps by offering guarantees of state purchase against the possibility of a fall in the market to those who are prepared to expand their capacity boldly. The principle of buying surpluses from the farming community in the United States has been pressed too far, but more moderate programs of government purchase—for stock piling or for buffer stocks—might be introduced to help the producers of basic materials. The state could also use these methods of stimulus and encouragement to persuade manufacturers to turn away from the mentality of the trade cycle in which everyone tends to expand and contract his enterprise under the influence of the same mood of hope or discouragement.

For instance, if the economy were heading for a boom, taxes—on income or on profits—could be raised and a check put in this way upon further expansion. On the other hand, if there were signs of slackening activity, the rate of taxation could be lowered and large concessions made to firms which undertook at that point to introduce new capital development. Taxation should in any case encourage the plowing back of profits into new equipment and greater efficiency, but in times of falling activity, the tax exemptions allowed on new equipment, new factories and new extensions could be made very generous indeed. Clearly such policies would be all the more effective if private business itself gave a lead in planning its replacements of equipment and its extensions of plant continuously rather than in fits and starts. If "round-the-cycle" planning became general in business, the need for government intervention would automatically decrease.

Another indirect method of securing something of the same result lies in government influence on the rate of interest. In Europe in the last three years, a sharp increase in the price people have to pay for loans has had a marked effect in checking the upward swing of the economy. In Italy, it turned inflation into deflation in a couple of months in 1947. And one of the factors in bringing the American recession to an end in 1949 was the easing of restrictions on credit.

The government can also intervene more directly in the economic process. In all the economies of the Western world—semi-planned or semi-free alike—the great bulk of production is carried on by private enterprise. Equally, however, there are many desirable things in each community that will not with any certainty be provided by private enterprise. The government can, therefore, help to keep the whole activity of the community taut and the demand for products of both public and private enterprise stable if it sponsors itself a large and steady program of investment. The idea is not new. For a long time past, the idea of public works—roads, bridges, land reclamation, drainage—has been generally accepted as a proper field of state investment. What has chiefly happened is that the concept of public works has grown very much larger. In a modern community, building of all kinds—cheap housing projects, schools, hospitals—are often handed over in part at least to the national and local authorities. In many countries, mining, transport, ports and harbors, public utilities, are also seen to be of public concern. All this has nothing necessarily to do with public ownership, but it has a great deal to do with state measures to ensure sufficient expansion, modernization and capital development. In predominantly free-enterprise France, for example, the Plan Monnet, largely financed out of Marshall Plan aid, has been devoted to the re-equipping and retooling of French industry. The Plan has not brought about any changes in ownership, but it has entailed state encouragement of a much higher measure of investment than industry could provide out of its own resources. Similarly, one of the declared aims of the Schuman Plan is to create an authority which will ensure adequate investment in Europe's coal and steel industries.

There is one field in particular in which a partnership between public and private enterprise for long-term capital development seems to offer particularly promising results and that is the field of basic economic development. In various parts of the world, in the British Commonwealth, in South America, in Asia, even in the United States, there are areas of known potential wealth which nevertheless have little or none of the equipment of successful economic activity—neither roads nor cities nor ports nor transport, nor even the food to feed new workers. Consistent development programs for such areas would call upon a great variety of resources in the older industrial regions. Heavy industry would be maintained in activity by the demand for constructional steel, for railway bridges, port installations, for new agricultural machinery and for the equipment of public utilities, the building trades would be called on for cement, for prefabricated parts, for household fittings, the consumer-goods industries for all the demands of the local population.

The primary investment would need to be supplied by governments or intergovernmental agencies. Private enterprise is no longer interested in the public utilities, the ports and tramways and electric light companies that drew private capital out to backward areas a hundred years ago. But once the basic installations had been supplied, private capital would find a new field of operation. Australia has embarked on an ambitious scheme of basic development with the financial backing of the International Bank. Another scheme of the sort is under consideration in Italy for the ten-year development of the backward but potentially wealthy Italian south. The program includes not only the normal public works of road building or land drainage, but also hydroelectric schemes, the building of subsidiary industries such as canning and food processing, reafforestation and the introduction of enterprises based upon the exploitation of timber. Similarly, the Clapp Mission to the Middle East has drawn up a comprehensive scheme of basic public works for increasing water power and irrigated land.

These, then, are some of the measures whereby government, with the co-operation of management and labor, can bring stability into the economy. But they are not policies that exist in a vacuum. They must be based upon an accurate estimate of the nation's resources from year to year and their successful implementation calls for a new approach to the problem of the annual budget. In the past, the state has usually been content to see what its inescapable minimum expenditure would amount to and then has estimated the taxation necessary to cover it. Today, a budget designed to underpin a full and expanding economy must be based upon a full picture of the economy and the most accurate possible estimate of the extent to which real resources will be used and spent. Otherwise, it would not be possible to know whether the effective demand for goods would roughly equal the amount available on the side of supply, and serious instability might creep in unnoticed and unchecked.

This idea of a budget based upon a review of the nation's total resources is not really a very revolutionary concept. With the growth of accurate records and statistics, Western governments have increasingly adopted the policy of presenting to their people year by year a full statement of the general state of the economy, of the movements within it—of employment, of investment, of wages and prices—of its prospects and achievements. The President of the United States now presents to Congress twice a year an assessment of the economic state of the Union. A White Paper on the British economy accompanies the British Budget. M. Monnet's Planning Office keeps a full account of the French economy and issues a regular report. Most central banks provide similar information. With these facts before it, a government can decide the general shape of its economic policy. Such a review does not imply total control. On the contrary, the more accurate the knowledge upon which intervention is based, the more securely it can be confined to essentials. In a democratic community, the general review of the nation's resources should be prepared with the co-operation of management and the unions, and the implications of the facts fully explored with them.

A more detailed example of how such a budget might look would perhaps be helpful at this stage. The hypothetical case of the United States has been chosen in part because the economy is only very partially guided and directed, in part because its economic prospects are not severely conditioned by factors beyond control—such as foreign lending or foreign trade. Let us suppose the President and his advisers have, in our hypothetical year, established that the country's total capacity to produce goods and services—its gross national product—is about $300 billion. If the economy is to run on an even keel in the coming years, something rather above $300 billion must be available in the shape of effective monetary demand. The extra money is necessary to absorb the economy's increased power to produce goods and to provide for a rise in population and an increased labor force—new mouths to feed, new hands to employ.

Having put the figure of necessary demand at some $300 billion, the government must then determine whether the economy is likely by its own unstimulated efforts to produce the necessary sum. We may assume that normal governmental expenditure would amount to about $55 billion, a figure which would include the containment program of defense and aid expenditure. Government spending would thus ensure the release of $55 billion of purchasing power into the community. Next, in collaboration with private business, an estimate would be made of the amount of investment private enterprise had in mind to make. A reasonable estimate might be 5 per cent of total resources for the replacement of old capital and 5 per cent of new investment—a figure, therefore, of $30 billion. It would then be clear that private domestic purchases would need to amount to about $215 billion for the economy to remain stable. An estimate of people's personal incomes after tax (their wages, salaries and dividends) would show whether in fact enough cash demand were in existence. (Actually in

1948, the people of America had $190.8 billion at their disposal and spent $178.8 billion on goods and services.) Let us suppose, however, that for our hypothetical year, private investment was planned at a level of only $15 billion and that the available personal incomes were not more than $190 billion. The government would then face a situation in which total demand in the economy might be short by some $40 billion.

It is at this point that special full employment measures would be necessary. As we have seen, the government could use a number of different expedients. It might encourage business to increase its investment by offering special incentives and rebates. It might increase taxation on the wealthier sections of the community where the failure to spend and invest would be more likely to be taking place (the poorer people inevitably tend to spend all their income), and then use the money collected by taxation to cover expenditure on unemployment relief, on old-age pensions, on veterans' bonuses, on new public works. It might borrow from the public and from the banks—as War Bonds were issued in the war—and use the funds placed at its disposal for similar purposes. Or it might simply increase its expenditure without covering it by new taxation or special borrowing and allow a budget deficit to become the source of new finance. This again is not a new departure. In 1949, the fact that Congress had reduced taxation while government expenditure continued at roughly the same level, made inevitable the emergence of a budget deficit of some $5 billion and this stimulus to expenditure was one of the factors creating the restoration of demand toward the end of 1949.

As an expedient, however, such procedure raises the question whether governments can afford deficits in this way. The short answer is that the government is not under the same compulsions as the private citizen or the private firm. It can always "create" money. Money is in essence a symbol of a certain claim on the community's resources and the government can always print the notes and stamp the pieces of metal that confer this claim. But this answer leaves the door wide open to the risk of inflation, to government printing presses working overtime, to the whole economy sinking to ruin under a whirling mass of paper notes. The real answer to whether or not the state can "afford" a deficit lies with the general level of economic activity in the community. If private investment and consumption is falling off, a budget deficit, which creates new monetary demand (since the government must issue new money to cover expenditure which is *not* covered by taxation) can have the effect simply of bringing effective demand back into line with the goods and services the community could in fact supply if the demand for them were active. It does not, in theory at least, upset the balance of the economy. On the contrary, it restores it. This process of unbalancing the budget when private demand begins to fall off can, however, be pursued with less risk if some reserves are accumulated during times of high economic activity when both production and demand are expanding and the general increases in incomes mean that taxation is bringing in more than the fiscal authorities forecast. If, for instance, in our hypothetical year, personal incomes were increased by a burst of prosperity, taxation might bring in more than was necessary to cover government expenditure. A budgetary surplus might emerge and could be used both to check a rise in monetary demand beyond the level which the resources of the economy could satisfy and to put in reserve a fund to be expended when private demand showed signs of slackening.

Some economists have, as a result of these possibilities, suggested that the state's budget should be expected to balance not in any one year—since a single year bears little relation to the normal rhythms of an industrial economy—but over a period of years (say five or ten), which would permit state surpluses and state deficits to have a genuinely stabilizing effect on the movements of the economy as a whole. In one sense, it is true to say that even without this balancing of accounts every decade, the state's finances can comfortably absorb quite large deficits. As we have seen, the existence of a growing national debt over the last hundred years has been virtually no obstacle to a steady increase in the wealth and productivity of either Britain or the United

States. Yet comparatively large peacetime deficits can cause concern. In a normal economy, the feelings and reactions of private individuals (private entrepreneurs and private investors) has immense influence upon the stability of the economy. The vast additions to a national debt made during a war are accepted as necessary and inevitable and when the war is over, everybody forgets about them. It cannot be said, in face of the evidence of the last hundred years, that they weigh in a discouraging way upon anybody. They are made and they are forgotten. Deficits in peacetime, however, do not slip so easily into oblivion. Investors, managers, bankers, trustees, become very concerned at the unbalanced budget and the failure of the government to put equilibrium into its accounts. And since it worries them, it effects their readiness to invest money themselves or—which is much more serious—even to keep their capital in the country.

If businessmen lose confidence and begin sending their capital to "safe keeping" elsewhere, they obviously decrease the effective purchasing power of the community with every cent or penny they send away. A painful vicious circle may develop in such a situation. The government's attempts to increase purchasing power to make good the vanished private capital may further increase the budget deficit and further increase the distrust of private capitalists. The "hot money" finds refuge in Switzerland or New York or South America and not only ceases to provide effective demand at home but increases the problem of the country's international balance of payments. It is sometimes possible to arrest this flight by a radical effort to balance the national budget and thus recreate confidence in the mind of the private entrepreneur. Something of the sort occurred in France at the end of 1948 and led in 1949 to a very important and successful repatriation of French capital. But such efforts may have the equally unfortunate effect of throwing men out of work and losing the confidence of the trade unions.

The truth is that much more education on these matters is needed on both sides of the industrial arena if the free economy is not to break down under the weight of accumulated distrust. Governments must do what they can to check the consequences of distrust. Strikes by workers for purely political ends can be discouraged by legal penalties. Strikes by investors and entrepreneurs—particularly the strike which takes the form of sending money abroad—can also, though usually much less successfully, be checked by legal action, by exchange control, even by confiscation. But all this is to attack the symptoms, not the disease and the disease is distrust. The worker in free economies has to be convinced—and it will take time—that a reasonable stability of employment will be his. The manager, the investor, the entrepreneur have to be as prepared to think freshly and courageously about the financial mechanisms available to free society as their own production engineers and research chemists are prepared to think about new products, new processes and new discoveries.

So brief an outline of possible policies for economic expansion cannot hope to counter all the doubts and criticism which the pursuit of full employment can still arouse. That there are risks in such a pursuit cannot be denied, yet often those who stress these risks do so as though the last thirty years had been a halcyon period of steady progress, sustained expansion and universal growth. They have been on the contrary among the bloodiest, beastliest, most inhuman decades Western man has ever managed to survive. Risks must be very great indeed to equal those risks of total deflation and depression which helped to bring Europe to Fascism, Nazism, and the world to the brink of destruction in total war. Risks must be very great to counter the despair which in the twenties and thirties made so many converts to communism and even today persuade the awakening masses of the East to turn a questioning eye to Moscow. Those who talk of the risk of inflation and the risk of expansion must at least remember that they are discussing at best an equality of risk and that the opposite road has already led mankind into an appalling blind alley of irrationality and war.

Yet the risks remain and the criticisms must be met. It is, for instance, a serious criticism to say that a policy of sustained expansion such as has been outlined here can lead to such a rigidity and distortion of an economy, such a piling up of unwanted goods, such a mass of unusable equipment, that at some point a collapse must follow.

This risk of glut is perhaps exaggerated. In any economy where purchasing power is reasonably stable, a vast mass of it is spent on daily consumption and even in the trough of a depression a large part of this contrives to continue. It is also true that the replacement of old equipment by new and the retooling of plants and workshops can be a reasonably steady process, demanding on an average about 5 or 6 per cent of a nation's resources each year. The risk of distortion and the misuse of resources is most obvious when new investment comes into question and the old yardstick of profit tends to weed out the ventures which can never pay their way. Nevertheless, it is difficult to believe that in the whole range of the Atlantic economy—quite apart from virtually undeveloped areas elsewhere—there are not sufficient profitable ventures waiting in the next ten or twenty years to keep an annual investment program of some 10 per cent of total resources in being. Compared with the immense flow of daily expenditures, the sum is very small. With populations rising, technological change continuing and the infinite possibilities of atomic energy still virtually unexplored, such a relatively modest sum can surely be found profitable employment.

In any case, the free nations can preserve a margin of flexibility by allowing a certain minimum of unemployed resources, both of manpower and materials, in their economies. It has been estimated that if 3 per cent of the working population are temporarily seeking employment, there is a sufficient slack in the economy to ensure competition and genuine effort. In their proposals for full employment policies, the United Nations experts suggest that automatic governmental devices for increasing demand shall come into play only when unemployment has exceeded 3 per cent of the insured population for a number of months in succession. Such a safety valve might give just the necessary check to inflation. And it is always as well to remember that it is really not difficult to check inflation. As the experience of Belgium and Italy have recently proved, governments can produce deflation almost overnight. It is the restoration of confidence, investment and aggressive expansion that can be the real problem. In the workings of an economy, as in so much else, it is easier to stop something than to set it going again.

One last criticism must be mentioned. Policies of full employment and full expansion are not difficult to imagine in large self-contained economies which are in control of their own resources, raw materials and reserves of manpower. But how do they work in economies which are essentially dependent upon foreign trade and which, therefore, do not control fully their own economic environment? The British economy has no certainty of being able to sell its goods steadily in Argentina or Canada or the United States. Yet declining sales in any of these markets would leave it without the food and the raw materials necessary to keep its workers fed and employed. Not a country in Western Europe is self-sufficient. All depend upon the general state of the world market for essential supplies. They cannot, in the middle of a general recession, hope to haul themselves up by their own bootstraps. On the contrary, a measure of deflation in one economy can communicate itself with painful speed to its neighbors. How, in these circumstances, can countries which depend upon trade plan for full expansion and employment?

Part of the answer lies naturally in the extent to which all the free nations are prepared to adopt policies of expansion. Above all, if both the United States and the British trading area—the sterling area—aim at stability and expansion, the larger part of world trade would be covered automatically. But this question of the international maintenance of economic stability carries the argument beyond the limits set by each national economy and belongs properly to the discussion of the international commitments and policies of the free world. That each nation should pursue stability and expansion is an essential starting point, but the full structure of a functioning Western economy depends upon the joint edifice of prosperity that is built above. In economics, as in politics and defense, there is no final security in isolation, and in the long run, the West will be nothing unless it is one.

# PART III · *Unity*

# 13

# *Can the West Unite?*

IN THE world-wide war of words, of propaganda and diplomacy, which the Soviets are waging against the West, one aim above all is at the center of their effort—to destroy the unity of the free world. This is the redoubt which they are determined to reduce, this the defense line they probe at every point to find its weak links and burst it open. The "peace campaign," for instance, is designed to confuse people's moral sense and to mobilize their deep desire for peace against the atomic bomb, the one weapon in which the West at present enjoys superiority. In Europe, the Communist Parties constantly portray the United States as an aggressive capitalist power intervening in Europe's internal affairs for its own imperialist purposes. The Marshall Plan has been a plot to dump American "surplus" goods and to capture markets for dollar goods which the slump-ridden, poverty-stricken American people cannot afford to buy. The Atlantic Pact and military aid are part of a devilish scheme to make mercenaries of the European states so that they can fight American wars. The old gibe once directed against the British, that they "would fight to the last French soldier" has been resurrected and flung at the Americans. They are the warmongers, their intervention is the only possible source of future war. Hence, in the interests of peace (the peace campaign once more) Europe must insist on the removal of the

American "invaders." "Amis, go home" is the Communist slogan in Western Germany. "Americans, clear out. Take your troops home. What are you doing on this side of the Atlantic? Stop meddling in other people's affairs." Those men and women in the United States who still long for the days when such strict nonintervention was the bedrock of American policy must find it somewhat disconcerting that Joseph Stalin should be among the keenest supporters of American isolationism.

The tale in Asia is no different. Everywhere Communist propaganda strives to present America as an imperialist power, trying either to revive the colonial control which the other Western Powers have largely abandoned or to prop up subservient and corrupt native regimes which will go along with "United States' monopolists and financiers" in the systematic exploitation of the Asian masses. When, for the month of August, 1950, the Soviet representative, Mr. J. Malik, returned to the Security Council to take over the Presidency, he used this forum to conduct daily tirades of abuse and attack on American "intervention" in Korea . . . "this beastly business, this colonial war" . . . and to demand that the American troops should take themselves home from Korea, from Japan and from every other Asian base and "leave Asia to settle its own affairs."

Mr. Malik's campaign was not without subtlety. Within a week of his return to Lake Success he realized that although the world had, outside the Soviet sphere of domination, unanimously approved of American action in support of the United Nations in South Korea, there were other aspects of American policy in the Far East which received anything but unreserved support. Opinion was sharply divided in the Security Council itself on the issue whether or not the realities of the Communist victory in China should be recognized and whether a Communist representative should take the place of the Chinese Nationalist delegate in the Security Council. This wider issue was exacerbated by the problem of Formosa. There the Nationalists were still in control, but in the early summer of 1950, a Communist invasion from the mainland had seemed imminent. Immediately after the North Korean attack, President Truman had taken the obvious military decision to prevent any further spread of Communist power in the immediate vicinity of the Communist onslaught in Korea. He announced that Formosa would be "isolated" from the arena. The American Seventh Fleet would safeguard the island against invasion from the mainland. Meanwhile, the Nationalists would cease their bombing attacks upon the Chinese coast. Unhappily for the clarity of this strategy some weeks later, General MacArthur, combining in himself the rôles of United Nations Commander in Korea and American Commander-in-Chief in the Far East, visited Formosa and the Nationalists were quick to seize on the opportunity to imply that the United States was now committed not to "neutralizing" Formosa but to actively defending it in support of the Nationalist cause.

Opinion in the non-Communist world, already divided on the issue of Communist China's representation, grew more disturbed lest the action that had begun as a clear United Nations defense of South Korea might be spread to include intervention in China's civil war. Mr. Malik was quick to seize the advantage offered by this wavering. He seized upon Pandit Nehru's earlier attempt to link the Korean war with the issue of China's representation in the United Nations and insisted that the Security Council should consider this question before dealing with any proposals for peacemaking in Korea. Day after day the wrangle continued but at least Mr. Malik had the satisfaction of bringing the issue of China to the vote and seeing the Council divided—with Britain and India voting for Communist China's admission to the Council, the United States against it. Even if only by an inch, the chisel had been inserted into the crack in the united front of the free nations. One success, at least, had been scored in the general Soviet strategy of confronting a squabbling, uncertain and interminably divided free world with the vast united strength and total unanimity of the Soviet monolith.

It would be unwise to belittle this Communist campaign. No doubt on the immediate issues of Communist China's representation and the future of Formosa, an agreed policy can be reached. The basis of the claim to represent a people must rest to a very great extent upon a question of fact—does the government's writ run throughout the country or does it not? On this basis, the Nationalist claim to represent China has become somewhat ridiculous and Asiatic opinion must tend to ask what deeper reasons the Americans have for pursuing a policy which seems contrary to reason and good sense. The Communists are, of course, delighted to provide their version of what those reasons are. The basis of accepting Chinese Communist representatives in the United Nations should be, as Mr. Trygve Lie has suggested, the simple physical fact that they are in control and can govern. Admittedly, however, Chinese intervention in both Tibet and Korea must undermine the readiness of other states to receive Communist China into the community of the United Nations.

The decision to "neutralize" Formosa is so obvious and sensible a strategic decision that, provided the ambiguities which the Chinese Nationalists try to attach to the policy are removed, it could become the basis of an agreed strategy among the free nations until such time as the Communist aggression in Korea has been brought to an end. Afterwards, the future of the island rests legally upon the final peace treaty with Japan, of which, in international law, Formosa is still a part. The correct solution, once treaty-making begins, might lie either in the transfer of the island to China or in a plebiscite to determine the wishes of the people who actually live in Formosa and to whom little attention has been paid by any parties to the dispute. Independence under a United Nations guarantee and with the certainty of economic aid from the free world might be a more attractive proposition than the control of Mao Tse-tung.

These issues, delicate as they seem, are, however, only one tiny segment of the free world's front of diplomacy and common action. This whole front is under constant Communist pressure and if a rift is mended here and agreement ends a difficulty there, the Soviet search for further uncertainties and disagreements will simply shift its direction and the relentless probing will continue just the same. It is the totality of the effort that disconcerts some observers in the West. "How," they ask, "can a group of free and independent states, loosely united by a number of common purposes some of which they would find it very difficult even to define, withstand the discipline and the unanimity of a world *bloc* held together by the strongest bonds of power and ideology? The methods that are open to the Soviets are not open to us. We cannot impose unity from above by making the national policy of the strongest among us the line which every other state must follow. The Soviet Union has subordinated the aims of all its satellites to the single aim of defending the Soviet fatherland by such measures as the Soviet fatherland shall determine. If it means turning foreign trade inside out, the present Czech regime will do it. If it means ruining the peasants in a total drive for collectivization, the Bulgarian government will do it. If it means accepting a Russian general as virtual head of the state and affiliating the armed forces with the Red Army, the Poles will do it. The new internationalism—which is the subordination of anyone else's nationalism to that of Soviet Russia—is an instrument that only the Russians can use. They can disguise it as a single Communist ideology. They can find converts to that ideology in each country. They can hang the Communists—such as Kostov or Rajk—whose nationalist prejudices remain too strong. Behind it all is the threat of mass deportation to Siberia which has already emptied the Baltic States of three-quarters of their inhabitants. Admittedly this policy can turn in the Soviets' hands. In Tito, they found a Communist unwilling to swallow the pill of Soviet imperialism, in spite of the coating of Marxist sugar. But even so, this fusing of nationalism and ideology, of imperialism and pseudo-internationalism is probably the most formidable instrument of unity and control mankind has ever seen. What have we in the West to set against it?"

The answer is, of course, nothing—of that kind. The

essence of the Western way of life, the essence of freedom itself is that there shall be neither enforced obedience nor enforced unanimity. The free world has a much more delicate problem of unity to solve. The only unity that will not destroy the way of life it is supposed to protect is a unity containing immense diversity, tension, discord, opposition and hairsbreadth balance. In a free society there are always some forces pressing against the outermost limits of unity and threatening to overstep them, there are always moments when, with their hearts in their mouths, men of good will must ask whether this time the rift has not opened too widely between conflicting ideas or interests and whether unity itself has not vanished into the abyss. If Communism is a loud tune played over and over again in violent unison by a band of trombones and tubas, the free way of life has the complicated harmonies of a full orchestra. The price paid for its variety and freedom and capacity to make all sorts of music is the miserable cacophony into which it can also fall. The same orchestra, the same players, the same leaders have it in them to give the world first a set of variations on the theme of appeasement and, within a year, a grandiose masterpiece in the spirit of Dunkirk. There is no solution to the problem of unity in asking every instrument in the orchestra of democracy to play the same tune. The task is the infinitely more testing one of letting their harmonies grow together.

In other words, we of the free world have to live with our differences and progress together and work together in spite of them. It is as well, therefore, to know where the differences lie and assess them frankly.

National divisions and antipathies run deep. Between the new world of nationally independent states that is struggling to birth in Asia and the older, wealthier and more stable community of the Atlantic lies a gulf which only ten years ago one might have called unbridgeable. Divided in culture and tradition, in race and history, the two groups had also to erase from their immediate memories two hundred years of colonial control of the East by the West. Not for nothing does

Communist propaganda to Asia hammer away, day after day, at the "imperialist pretensions" of the Atlantic powers. Not for nothing does the Soviet regime stress on occasion its Asiatic aspects. Stalin would no doubt not wish to be reminded of the day in 1941 when shortly before Pearl Harbor, he kissed the Japanese Foreign Secretary, Mr. Matsuoka, at Moscow railway station, remarking, "We are all Asiatics." But no one can deny that the development of the Soviet Union's industrial wealth beyond the Urals and its drastic plans for Siberian settlement have increased the Asiatic aspect of the Soviet community. Nothing meanwhile is left undone to point the contrast between Russia's solidarity as an Asiatic state with Asia's fundamental interests and the gross interference practiced by the non-Asiatic powers of the West.

As we have already seen, certain developments since 1945 have undermined the efficacy of this promising Soviet line. The Soviet Union has itself intervened in Asia in the manner of the old-style imperialist by annexing Port Arthur. The old-style imperialists themselves have very largely taken themselves off. India, Pakistan, Ceylon, Burma and Indonesia are now fully independent Asian states each ready—with greater or lesser efficiency—to deal with their own local Communists and to turn a wary eye on Russia's pretensions to Asiatic leadership. Much has therefore been gained, but the relations between Asia and the West remain as delicate as exacerbated nationalism, mutual incomprehension and Western overconfidence can make them. One reason for the dangerous situation that has arisen in the Far East is that Asian opinion on the whole accepts Mao Tse-tung's victory in China as a genuine expression of the Chinese people's will and tends to see in American support for Chiang Kai-shek an "interference" in Asian affairs that recalls the older imperialism. That this view is encouraged by Communist propaganda is not in doubt, but it is essential that no Western policy should be capable of receiving such a twist. No non-Communist Asian nation, for instance, has criticized the American action in Korea. On the contrary, each one has openly supported it, some to the pitch of sending troops. This approbation has been a severe blow to Moscow and the strongest possible reinforcement of the United States' moral position. In Asia, it is not enough that Western policy should be disinterested. It must also appear so. When Pandit Nehru complained, during the discussion of China's representation in the Security Council last August, that the Western Powers took too little account of Asian opinions and susceptibilities in reaching their decisions, he was reminding them of a habit which might, if pursued, shatter the narrow bridges of growing confidence which since 1945 have been thrown across the gulf between East and West.

Some critics are inclined to scoff at the idea of Asian opinion. "What is it," they ask, "but the outlook of an infinitesimally small group of intellectuals and politicians who have no conceivable claim to be representative?" Yet this same opinion has remade the map of Asia in the last ten years, and however little of the world's great debate may trickle down to the rice paddies and the plantations, some obscure ferment of ideas is at work there so that when their leaders speak of national independence, the masses understand and when they are offered bread and land, they follow. These are the forces which the Communists hope to harness to their revolution and which even the new native leaders of Asia must take into account. Do the Western Powers suppose that they can simply wish them out of existence?

It is likely that in the next twenty or thirty years—crucial years for containment—the difficulties impeding confidence and understanding between East and West will prove the most dangerous and hampering to the creation of a united free world. But they are not by any means the only difficulties. The Western world itself has its divisions and its misunderstandings, and often they seem more violent and more unbridgeable because everyone's idiom is the same. Everyone expects the same standards of behavior and norms of judgment. We cannot say of our Western neighbors, "Ah, but you must expect the Eastern or the Asian or the Oriental view of life to differ from ours." We do not expect our view of life to be radically different from that of our next-door neighbor—across the Channel or across the Atlantic—and the amount of heat we put into our local disputes is proportionately greater. Certainly by any standard of measurement, the new Asian governments are daily excused errors of policy and outlook which would double-damn any European or American statesman caught out in the same misdeeds. This unrelenting vigilance of criticism reaches a really remarkable pitch in the relations between Great Britain and the United States, whose citizens talk each other's tongue and read each other's newspapers perhaps too avidly for peace of mind on either side of the Atlantic.

The starting point of all these national difficulties and frictions is the fact that the mature, distinct, long-established and somewhat ingrown national states of the West would in their hearts rather be left alone. An immense fund of natural isolationism underlies most national reactions and it takes very little to change it from a passive preference for one's own ways and interests into an active dislike of other peoples'. Opportunities for isolationism, however, vary from state to state and the tug of war between the need for external support and co-operation and internal resistance to the very idea of it makes up a large part of the daily drama of Western diplomacy. When the war ended, there were, in addition to each local isolationism, some broader trends of separatist policy which had the effect of holding the West apart for at least eighteen months after victory. It is an ironic thought that in 1945 there was a tendency both in the United States and in Europe to believe that each could better come to terms with Russia than the other. President Roosevelt had the presentiment that the "new forces" in the Soviet Union might be ready to build "one world" more quickly than Mr. Churchill who had "not been His Majesty's First Minister in order to preside over the dissolution of the British Empire." The return of the Labour Party to power in Britain in 1945 and the strength of the Left in Europe at that time created the opposite view that "Socialist Europe" could make terms with the Soviet Union more speedily than "capitalist America." This belief has even lingered on under the guise of the Third

Force—a social democratic bloc in Europe which, in full neutrality, would "mediate" between the rival extremes of American capitalism and Soviet Communism.

So long as such views prevailed, there could be no working Atlantic community. They were, as we now see, based on precisely the same fallacy—that there was something the Americans called "progress" and the Europeans "socialism" which both could share with Russia but not with each other and that there was something called "imperialism" which the United States saw in Britain and a "reaction" which the Europeans saw in America which could prevent the Western Powers from working with each other. All of them missed the point which has since proved decisive—that the Western Powers shared the fundamental attribute of freedom and the Soviet Union represented the opposite and irreconcilable principle of totalitarian dictatorship. [1]

The West must thank the Soviet Government for the enlightenment that has since revealed the fundamental alignment between the enslaved and the free. They might, of their own free volition and insight, have understood the division in the end, but by that time, the process of indirect Communist pressure and infiltration might have left nothing in Europe to save. As it was, the tide was turned by the inability of the Soviets to bide their time and leave the natural isolationism of the West to grow. Perhaps their most signal error was their failure to perceive how ready the United States was in 1945 and 1946 to do all the things the Communists clamor for now—withdrawal of troops, retreat into a purely national view of policy, abandonment of Far Eastern interests, retirement from world responsibility. But their mistakes in Europe were as great. They destroyed socialism in Eastern Europe and snubbed it in the West, they fought in the trade unions, they sickened the workers with political strikes, they outraged liberals by their treatment of liberals in the East, they alien-

[1] The author recalls a lunch in 1942 with that remarkable writer, the late George Orwell, in the course of which he banged the table and repeated again and again, "After the war you will not be able to work with Russia because it is a dictatorship. You will be able to work with America because it is a democracy."

ated scientists by their dragooning of science, they wearied everyone with screaming propaganda. It is hard to think of an error that Soviet policy did not commit.

The first victim of all these efforts was the deep isolationism of the West. Reluctantly but decisively the United States abandoned the predominant concentration upon its own interests which was typical in 1945 and 1946; in 1947 came the turning point of the Marshall Plan. The desire for a Third Force lingered on in Europe and, as evidence of Russia's military strength increased, was reinforced by a desire to be neutral and not a battlefield in a possible war between the United States and the Soviet Union. But this mood, too, began to fade as the Russians proved how "neutrals" fared in Soviet-occupied Europe. By 1949, there was little trace left of the confusions that had followed victory in 1945. An Atlantic community of interest was beginning to take shape.

There is no denying, however, that this community was and is still confused. At the risk of considerable oversimplification, one can say that the root of the confusion lies in the peculiar position and predicament of Great Britain. In the community of the Atlantic and in the wider fraternity of free nations, Britain is a member of three distinct groups of powers. First in sentiment, tradition and age comes its membership in the British Commonwealth. It has the closest possible relationships with the two Pacific Dominions, Australia and New Zealand, relations hardly less close with Canada, and a link—now weakened by the racial issue—with South Africa. In British eyes, the value of the Commonwealth has been greatly enhanced by the decision of three independent Asian nations—India, Pakistan and Ceylon—to remain within it. This development has encouraged the hope that when independent nations have grown to maturity in the West Indies and in Africa, they too will decide to remain within the Commonwealth family. This political system is to a limited extent reinforced by a loose economic grouping which is roughly coterminous with the Commonwealth but excludes some Dominions, such as Canada, and includes some non-Commonwealth states, such as Iraq. This is the sterling area, a group of states which conduct with each other full multilateral trade on the basis of sterling and keep a single dollar pool of all the dollars it earns in London.

In the second place, Britain is a willing and eager member of whatever Atlantic community can be brought into being. The lesson of 1940 has been well learned. The British know that there is no security in the world for them without the partnership of the United States and Canada. Moreover, they are little by little overcoming the prejudices and obstacles that have in the past rather damped their desire for close association with the United States. In some circles, a critical mood remains. It is not a hundred years since Britain held the position of arbiter of the world, now occupied by the United States. To lose freedom of action and decisive leadership and to see them pass to another power is always galling and it is particularly so among those trained in the habit of command. It is for this reason, perhaps, that it is in British administrative circles—in the Foreign and Colonial Offices, for instance—that the instinct to dislike Americans as inexperienced upstarts seems to persist. In general, however, the fantastic speed with which the United States has settled to the tasks of world responsibility and leadership and the tact with which on the whole its duties have been discharged—did any plan ever impinge less on the people it assisted than the Marshall Plan?—have produced a new mood of respect and gratitude in Britain. America's ability to aid without intervening has also brought about a complete revolution in the thinking of the Labour Party and the trade unions. When one reads the successive programs of the Labour Party since 1945 and notices increasingly cordial references to American assistance and American partnership and the gradual disappearance of all mention of the Soviet Union, one has an uncanny feeling of watching an entire ideological revolution occurring in the space of five years.

Last of all, Britain is a member of the European community. Here the lesson of 1940 applies in reverse. The British who have seen the sites for guided missiles built on the Channel coast do not imagine that affairs across the twenty miles of water are no concern of theirs. Nor is their interest simply the narrow interest of fear. Since the war, the recognition of the need for the closest relations with Europe has grown remarkably and is now accepted with enthusiasm by many Conservatives under Mr. Churchill's leadership and, somewhat grudgingly, by the Labour Party. This pressure of public opinion has been enough to bring about Britain's participation in the Council of Europe and has led, for the first time in peacetime, to British willingness to join in setting up a completely integrated European High Command.

On the face of it, this position occupied by Britain at the intersecting point of three communities does not appear either very complex or very disadvantageous. In theory, it offers a unique opportunity for constructive action and numberless occasions for progressive and co-operative diplomacy. The aim of the three communities is, after all, the same—the pursuit of unity, the containing of Russia, the building of a free and expanding world economy. Can it not be argued that it is Britain's supreme good fortune, at a time when in point of strength its influence has passed its zenith, to find that this accident of politics and geography has left it such a vital rôle to play on the stage of the free world? And, indeed, the argument would be convincing and conclusive if only all three communities had the same notion of how unity and defense and strength can best be secured. To be the center of three revolving wheels can be an influential and even exhilarating position if all the wheels are going in the same direction and at roughly the same speed. But what if they are not? The British position then becomes about as uncomfortable as any position a state could occupy. Everything that gets stuck in the wheels, every failure to advance, every jamming and every useless revolution will be blamed on the one power which sits in the middle and which, because it cannot follow each wheel in its separate gyrations, ends by looking like a brake upon them all.

This is, in fact, what has occurred. Britain's partners in the United States and Europe have put a different emphasis upon Western unity than the British do themselves. Influential opinion both in the United States and in Europe has come to believe that political federation is the right method of securing unity and that Western Europe is the right place to try it out. Two points have influenced American thinking. The first is their own constitutional experience. One hundred and fifty years ago the federal experiment was begun in the United States and no state that had experienced the phenomenal growth and freedom and unity-in-diversity of the United States could fail to believe that the experiment was worth repeating. It is true that in its latter-day relations with sovereign states in its own hemisphere, the United States has followed the practical and empirical rather than the federal approach. The Pan-American system is one of independent sovereign states meeting together to concert policies of mutual interest. With Canada the useful experiment of joint defense under two governments has been a proved success. But federation in Europe would not need American participation, only its enthusiasm and support.

The other American argument is the immense economic strength that has been built up in the United States as a result of its single market. Take away the twenty-odd separate boundaries of Western Europe, the federalists argue, and in the unified market that would result, production would expand and productivity increase as it has done in the United States. This argument for economic integration is not confined to the federalists. Many whose minds on constitution-making are completely open see no economic future for Europe save in the breaking of its narrow nationalist bonds of autarchy. The arguments reinforce each other, however, when the difficulty of realizing economic integration without political union is fully grasped.

The response in continental Europe to this order of ideas has come in part from the traditional strength of the European idea, in part from the postwar revolt against economic regulation and planning on a national basis. But where the mood for federalism is strongest—in France, Germany and Italy—it springs from another source. All three countries have been wrecked and drawn into catastrophic wars by their national rivalries. In the course of these wars, they have been occupied by the enemy, the central administration has been broken to pieces (at one time in World War II four separate authorities ruled in different parts of Italy), they have lost confidence in governments made up of party coalitions. Many of them no longer believe that a central national authority can either protect interests or secure loyalties. In a word, they are disillusioned with the idea of national government as such and believe that only a European government can recreate their moral and political stability. This mood is reinforced in France by the belief that Germany can be drawn into the Western community without risk of renewed domination only if the framework of that community is federal. Thus to American promptings toward integration and federalism, many Frenchmen, Germans and Italians, and to a lesser extent, the Belgians and the Dutch have made an enthusiastic response. In the last two years, more and more of their plans have had a federal undercurrent and in the Schuman Plan the aim of making the project the first step toward a federal Europe is stated explicitly.

The British, who have been spared the harrowing experiences of occupation and have a political system of venerable age and incomparable stability, do not feel this federal urge (nor, incidentally, do the Scandinavian powers, who in the main have also avoided the worst consequences of war). Neither the Conservative nor the Labour Party accepts the idea of strict federal union and although no one would refuse Mr. Churchill the title of "good European" or deny that he, more than anyone else, had brought the Council of Europe into being, it is clear that, in common with all other responsible British leaders, he does not accept either the federal method or its application to a union of Britain with Western Europe. The reason is in part the difference in emotional climate already described, in part it is a British preference for the methods which have held together both the independent Commonwealth and the sterling area—the methods of intergovernmental co-operation and of a steadily tightening mesh of agreements on specific points. But the chief reason is the fear lest a close and exclusive association with Europe would cut Britain off from its links with the Commonwealth and weaken its relations with the United States. For Britain, Western Europe is only one small part of the great community in which it feels itself to be an essential partner. No political leader, no political party is prepared to sacrifice the whole for the part.

It is no use denying that many people in both the United States and Europe find this a very tiresome attitude. Wherever on either side of the Atlantic there still lurk traces of isolationism, the reaction is frankly angry. If only Britain would settle down in Europe and drop these trans-Atlantic aspirations, America could get on with its own affairs and Europe would be left in peace. Fortunately, Russia has left so little of this outlook in peoples' conscious thinking that probably it does no more than produce small bursts of irrational irritation. Nevertheless, these small bursts tend to get into print.

A more widespread difficulty, especially in America, is the inability to understand the store Britain sets by its Commonwealth links. Only five or six years ago, the distrust of the Commonwealth as the creation of British imperialism was widespread; dislike of the sterling area as a "plot against the dollar" is still current. It would take little short of a revolution to cause American opinion to see both as two of the few remaining mechanisms that underpin the little stability left in the world. There are some signs that the revolution is taking place. The vital importance of Australia to Pacific defense and the rôle of Canada in the Atlantic are recognized. India's decision to remain in the Commonwealth has undoubtedly influenced American opinion to which, before 1947, British imperialism in India was only slightly less abhorrent than Hitler's in Europe. But even where the contribution that individual members of the Commonwealth can make is recognized, the conclusion does not necessarily follow that the Commonwealth as a system has any particular value or that it has sufficient importance to be allowed to stand in the way of the overriding advantages believed to exist in a European federation. In some circles in both the United States and Europe, it is held that Britain should be forced to choose between the "solid reality" of Europe and the vague, amorphous relations it maintains with distant Dominions which, in any case, might easily prefer to be linked with the United States—Australia and Canada are often indifferently assigned to this category.

What can the British say to explain the precise relations which hold together their Commonwealth? They hardly know themselves. Its essence is its lack of constitution, its minimum of binding force. Yet they know that they can work mutually useful financial arrangements with their Dominions which, if tried out with France or Belgium, would collapse in a week. They know that twice in a lifetime, Australia, New Zealand and Canada have joined them without a moment's hesitation in their struggle against one of the states which is now to form the "solid reality" of Europe. They believe—they cannot know yet—that the relationship between the English-speaking Dominions and the new Asiatic Dominions will do more than anything else to create self-respect and mutual respect in the dealings of East with West. Even if all these things cannot be reduced to the lawyer's draft of a federal document, the British cannot but weigh them in the balance of their choice—if they are forced to choose.

Unhappily for understanding and good will between the Western partners, criticism of Britain's political hesitation *vis-à-vis* Europe has been intensified by the suspicion that the real reason for it is not a genuine preference for a wider Atlantic community or deep loyalty to Commonwealth ties but plain economic isolationism. There are three threads in this distrust of Britain's economic policies. The first is an old thread woven many years ago into the American attitude toward the Commonwealth. In American trading opinion, "discrimination," the granting to one nation of advantages not conceded to others, has always been the cardinal sin. This the British committed at the bottom of the Great Depression when, at the Ottawa Conference, they introduced imperial preference and gave the Dominions and received from them trading advantages not extended to other states. The second thread is the issue of convertibility. Since the war, the dollar has been so scarce and so sought after that the British have only once—during the disastrous summer of 1947—permitted the free conversion of sterling into dollars. Throughout the sterling area, sterling may not be converted into dollars and the dollars earned are paid into a central pool controlled by the monetary authorities in London. It is true that every dollar earned is spent and that no amount of converting sterling into dollars would increase the flow of dollars into the world's markets. That figure is fixed by American purchases, loans and gifts abroad. But traders—among them American traders—holding unconvertible sterling and unable to secure dollars for it, easily come to attack the sterling area system as a vast device to protect British interests.

The last thread is the belief that British economic policy has used its controls, its sterling area, its unconvertibility and its close system of bilateral trade pacts to promote its socialist planning at home. All attempts to free trade in Europe, the argument runs, have broken on the obstinate refusal of the British to risk interference in their planned economy. They maintain full employment by pouring sterling into the world and they ensure that it will all be spent on buying British goods by keeping it unconvertible. Thus they sacrifice all change, movement and progress in the general economy to their own narrow interest in national planning. It is economic isolationism, reinforcing political isolationism, that keeps them from joining with Europe. They will not expose their inflated economy to competition. They will not test the value of their currency in the open market. This is the very system of Dr. Schacht himself masquerading under the name of social democracy.

The visitor from the moon, reading so far, would no doubt conclude that the Western community is a myth. In its place he would see a group of angry powers bandying criticism backward and forward, glaring at each other in unconcealed irritation and obviously quite unable to discover any inner principle of harmony and cohesion. When Sir

Stafford Cripps is not lecturing the French, Mr. Foster is lecturing him. When M. Petsche stops attacking Mr. Gaitskill, M. Frère weighs in with his criticisms. And every now and then, everyone joins together in a chorus of mutual recrimination. Is this too fanciful an account of some aspects of the relations between the United States, Britain and Europe in recent years? In fact, the outlook is not so tragic as these exchanges might suggest. The differences and difficulties remain, and it is the purpose of these chapters to examine them further, but it can be said quite dogmatically at this stage that they are not sufficient to check the further growth and consolidation of the Western world. In the immediate future the chief political issue will be defense and on this there should be no real division of opinion between the United States, Britain and Western Europe. When the defense of the free world is at stake, no one suggests that anything less than a full Atlantic partnership will suffice and the creation of such an Atlantic defense system now has the first call on all the energies of the West.

Economic differences, too, have been growing less acute in recent months. This is an issue to which we must return later. Here it is sufficient to point out that both in its domestic and in its international policies, the British government has reconsidered the rigid planning that was its ideal in 1945. The Labour Party program of 1950, *Labour and the New Society*, places a new emphasis upon competitive efficiency, costs, productivity and the lowering of export prices, admits the rôle of dynamic private enterprise and makes no new proposals for nationalization. In its international policy, Britain, by signing the European Payments Union and taking a lead in the removal of all quantitative restrictions in about 60 per cent of its trade with Europe in the course of 1950, has restored convertibility and competition over a large sector of British trade. Nor has the modification of policy come only from the side of the "planners." The long discussion of full employment at the summer session in 1950 of the Economic and Social Council underlined the need for the less managed economies to introduce stability into their domestic and foreign trade and in the course of 1949 and 1950, it was the American authorities in the ECA missions that urged more expansive policies upon Belgium, Germany and Italy. Beneath the surface of economic dispute, there seemed to be appearing for the first time a certain minimum economic strategy upon which the West could agree.

The chief reason, however, for remarking but not fearing the differences within the Western world is the new mood of urgency and realism introduced by the Communist onslaught on Korea. Much that seemed vital before June 1950 now appears the very luxury of argument. In the new mood of unity and determination, obstacles exist only to be overcome.

# 14

## *The Next Two Years*

◇◇◇◇◇◇◇◇◇◇◇◇◇◇◇◇◇◇◇◇◇◇◇◇◇◇◇◇◇◇◇◇◇◇◇◇◇◇◇◇◇◇◇◇◇◇◇◇

THREE tasks have already been suggested as the immediate target of the Western Powers, as their absolute priorities in the effort of containment. The first is the building of an effective system of joint defense, the second the maintenance of stability and expansion in the United States and Europe, the third a new, systematic and much more ambitious effort to raise the standards of backward peoples, particularly in Asia. The basis of this triple policy is, naturally, the maintenance and expansion of economic strength in each co-operating nation, and some of the possible means for achieving it have already been suggested. But the Western Powers also need to pursue a joint economic strategy and achieve a wide measure of practical economic co-operation, since, apart from the United States, none of them can make its contribution, either to defense, stability or expansion, unless it can count on the support and collaboration of the whole Western team.

Of the three tasks the first is in some ways the easiest. It is in the field of defense that governments find it most natural to sacrifice their sovereign powers where the pretensions of total sovereignty look most absurd. The West has also had the recent and successful experience of integrated armies under a single international command in the shape of SHAEF, the Supreme Headquarters of the Allied Expeditionary Force, set up for the campaigns of the last war. When within three years of victory, Russia's military preparations compelled the Western Powers to look once more to their defenses, it was to this earlier model that they turned. In 1948, Britain, France and the three nations of the Benelux Union—Belgium, Holland and Luxemburg—signed the Brussels Pact of Western Union and at once set about the establishment of a single military headquarters. Under the supreme command of Viscount Montgomery, the land forces and the naval forces of Western Union were allotted to French commanders, the air force to an Englishman. A completely international staff was created at Fontainebleau and defensive plans began to be prepared in which the functions of the military forces of each nation were worked out on a completely integrated basis.

By the following year, Soviet diplomacy had achieved the development which of all others it should have most striven to prevent—the decision of the United States to enter in peacetime into military engagements with other powers. So rapidly have the currents of history poured past the Western door in recent years that it is already difficult to remember what a turning point in the destiny of the free world was reached when the United States signed the Atlantic Pact and committed itself to the defense of its neighbors in Europe. But it is essential to keep the perspective of history and to remember, particularly when progress seems to be slow and the temptation to criticize strong, what a revolutionary change in Atlantic relations the American decision of 1949 brought about.

The shaping of the new alliance brought into existence three defense regions—a northern, covering Scandinavia and the Baltic; a central region, coterminous with Western Union; and a southern, concerned primarily with the defense of the Mediterranean. No supreme headquarters was established for the new pact, however, and its chief military organ for the time being was the Standing Group composed of three high-ranking officers representing the United States, Britain and France in Washington. An informal Anglo-American Joint Chiefs of Staff organization had remained in being after the war. The Standing Group was formed by the co-option of a French member. The actual authority controlling the Pact has come to be called the North Atlantic Defense Council. Its members are the twelve Foreign Ministers of the treaty countries who meet from time to time to decide major matters of policy. Early in 1950, the obvious need for a more sustained organ of supervision and development led to the appointment by the Foreign Ministers of deputies to represent them on the Atlantic Council which was thus able to remain in more or less constant session.

Such was the shape of Western defense when the Communists opened their invasion in Korea. In the clear light of actual aggression, the shortcomings of the structure became suddenly and painfully obvious. It was something gained that a co-operative framework at least existed but the more it was examined, the less was found inside. Of committees and councils and liaison officers and deputies there was no end. Of armed forces and tanks and genuine strategy there seemed almost no trace at all. The Korean campaign thus ushered in a period of severe stock-taking in the sphere of Western defense and especially in the crucial Western Union or "central region" where the loss of hardly a mile of territory could be risked in the event of war. The first need was clearly to get fully armed and equipped units into Europe. A garrison on a scale sufficient to check a Russian advance and give the Atlantic Powers time for general mobilization would, it was estimated, require between 50 to 70 divisions on garrison duty in Europe. Available for Europe from all sources were about a dozen, and those were under strength. The expansion of each national army had, therefore, the first priority together with the expansion of its military expenditure to something comparable to the new American level of over 15 per cent or to whatever higher percentage a strict judgment of military necessity might decree.

The second need was a radical change in strategic thinking. Although in principle, the Atlantic Powers had agreed to "balanced forces" in which each nation would contribute its share to each of the fighting services, in fact, a certain division of function tended to underlie the discussions and this division was, to say the least, extremely disconcerting to the French. The natural forces of geography and history seemed to be pointing the way to the provision by France of the chief land forces while Britain and America would concentrate on sea and air support, the Americans in particular preparing themselves for long-range strategic bombing, presumably based upon the United States. The outline of such a defense scheme meant one thing and one thing only to the French—that a wholly inadequate French army would bear the brunt of a Russian offensive, that Europe would be occupied and then, after years of strategic bombing by its distant ally, would be submitted to the renewed agony of liberation by forces advancing from the presumably still impregnable British Isles. That there would be nothing left to liberate and that liberation itself would be little less a disaster than attack was the common belief of all educated Europeans.

The chief change necessary in Western strategic thinking was therefore not only to increase the size and fire power of the national armies but to station more of them in Europe. The Allies' armies in Germany were already outposts of Western defense rather than armies of occupation. Europe's passionate hope was that they would now be mightily reinforced, particularly by American troops. Indeed, in the case of France, so violent had been the shock administered by occupation in the last war and so uncertain the state of national morale with a certain Communist Fifth Column in its midst that a really effective French contribution to European defense could probably only follow the arrival of British and American reinforcements. French manpower, French resources, French energies would be added to the growing snowball of defense, provided France's allies supplied the original ball and started it rolling.

The third development followed logically upon this need to bring more American and British troops into Europe. A growing body of opinion reached the conclusion that the parallel and overlapping military structure of Western Union and Atlantic Pact had become both cumbrous and unnecessary.

The division existed simply as an historical accident—that the Western Union powers had reached agreement more speedily among themselves than with their great neighbor across the Atlantic. But no single member of the Western Union group would have pretended for a moment that the defense of Europe could be achieved without full American participation. The "central region" of the Atlantic Pact, not Western Union, was the vital military basis of planning and, frankly, Western Union itself had become no more than a duplication of military and staff arrangements that could be more efficiently secured on an Atlantic basis, once the United States and Canada had taken the decision to commit more troops to Europe. As it was, a frightening amount of overlapping and wasted effort appeared to be arising from the multiplication of authorities. The Foreign Ministers and Defense Ministers of the five Western European Powers seemed to be continuously on the move from one international meeting to the next, all with similar agendas and all tending to reproduce the decisions taken elsewhere. The proposal, therefore, began to be put forward with increasing insistence that the whole structure of European defense should be reconsidered.

Some enthusiasts at the summer meeting of the Council of Europe in Strasbourg in 1950 suggested the creation of a single "European Army." Those who foresaw what confusion such a totally unified force might cause in terms of organization, discipline, language, command, and differing military traditions proposed a more sober solution—that the Western Union Pact should be totally absorbed into the Atlantic Pact, that the supreme political authority should be the Atlantic Council composed of the Foreign Ministers of the twelve member states, that deputies of higher political status should be appointed (Ministers of State rather than career diplomats) and that a Combined Chiefs of Staff should be set up in Washington to direct the general strategy of the Atlantic forces. In Europe, Fontainebleau should be transformed into the headquarters of an Atlantic army with an American of the caliber of General Eisenhower in supreme command. For the time being each government should allot to this Atlantic command complete control over agreed national contingents, but would retain responsibility for recruiting, supplying and financing the national armies themselves. Later, perhaps, from the experience of a completely integrated general staff, a single army recruited impartially in all the Atlantic countries and under the direct control of the Atlantic Council might follow. For the present, however, speed remained essential and the allotment of separate national contingents to a central unified command seemed to offer the most rapid line of advance. These various decisions—to station more British and American troops in Europe and to appoint an American Commander in Chief to the Atlantic force—were agreed to by the Foreign Ministers in the autumn meetings of 1950.

The formulation of such a policy clearly raises the problem of Germany's part in a new effort of defense and the United States was convinced that a small German army would have to be created.

This suggestion, however, aroused all France's worst fears and memories—memories of defeat and occupation, fears of a revival of German military might. The British, after some initial hesitation, were ready to admit German divisions under a completely international Atlantic General Staff. The French, unhappily, came to a different conclusion and refused to move forward on the question of German rearmament unless the idea of the "European army" was revived. Each national contingent should be no bigger than a battalion and battalions of mixed nationalities should serve in single divisions, the whole being under a "European" Minister of Defense. In this way, they continued once again to retreat from the "Atlantic" to the purely "European" context and incidentally to place Britain once more in the position of appearing to have to choose between an American-Commonwealth orientation or a European one. More dangerous still was the likelihood that American public opinion might become exasperated at the delay introduced by the French proposal and tend to write Europe off as incorrigible.

At the time of writing, no solution has been found and it can only be hoped that the French Government can be made to realize speedily that the best defense against both Russia now and Germany hereafter lies in full American participation in Atlantic defense. To throw away American support, to delay the appointment of an American Commander in Chief, to weaken the interest of American public opinion and all for the pursuit of a federalism which cannot be secured from one day to the next can only be called folly. The difference between a German battalion and a German division is not worth the risk of failure in the broad field of Atlantic strategy.

The creation of an Atlantic Army would close the most dangerous breach in the defenses of the free world, but Europe is not the only possible scene of aggression. It was suggested in earlier chapters that the number of areas in which Russia could practice "aggression by proxy" is limited. Yet they exist, especially in the Far East, and there, too, defense arrangements need to be both adequate and planned on more than a day-to-day basis. The general control of such a defense system could still be the responsibility of the Combined Chiefs of Staff in Washington, provided the whole British Commonwealth were represented on it and not simply Britain and Canada. The analogy of Korea suggests that the need is for a number of small highly armed, highly mobile armies, drawn from contingents of the co-operating Atlantic and Pacific powers and able to move with all speed to any threatened spot in order to reinforce local resistance. Such an army has come into being in Korea and, provided the constitutional obstacles can be overcome, it would be an immense advantage if the West's mobile defense forces could be placed at the disposal of the United Nations—the point will be discussed in a later chapter.

One last responsibility of any joint military authority must be mentioned—to make sure that, should the worst occur and a general war break out, in spite of all the free world's endeavors, the schemes ready in each nation for full mobilization would be adequate and complementary. A plan for industrial mobilization and the building up of a trained reserve of manpower for the armed forces, which implies some form of universal military training, are as vital to successful defense as joint strategy and joint command. Unmobilized resources, however vast they may be, do not win wars. The Atlantic Council has few heavier responsibilities than to urge, persuade and direct its member governments to ensure that Western defense both in time and resources is defense in depth.

It is at this point that the immediate problems of military defense begin to impinge upon the second task of the Atlantic community—to see to it that in the process of building up its defenses, Europe's economic stability and progress are not put in jeopardy. There is no disguising the fact that the need for greater expenditure on defense and preparedness has come at a most inconvenient time. With the massive aid of the Marshall Plan, Europe had by 1950, reached the brink of stability. An export drive, which had taken British exports to 170 per cent and French exports to 150 per cent of their respective prewar levels, was responsible for part of the improvement. The steady increase in productivity—production at a level of 25 per cent above prewar—also had a hand in it. The ending of inflation had helped. Yet the precariousness of all this was illustrated by the fact that Western Europe's standards of consumption were still well below those of 1938 and that it still needed nearly $3 billion Marshall aid to balance its international account for 1951. Worse still, it looked, on the most optimistic assumptions, as though Europe's trade budget would be out of balance to the extent of over a billion dollars when the Marshall Plan ended in 1952. How, then, could such unstable economies carry the new burden of a defense effort which would reduce their exports, divert production from civilian to military use and everywhere restore the risk of inflation?

A possible answer has already been suggested in the case of the United States—that of a spurt in production to increase national income to the levels necessary to absorb the extra military expenditure. But this solution could not be adopted by Europe simply on its own initiative since the machines and the raw materials necessary for such an increase could not all be procured inside Europe. Indeed, most of them could only come from the United States. They would therefore be unobtainable, except in return for further exports, or further American aid. Exports would now be cut. Could the European nations reasonably expect yet more assistance from the United States?

In fact, as we know, American aid has been extended with the utmost speed to cover the new emergency. The full sum of Marshall aid for 1951 was voted by Congress. In addition, the money available to provide armies for the United States' allies under the Military Aid Program was increased from a billion dollars to $4 billion. In return, the American Government only asked—in a series of official notes to each member of the Atlantic Council—that the defense expenditure of its partners should be adequate. What is emerging is, in fact, very much the pattern of the last war in which, for all war supplies, the rule of "to each according to his need and from each accordingly to his capacity" was adopted. The scheme of Lend-Lease which, with the introduction of return Lend-Lease, became the policy of mutual aid was based upon the idea of removing the dollar sign—and every other money sign—from the war effort of the Grand Alliance. Although a formal return to Mutual Aid has not been announced in the new conditions of containment, something very like it is in fact coming into being. Provided each partner places in the common pool an agreed share of its wealth and work, the United States, as the most powerful member of the group, sees to it that the balance is made up and the local economy held steady. In a segment of each Western economy, which may vary from 10 per cent to 15 per cent of the whole, the earlier conditions of mutual aid are being restored. Nor is it possible to think of any other way in which the immediate effort of containment could be successfully financed.

The fact, however, that the various economies are not and need not be totally engaged in the defense effort must create some very delicate problems. The truth is that the Western world has now to try to work an economic system which is to 15 per cent, co-operative, and for the rest, competitive. The position is not, of course, new. Ever since the war, the American as taxpayer has been assisting the European nations to compete in his own and other markets, while as businessman and exporter, he has been trying to keep them out. But the experience of the last war suggests that in the interests of allied unity, this Janus-headed aspect of Western association, part co-operative and part competitive, should be recognized and kept under continuous review. In general, Lend-Lease and Mutual Aid were triumphant examples of how completely and loyally nations can co-operate. Even so, the British have uncomfortable memories of the harshness of American criticism when steel supplied under Lend-Lease was thought to be reappearing in British exports sent to the Argentine. The problem of exports is all too likely to prove a stumbling block in the new phase of limited Mutual Aid. One of the consequences of greater European rearmament may be the loss by British or French firms of overseas markets already lost once in the last war and only just recovered after five years of painful effort. One reason why German industry must be drawn in to play its part in rearmament is that German firms could hardly be left to take over Belgian and French and British markets while the Atlantic powers switch to armament-making. The completed weapons need not be made in the Ruhr, but steel and other components should be drawn from German industry. The British and the French can hardly complain if American firms move in to fill the gap left by a decline in European exporting, and many American firms will in any case also be temporarily diverted from foreign to domestic production. But the opportunities for misunderstanding and friction are obvious enough. It is not possible to suggest a general rule for meeting this difficulty, but clearly it cannot be left to the workings of chance and the risk of recrimination. Given the far greater understanding of Europe's economic needs now enjoyed by American officials and given the essential nature of exports to European recovery, it should no doubt be possible to give the maintenance of some European exports a priority equal to the military programs. Or, at least, it *would* be possible, if a joint body for determining priorities did, in fact, exist.

This, surely, is a weakness in the present phase of the Atlantic effort. In the autumn of 1950, the economic relations between the partners were still under the control of two separate bodies whose purposes tended at many points to be positively contradictory. The aim of European recovery was the responsibility of the Economic Cooperation Administration in Washington and Paris and of the various ECA Missions in each European capital. Its opposite number in Europe was the Organization for European Economic Cooperation in Paris in which nineteen national delegations worked together with the help of an international secretariat. As a first step toward creating greater unity of effort, American and Canadian representatives were invited to join the OEEC as full members in the course of 1950. The military commitments of the powers and the economic resources necessary to fulfill them were, however, under the review of the Atlantic Council and its deputies. Expert sub-committees had been called into being to assess economic possibilities and difficulties and to work out a practicable program of the scale of local effort that could be achieved and the extra American assistance that would be necessary.

It seems virtually impossible that such a diffuse and unco-ordinated machinery of economic co-operation can produce the best and smoothest results. In the first place, it means a perpetual attending of committee meetings by responsible ministers who, moving from one green baize table to another, must be pardoned if they have no time to think at all. The dovetailing of military effort into sustained economic progress also risks being a very haphazard process so long as entirely distinct bodies are dealing with two sides of the problem. Above all, this division of machinery suggests a distinction between the effort of recovery and the effort of containment—a distinction which is wholly false. Defense and stability are two sides of the same coin of containment. It would, therefore, seem that the economic structure of the Atlantic partnership would, like its military structure, stand to gain very greatly if it could be simplified and unified. The invitation of American and Canadian officials to join the OEEC has shown the way. The next step would be to fuse this body with the ECA and to form from them a new Joint Production and Resources Board of the Atlantic Council. The experience these men have gained of the entire Atlantic economy is unequaled. Their knowledge of how allocations can be made between different claimants and of how a balance of interest is to be maintained is second to none. The secretariat should be strengthened by the addition of men who worked in the wartime Combined Boards, and the Atlantic Council would, no doubt, in making the transfer of powers and responsibility, take steps to create a smaller and more compact organization. But quite apart from internal reorganization, the mere fusion of three different bodies would of itself prevent the confusion and duplication and faulty staff work that has dogged the Atlantic Council so far.

A further task of the new board should be mentioned. The immense increases in price for some primary products such as tin, copper and rubber which occurred in the summer of 1950 suggest that a system of procurement and allocation should be introduced at once to prevent rocketing prices and cutthroat competition for supplies. The Atlantic powers are no strangers to such a system. They worked it well in the last war. As a temporary expedient, during the years of greatest economic expansion, they may need to restore some such machinery under the aegis of their Resources Board.

There remains a third undertaking—the creation of a fund and an organization for economic development in backward areas. The two fields of joint action that have been examined so far are simply logical extensions of policies already introduced and accepted in the Western world. No such general agreement exists in the case of economic assistance to backward areas and no organizations have so far been brought into existence to co-ordinate a Western effort or expand it to the necessary scale. The issue has remained on the margin of men's effort and attention and in the last two years it has been more discussed than acted upon. True, a few first steps have been taken which were outlined in an earlier chapter but the various hints and essays and declarations do not add up to a consistent policy. Least of all, do they amount to anything like the scale of action already advocated—that 2 to 3 per cent of the Western Powers' national incomes should be earmarked annually for the financing of development plans and for general economic assistance in Asia and elsewhere. The first step is, therefore, agreement between the Powers but this or some more modest program is essential to their joint effort of containment. Once the decision is reached, there is everything to be said for setting up some machinery to direct expenditure, prevent overlapping and see that separate programs support each other. For a time at least such programs would compete for manpower and raw materials with the defense effort and with plans for European stability. Their co-ordinating body should therefore work in the closest possible co-operation with the proposed Production and Resources Board and the most suitable method would seem to be to set up a third committee under the Atlantic Council—an Economic Development Board.

Even in the limited field of assistance and development explored so far there are already some signs of conflict and misunderstanding between the multitude of different bodies surveying the possibilities. Anglo-American misunderstandings have arisen over the desirability of using dollar investment in Africa. The British Colonial Development Corporation has indulged in a public misunderstanding with the International Bank. The Commonwealth officials at work on the Spender Plan have not yet worked out a satisfactory *modus vivendi* with American administrators at work on plans for the President's Point IV. And behind all these differences lies the question of the relationship of each national effort with that of the United Nations. It is already clear that without some central body there will be not only confusion of plans and competition for resources but a gross waste of the very limited trained manpower available for the arduous work of educating, guiding and training technicians and mechanics and skilled workers in backward economies. Provided the Atlantic powers decide to give the economic development of backward areas the priority it deserves, nothing could be more timely than that they should set up a single body able to review such programs, suggest the gaps that need to be filled and keep the total effort in reasonable shape.

This, then, could be the structure of a full Atlantic alliance, bent upon an effective policy of containment and determined to maintain the strength and unity which alone can make it succeed. The main executants of policy would remain the governments, but control over a number of matters of vital strategic and economic concern would have been translated to common organs of discussion and decision. At the apex would stand the Atlantic Council, a body of Ministers in almost continuous session, acting in effect as a Cabinet to the entire Atlantic world. Under its immediate authority would be a Combined Chiefs of Staff in Washington and a unified supreme command in the field in Europe. The preservation of economic stability and the achievement of military mobilization would be under the oversight of a Joint Production and Resources Board. Finally a new organ—an Economic Development Board—would undertake the extension of Western standards of wealth and well-being to less fortunate areas of the world. Of these, only the last represents a new departure. The others grow organically from the cooperation already achieved and if they are allowed and encouraged to do so, the Atlantic world will have at its disposal a machine of unity and effective strength such as no coalition of free states has enjoyed in history before.

# 15

## *The Roots of Instability*

THESE three agencies of the Atlantic world should not be thought of as temporary expedients. The kind of problems with which they are designed to deal will not vanish from the free world for a generation to come. The holding of the frontiers of freedom—which is the essence of defense policy under containment—may last as long as Britain's "Eastern Question" lasted. It may even have to endure as a permanent feature of our civilization—as the Roman frontier endured through hundreds of years. No society can expect as of right to be preserved from external threats and the watch on the marches of the free world must continue so long as an alien and hostile system continues its pressure for world dominion. We do not know how long that will be.

Nor will the economic agencies become redundant within the next ten years. The immense combined operation the West must set for itself—that of creating an expanding world economy—will not be achieved by mistake or by accident or by automatic means. In its way stand three obstacles all of which will with fateful certainty grow larger if left to themselves. Europe will relapse into instability if the effort to create a balanced European economy is brought to an end before the goal is reached. The backward areas of the world, menaced by communism and distracted by new national aspirations, will not draw in capital for their development unless special steps are taken to guide it there. And these two difficulties are in a sense different aspects of the third—the world's inability to earn or obtain sufficient dollars to create a stable relationship between the United States and every one of its neighbors. But if these are the main problems—and who will doubt that they are?—the proposed Combined Boards would be singularly well fitted to deal with them, covering as they would the main aspects of the problem and bringing together the governments whose sustained co-operation is the only possible key to success.

The chief reason why there can be no speedy or automatic restoration of an expanding world economy is that the roots of the present lack of balance go deep down into the history of the West in the last hundred years. If an oversimplification may be permitted, it is probably true to say that almost every development in those hundred years has made a free, prosperous and self-adjusting international economy more difficult to secure. The evils which made the Marshall Plan necessary, which have impeded its progress and still leave the Western Powers with an enormous question mark over their future stability are in large part the results of a steady growth of the world economy *away* from conditions of stability and expansion. The Marshall powers are, with the utmost gallantry, swimming against the tides of history. We shall have more pride in their achievements and a healthier respect for their difficulties if we realize that "the wave of the future," left to itself, would probably drown them all.

Modern industrialism began in a blaze of confidence in the beneficial combining of automatic forces. These were in the main the forces of competition and of profit and loss in the market place. If each man was left to produce where conditions were most favorable to production, his goods would be the cheapest in terms of labor and materials, they would undercut other producers in the free market and, provided no artificial barriers were set up, production would tend to settle where it could be carried on most cheaply.

This, briefly put, was the fundamental "law of comparative advantage," which, operating through a free market economy, would give the best—because cheapest—economic results. Every man, every group, every country would profit by the operation of the law. Each would concentrate on what he was most fitted to produce and this division of labor would provide mankind with the maximum amount of goods at a minimum of real cost.

Like most theories, this law of comparative advantage contained a hard core of truth together with a number of quite remarkable assumptions. It was and is true that, all other things being equal, it is best for society to divide up its activities and let those most fitted to produce an article do so. It is also true that a good way to discover who is most fitted is to submit him to the test of selling his goods in competition with other would-be producers. But even in its simplest form, the law of comparative advantage made some formidable assumptions about the nature of man and society. It assumed, for instance, an almost complete mobility of labor. Men would go where goods were being produced, but if that center of production was driven out of business by cheaper production in other parts, the men would move on. They would move on, even if it meant moving to another country altogether.

A similar mobility was assumed for capital. It was thought of as an abstraction, a power-to-produce-wealth, which, failing in one place, could be transferred somewhere else. In fact capital was and is buildings and plant and fixed equipment of all kinds and its mobility is strictly limited. Adam Smith, the classical exponent of the law of comparative advantage, had his suspicions that capital might be inclined to insufficient flexibility. He foresaw the temptation that would arise to safeguard existing installations by price agreements and other attempts to evade competition. In fact he said that he never saw a group of businessmen together without suspecting them of some conspiracy in restraint of trade. Nevertheless, the picture of an open economy in which capital and labor moved freely in search of "comparative advantage" remained the theoretical basis for the belief in automatic expansion and general beneficence.

It is particularly important to notice the application of the law of comparative advantage to trade between the nations. The same fundamental rule was to apply. Each nation would produce what it was most fitted to produce and maintain its position in the world by selling only those goods it could produce most cheaply. If other nations undersold its products, it would have to change to other forms of production. If—an unlikely event—it could produce nothing more cheaply than any other country, then, in strict theory, its inhabitants, in their primeval mobility, would have to move somewhere else. This law of comparative advantage would work between nations, however, only if three conditions were maintained. The first was that national currencies could be freely converted into any other currency at agreed and stable rates. The device which came to be adopted was that of the gold standard. Each currency had a given value in relation to gold and could be exchanged into any other currency on that basis. Gold could also be used to settle trading debts if at any point a country found itself a general debtor. But it was assumed that these instances would be marginal, for the same law of comparative advantage would tend to keep the sales and purchases of nations in balance. If a nation was buying more than it sold, money would leave the country to pay for the import surplus. This decline in the amount of money available would cause prices to fall in the country buying too much and correspondingly to rise in the country selling too much. This fall in prices would make domestic goods cheaper than imports. Less imports would therefore be bought while exports would have become less costly and more able to compete. Imports would therefore decline and exports increase and a new level of exchange be established at which purchases and sales balance. Meantime, the temporary debts could be settled in gold. Such was the theory.

The second condition for the working of comparative

advantage was that capital should have the right to move freely across frontiers. The third was that the local government should not discriminate in any way against producers in other countries. This last point of discrimination is important, for it still plays a large part in the discussion of international trade. Discrimination occurs if a country gives to another country a trading advantage it does not automatically extend to all others. For instance, if Sweden had decided a hundred years ago to buy its wine in France and to exclude all other wines even if they were cheaper, discrimination would have taken place. The decision to buy wine would have been based not on its cheapness but upon some other possible political criterion. But once the economic yardstick of price was left behind, the law of comparative advantage would cease to work. This principle of nondiscrimination became very important after the first successful undermining of the law had taken place in the shape of tariffs. By the middle of the nineteenth century, it had been generally accepted that a government might flout the law of comparative advantage to the extent of protecting local production and putting a tariff on imports from abroad. Once these tariff walls had come into existence, nondiscrimination became a way of lessening their effect. To return to the instance of Sweden, let us suppose that the government sought to give an advantage to French wines by lowering Swedish tariffs on the import of wines from France, but by maintaining them for everyone else. This would be gross discrimination and the nations would seek to defend themselves against it by including in their commercial treaties "most-favored-nation" clauses by which any lowering of tariffs conceded to one nation would automatically be extended to all other traders. In this way, nondiscrimination did act, at that time, as a means of reducing the obstacles to international trade. So long as tariffs were the chief impediment to free trade, the doctrine of nondiscrimination clearly had a liberalizing effect.

For its full working, the law of comparative advantage clearly stood or fell on the extent to which resources and manpower could be moved in response to competition in the free market. If for one moment one stops thinking of "labor" and "capital" as abstractions, the limitations of the law seem obvious enough. "Labor" is men and women and their families, living in homes and towns and countrysides, bound by sentimental ties to the place of their birth, shaped by language and national tradition and capable of deciding their movements on any but economic grounds. "Capital" is all the installations of a business concern, the plant, the equipment, the local skill of its managers, their experience of particular markets or particular national conditions. In other words, the supposedly movable factors, whose quick response of the price mechanism would, it was assumed, tend to concentrate production where goods could be produced most cheaply, were potentially highly immovable and inclined of their very nature to seek to protect existing positions rather than move on to new enterprises under comparative pressure or in search of greater profits. As Lord Keynes once suggested, the law attempted to apply "the theory of fluids to what is in fact a highly viscous mass."

One may ask how it was, given this gap between the idea and the reality, that the belief in a fluid economy retained such a hold on man's thinking for so long and is still today at the back of people's minds when they speak about the necessity of creating a "single market" and of "integrating the European economy." Part of the answer lies in the theory's core of truth. Goods can be produced more cheaply in some areas than in others. Comparative advantages do exist and the world's resources are still so scarce in comparison with the infinity of human needs that it is in the interests of the whole human family that the cheapest production should be achieved. Waste is not yet a luxury mankind can afford. To build a large high-cost steel works, say, in Italy that has neither steel nor coking coal while cheap steel is going into surplus in the Ruhr is a clear example of a misuse of Europe's resources. But even this core of truth depends upon the ability of men and capital to move in search of competitive advantage and there are such obvious limits to this assumption that one is still left wondering how the doctrine came to be accepted in such an unadulterated form.

The chief reason is undoubtedly that when the industrial revolution began and the new possibilities it opened up first broke on the dazzled mind of man, the economy was considerably more fluid than it has since become. However unreal the idea of men and capital moving in complete freedom in response to competitive pressures may seem to us now, it could practically be taken for granted in the first half of the nineteenth century. The British industrial system had the supreme mobility which belongs to the pioneer in any field. During the thirty or forty years' start given to it by its lead in the Industrial Revolution, British manufactures could be sold in any market more cheaply than the products of artisans and handworkers, and British capital could move anywhere since it was virtually the only capital in the field.

Britain's peculiar structure—that of an island not very lavishly provided with raw materials apart from coal—compelled it from the start to look beyond its frontiers and to send its goods and its capital overseas in return for purchases of food and raw materials. This natural balance of trade reinforced men's confidence in the automatic workings of the gold standard. As we have noticed, the use of gold was theoretically designed to cover temporary lacks of balance in traders' international account. So long as the bulk of the world's buying, selling and lending was carried on in sterling, the disequilibrium in trade always tended to be marginal. The British economy of selling manufactures, lending money and taking payment for them in primary materials pumped sterling through the system as a heart pumps blood through the body. A general circulation was maintained. Thus the apparently automatic balance between manufacturers and primary producers, sellers and purchasers, and borrowers and lenders, reinforced men's belief in the capacity of the law of comparative advantage, working through competition and the pursuit of profit, to produce a balanced economy.

At about the same time, the same confidence in free

competition and free movement was being triumphantly vindicated on the other side of the Atlantic. True, the Americans were no believers in free trade in the world at large, but the miracle of the United States in the second half of the last century was that it presented as nearly as possible the *tabula rasa*, the open fluid economy which the law of comparative advantage required in order to show its best results. The industrial system of the United States moved out into virgin territory. Virtually no obstacles of history or settlement or earlier industrial location stood in the way of capital and manpower as they moved out in search of the best and cheapest areas of production. The vast continent offered incomparable mobility which a new generation, in the main unshackled by the thousand inhibitions of class and race and nationality of older continents, was prepared to exploit to the top of its competitive bent.

Yet neither the British nor the American experiment of a mobile economy would have been conceivable had it not been for the fact that, during the crucial decades of their progress, their labor force was, to an extraordinary and indeed dangerous degree, mobile. The workers who poured in from the countryside into the new industrial slums of England were mobile indeed. They were reduced almost to the bare essentials of humanity. They had neither rights nor possessions nor—often enough—places to lay their heads. To their employers they were "hands," disembodied elements of working power. They could be mobile, for few people in civilized history have traveled so light. The factor of free land and the frontier in the United States preserved it, perhaps, from the worst horrors befalling the urban working class in Europe. But the mobility of labor was strong enough to bring nineteen million across the Atlantic from the old world and to send a steady stream of new settlers outward across the continent toward the Pacific shore. Once again, these men and women traveled light. Even their homes went with them in their covered wagons.

These conditions of natural balance and mobility were enough to fix the law of comparative advantage in men's minds with the strength of a dogma and a myth. It belongs to the golden age of the free economy to which the more fortunate groups in Western society still look back with nostalgia and with an underlying query whether the conditions could not, after all, be recreated if only all the regulations and controls and paraphernalia of regimentation could be removed from modern economic life. The industrial economy appears to them to have had its age of innocence, its Garden of Eden, before the serpent of planning tempted men to sin. But precisely because this nostalgia for the past is so strong, it is essential to set reason against the myth and to realize that man's fumbling attempts at regulation and direction did not end the golden age—it ended itself. The subsequent efforts at control have been practically without exception attempts to repair the damage the system had begun to generate on its own initiative and momentum.

The first break in the defenses of the "free economy" and in the validity of the law of comparative advantage virtually grew up with the Industrial Revolution itself. As we have seen, Britain's industrial supremacy gave it free entry into every other economy by virtue of the cheapness of its new factory-produced wares. Neither the United States nor Europe was prepared to accept this consequence of Britain's capacity to produce more cheaply. One of the baits with which Alexander Hamilton persuaded the Confederate American States to accept the idea of full federal union was a high protective tariff against Britain. The plea that no local industrialism could be started unless "infant industries" were protected against foreign competition marked the first introduction of discrimination and rigidity into the supposedly fluid international economy.

American tariffs grew steadily with the nineteenth century and the same process was repeated in Europe. The reasons for it were the same. Local handicrafts, local centers of manufacture were unwilling to be wiped out of existence by the new flood of cheap goods from Britain. If this was the implication of the law of comparative advantage, the law itself had to go. Europe was no virgin continent. It was a closely settled, fully worked, highly sophisticated collection of self-conscious national units and local interests. Capital and labor, even if they represented no more than the traditional crafts of a city or a rural area, began to show that they could choose to be immobile and expect protection. Since only governments could give such protection, the foundations of economic nationalism were laid and the tariff walls began to rise in Europe not, certainly, to the height of the American tariff, but in a more damaging fashion, since the areas they protected were so small and the pretensions of economic sovereignty they fostered so ridiculous. But the absurdity proved no barrier to their adoption. It is a hundred years since the building up of tariffs began the atomization of a European economy.

The next breach in the defense of unfettered trade came from the side of labor, and it was reinforced by the conscience of Western man. The workers asked and received protection against the rigors of economic law. Through their own trade unions and by governmental action, they began to acquire a stake in the community—better houses, better conditions of work, rights to education—and, as the word "stake" implies, with each advance they acquired a little more stability. The stakes were really driven into the floor of the economy. Their desire to be protected from the competition of men with fewer stakes—men still traveling light in the old sense—was one of the chief forces behind the momentous decision taken by the United States after the First World War to put an end to free immigration. Between the wars, the desire that the homes and settled interests of the workers should not be sacrificed to the needs of industrial mobility led to the growing demand that work should be taken to the workers. It was, for instance, a Conservative, not a planning, government in Britain that compelled Messrs. Richard Thomas to site its new strip mill at Ebbw Vale in the heart of a distressed area and not where comparative economic advantage would have dictated.

The protection of the workers' interests against the hardships imposed by the unchecked workings of economic laws, has, of course, been the mainspring of Western socialism. The belief that this protection could best be afforded by turning over "the ownership of the means of production" to the state was a Marxist gloss upon social democracy and it never took much root in such typically social democratic parties as those of Scandinavia. But all socialist parties believed that the government should be used in one way or another to secure more stable conditions for the workers and since the writ of government runs only as far as the national frontiers, government planning and intervention were bound to increase the divergences between different national economies and the barriers between them.

It should not be thought that the workers alone tried to protect themselves. Capital, too, looked to government or to its own efforts to secure greater stability. Thus the growing immobility of labor both within the economy and between economies was matched, particularly in Europe, by a growing rigidity in capital. It took the form of abandoning competition and putting in its place cartels, trade associations and price-fixing rings all designed to circumvent competitive pressure and leave existing industries in production whatever their level of costs. Agreed prices were fixed high enough to cover all but the most inefficient producer and the market was divided between the various firms on a quota basis. The whole of German heavy industry was built up on a foundation of interlocking cartels; sections of French and Belgian industry conformed to much the same pattern. Britain tended more toward the price-fixing trade associations.

Nor did the arrangements stop at national boundaries. After 1933, a European iron and steel cartel covered the foreign sales of practically every steel product through its various *comptoirs*. Britain entered the cartel in 1936, and in 1938, some American exporters of steel also joined the association. Thus, from a large part of the prewar international trade in steel, the law of comparative advantage had been entirely banished. This trend toward the immobility of capital did not, it is true, go so far in the United States. The various

American antitrust acts have had some influence upon the competitive tone of industry but the decisive factor is no doubt the thrust and drive of American management and the general temper of American society. Yet, on the whole, American standards of competitiveness became, as the century advanced, the exception. Elsewhere the rigidities of an immovable labor force and necessarily static and uncompetitive capital made more and more nonsense of the old law of comparative advantage. Protection, not competition, the status quo, not movement, security, not advance—these were becoming the watchwords of the European economy.

# 16

# *Recipe for Chaos*

THE date—1933—of the organization of a fully functioning European steel cartel is significant. It was a year of depression, following three other years of the worst collapse in trade and production the free world had ever seen. It is thus a reminder that every trend toward great immobility and greater protectiveness both inside national economies and between them was reinforced and exacerbated by the tendency of the free economy to progress in a steady rhythm of contraction and expansion. The trade cycle, a phenomenon which had not been foreseen in the early days of unbounded optimism in the national harmonies of demand and supply, was a deathblow to general confidence in automatic adjustments. Earlier chapters have attempted to show how the "natural" unchecked movement of private investment tended automatically to produce the ups and downs of boom and depression. These fluctuations also had their automatic consequences in the sphere of international trade. Once domestic demand begins to decline in one nation, in other words, when a period of deflation sets in, the consequences can be very troublesome for its trading partners. The deflated nation will begin to buy less abroad, yet the slackening of domestic purchases will make it all the more eager to go on selling its exports. Yet, if a nation begins buying less and tries to sell the same amount or more, two things happen in the markets of its neighbors. If they keep up their purchases, they will have to begin to pay for them in other currencies, perhaps even in gold. Their own sales will have ceased to provide them with enough of the deflating country's own currency. There is, therefore, a temptation to some governments to deflate their economies simply in order to increase their supplies of foreign currency and gold. In so doing they risk internal unemployment and pile up a bigger reserve.

The second consequence of deflation is that "unemployment is exported." Exports are pushed out into foreign markets to keep men at work, since domestic demand has fallen off. But the exports arriving in another market compete with domestic production there and, especially if local demand is falling, force men out of work in domestic industries. These international consequences of internal deflation can, of course, be counteracted and absorbed by the various economies in the short run. A nation's balance of trade is not static. Britain, for instance, had a surplus in its trade with Europe in 1948, a deficit in 1949 and a surplus again in 1950. But the consequences become widespread and even devastating if the outward movement into deflation lasts too long and takes too many economies down with it. And unhappily the old automatic workings of free trade have tended to extend and aggravate the movements toward depression rather than to correct them. Let us suppose that the slackening of demand which ushers in the downward phase of depression occurs first in France. French demand for imports from abroad will begin to fall and the supplies of French francs made available to other countries by French purchases abroad will shrink. This shrinkage reduces the amount that other countries can purchase in France. If the reduction of trade went no further and the countries now finding it difficult to export to France could simply balance their books by cutting down their purchases in French francs, the disturbance would be real, but local. But the workings of nondiscrimination and the network of "most-favored-nation" clauses forbid this limited action. If a nation introduces cuts in its purchases from one country, it must in the name of nondiscrimination introduce them all around. A recession starting in one country can therefore be spread within a comparatively short time to all its trading partners. "Automatic" forces make the slump in world trade all the more complete, once it begins, and the more important the position it occupies in international trade, the quicker the deflationary process will spread.

In fact, the nations have attempted by all manner of expedients to protect themselves against these tides sweeping across their economies. As domestic production sank in the down-plunge of the cycle, some governments raised their tariffs to new catastrophic heights. One of the first American reactions to the 1929 crisis was to introduce the Smoot-Hawley tariffs which gave the United States tariff protection on an average three times higher than that of any other state. Britain, until 1932 practically the lone surviving exponent of free trade, introduced tariff protection for the first time in that year.

In Europe, the thirties brought with them a tremendous variety of expedients for countering the automatic and disastrous movements of world trade. Most of them had the double aim of protecting local employment and preventing a complete loss of foreign reserves and gold. One set of expedients tried to limit the flow of imports from outside. Quotas were fixed beyond which imports were forbidden. Licensing systems were introduced to compel merchants to secure permits before they could import goods. Bilateral trading agreements were signed, according to which one nation undertook to buy so much from its neighbor provided it undertook to buy the exact equivalent in return. It was as though in a city, the baker could buy from the candlestick-maker only if the candlestick-maker needed bread when the baker needed candles. It was equivalent to the virtual extinction of the use of money in international trade. It was, in fact, barter.

Another set of expedients sought to control the possible loss of foreign reserves. Freedom to send capital out of the country was restricted (even so, foreign capital escaped to the United States to the extent of $113 million a year from 1934 onward). Currencies were declared to be inconvertible—in other words, they could be spent only in the country issuing them. Traders were allowed foreign exchange to buy goods abroad only under the most rigorous safeguards. Thus, with quantitative restrictions on imports and every sort of obstacle to the convertibility of currencies, it is not surprising that world trade all but came to a standstill in the trough of the depression and that, as the upswing slowly occurred, only a partial return to free international trade proved possible. Not every nation maintained the complete battery of protection introduced into Germany by Dr. Schacht—protection employing every one of the expedients mentioned above and even others springing from the Nazi Finance Minister's ingenious mind—but Europe remained crisscrossed with tariffs, quotas, restrictions and inconvertibilities of every sort and it was in this condition that much of the Continent entered the last war.

Such then was the balance sheet of a hundred years of international trading in the West. Internal and international cartels, an increasingly immobile labor force, currency regulations and trade restrictions reinforcing every frontier—these were the results of a century of submission to and reaction against the workings of automatic economic laws. Up to a point, the system still worked. A wide area of multilateral trade was still underpinned by the ability of Britain and Europe to buy extensively in the United States and to pay for their purchases in part out of their investment income and in part by selling to America colonial products such as tin and rubber from their Far Eastern dependencies. But even behind this pattern of relatively stable trade, there lay yet another obstacle to freely moving commerce, yet another difficulty which the original exponents of comparative advantage could not have foreseen.

The fact that Britain's dominance in world trade in the nineteenth century created a natural balance has already been mentioned. Its sale of goods and its loans of capital could be repaid in food and raw materials. The world was never short of its chief means of exchange because Britain, through natural circumstances, adopted the only policy compatible with being a creditor. It had an import surplus. It accepted its debtors' goods and did not demand payment in their currencies or gold. When, however, the United States took Britain's place as the principal economy in the world, it could not, of its very nature, fulfill the same balancing role. It did not need to buy extensively abroad, its economic system had been built up behind a high wall of tariffs, it gradually became the best and most prolific producer in the world not only of machines but of foodstuffs as well. Its need to import, unlike Britain's, was almost negligible. Its ability to sell and still more to lend became rapidly unique.

This disparity was masked in the twenties and thirties by the workings of the gold standard. It is true that in earlier days men had always thought that only marginal debts would be settled in gold. It says something for the strength and flexibility of the system that between 1919 and 1939 $11,000 million in gold could be sent to the United States to cover unpaid debts. But clearly, such a degree of disequilibrium could not continue indefinitely. Yet there were no "automatic" ways of rectifying it. One of the main reasons for the lack of balance in the thirties was the flight of foreign capital from Europe to the United States. Yet control of capital movements was not compatible with the ideal of "fluidity." Restrictions on dollar purchases might have been a possible expedient, but they would have offended against the cherished rules of "discrimination" unless they had been extended to every other nation. A reduction in the value of non-American currencies would, in all probability, have been followed by devaluation in the United States—as it was in 1934—and competitive devaluations are certainly not the key to world stability. The war intervened before this process reached its logical end—the transfer of practically all non-American supplies of gold to the United States' vaults at Fort Knox. In 1939, very few people foresaw that the worst obstacle to postwar trade would be a universal dollar shortage. But the roots of the problem were already apparent in the world's sustained inability to balance its accounts with the United States and the problem was there waiting as a rod in pickle for the victors once the war was won.

But even the few who did foresee the world's future dollar shortage could not possibly have guessed what the scale of that gap would turn out to be. When the fighting ceased, the European industrial machine was at a standstill, and with it, temporarily at least, Europe's capacity to produce and export had vanished. The Far East, a former rich source of dollars, had been ruined by the Japanese war and was now under the ban of civil war. The old overseas investments of Europe had been largely liquidated to finance the war. Yet the materials, the food, the machines Europe desperately needed to recover its lost strength could be procured only in the United States. The result was inevitable and in 1946 and 1947 the gap between the dollars Europe could earn and the dollars Europe needed to survive at all was in the neighborhood of $9 billion a year. Not even the worst pessimist had foreseen such a shortage.

It would also have been quite impossible in 1939 to foresee that the dollar deficit could be flanked by another and opposite obstacle to the return of free trade. When the war ended, in addition to its need for dollars, the world found itself saddled with a surplus of sterling. Britain, as a creditor country, had long maintained a deficit in its actual trade. It regularly imported more than it exported and the balance was paid by the income on its large overseas investments, amounting to some £4 billion (in predevaluation prices). During the war, many of these assets were spent on the war effort. In particular, most American investments were liquidated to finance "Cash and Carry." Britain also permitted India and Egypt to charge it—at inflated wartime prices—for all the services and installations provided on their soil. The result was that Britain came out of the war loaded with a war debt of between £3 billion and £4 billion—the so-called sterling balances.

The implications of this fantastic revolution in Britain's position, changing it from an important creditor to a general debtor in six short years, was recognized—but only up to a point. The British Government set itself the target of increasing British exports by 50 per cent and by 1950 the level had reached 70 per cent above prewar. The American Government saw that special aid was necessary and extended a $3,500 million loan. Yet neither government foresaw the real scale of the crisis and this fact is very clearly illustrated by the trend and content of the plans they made in 1944, before the war was over, to restore equilibrium to international trade once the victory was won.

When the nations assembled at Bretton Woods, their deliberations were dominated by the American and British delegations and it is no secret that in the final conclusions reached by the Conference, American views on the whole prevailed. The governments recognized that some special measures would be necessary. Not even the most optimistic thought a return to the gold standard would be possible and in all the plans, allowance was made for a transitional period during which the exceptional strains of war would abate. But the optimism of the American outlook is written into every line of the constitutions of the two new international agencies which were set up as a result of the Conference. They were both based on the assumption that transitional difficulties would be overcome and that a "natural" state of equilibrium could and would be speedily restored. The two new bodies—the International Monetary Fund and the International Bank for Reconstruction and Development—were designed to work in a world in which automatic forces would ensure general and normal stability. The bank, it was carefully laid down, was in no way to take the place of private international investment. Its chief duty would be to encourage and reinforce it. The Monetary Fund's declared task was to tide the nations over temporary fluctuations in their balance of payments. A fund, jointly contributed, was set up on which member nations could draw if, for one reason or another, they become short of another nation's currency. But the provisions of the IMF's charter were clearly dependent on a quick re-establishment of equilibrium. For instance, the amount of dollars placed at its disposal was $2,750 million. This would be virtually the extent of the funds upon which other nations could rely to tide them over temporary shortages of dollars. Could there have been clearer proof that the scale of the postwar gap, which between 1946 and 1949 amounted to well over $20,000 million, was completely unforeseen?

A similar insufficiency underlay the Fund's mechanisms for dealing with obstinate debtor–creditor relationships. Its charter placed the strongest possible restrictions upon any tendency on the part of governments to remain in debt. But only in the most complicated circumstances could the nations take steps to deal with a permanent creditor. The Fund's rules did include a provision for declaring the currencies of permanent creditors "scarce" and for permitting debtors in those circumstances to apply special restrictions on them—in other words, to discriminate against them—but this state of scarcity was to be reached only after such cumbersome negotiations that debtor governments would in all probability have had to introduce their own restrictions and discriminations meanwhile.

In a word, neither the Bank nor the Fund was designed to deal with more than marginal insufficiencies, the Bank with small fallings-off in the level of international lending, the Fund with temporary maladjustments in the nations' balance of payments. What neither were built to prevent was the state of near-chaos in international economic relations with which the victors were confronted when victory had crowned their arms.

The chaos was, no doubt, the inevitable aftermath of war. Even so, it dangerously reinforced the old barriers and rigidities first experienced in Europe in the Great Depression. Every European nation was busy protecting itself with quotas, licensing systems, inconvertible currencies and frozen capital accounts. Such trade as could be revived quickly was conducted almost completely on a bilateral basis. Old sources of trade in Eastern Europe were cut off by the Soviet occupation. Germany, a former pivot of European trade, was ruined and divided. Overseas income had vanished, the Far East was in flames. All these separate problems fused together in the single universal hunger for dollars and this deficit reacted in its turn upon the British surplus of sterling. Neither British efforts to increase its exports nor American generosity in gifts and credits was sufficient to bridge the gap. Nearly every nation needed dollars. Nearly every nation had too much sterling. Under such conditions, there could be only one result. When one currency is in universal deficit and another in almost universal surplus, the holders of the surplus currency will always attempt to convert the currency of which they have too much into the currency they need. All round the world, nations holding sterling set about converting it into dollars. The British Loan from America began to be the source of dollars for every country that could circumvent Britain's attempts to keep sterling inconvertible and the sterling balances safely blocked. When in the summer of 1947, Britain, complying with the terms of the American loan, made sterling convertible, its whole reserves of gold and dollars began to vanish down the funnel of universal demand for dollars.

This crisis of 1947 coincided, as we know, with a new attempt to deal with the drastic conditions prevailing in the world after the war. The Marshall Plan opened a new epoch both in men's understanding of the free world's economic ills and in their determination to deal with them. But before the great experiment is looked at in greater detail, one point needs to be borne in mind. The evils of blocked currencies, tariff barriers, bilateral treaties and the throttling of all free trade and movement were all aggravated by the last war, but not one of them was caused by it. Their roots go further back, back into the last hundred years of economic development, back into the transfer of economic power from Britain to the United States, back into the loss of mobility, the growth of economic nationalism, the rigidity of the whole economy which has grown steadily and in many ways disastrously for over a century. Any experiment to restore mobility is thus a very audacious experiment. It means reversing the habits of more than a lifetime. This fact must be constantly held in view in examining the profit-and-loss account of the Marshall Plan.

# 17

## *Background to Marshall Aid*

THERE is a danger, when men consider a great economic venture such as the Marshall Plan, to get lost in its details and intricacies and lose the significance of the policy as a whole. The details are important—there is hardly one that does not throw some light upon the obstacles to full unity and co-operation between the free nations, hardly one that does not also suggest what might be possible in the way of advance and expansion if unity were achieved. But the chief significance of the Plan does not lie in this particular payments scheme or in that specific dollar allocation. It lies in the fact that the Plan could happen at all. The political and moral significance of the American gesture far outstrips any economic consequences the Plan has had. As we have seen, there was no external compulsion on the United States to act as it did. It could have responded to Europe's collapse and communism's pressure by turning its back on both and concentrating blindly on its own defense. In other words, the American position in 1947 was one of freedom—to act well or ill, creatively or negatively. By choosing the positive response of vision and generosity, the American people broke with the supposed fatalities of history. They exploded the Marxist fallacy of inevitable imperialism. They exposed the cynics' belief in the triumph of narrow nationalism. They remade history since their action brought into being a new range of possibilities for which men could hardly have dared to hope. The defenders and exponents of free society took up their task with new enthusiasm, the propagandists of communism found themselves suddenly and surprisingly on the defensive. Free men everywhere held their heads higher, the doubters began to wonder, the waverers to be convinced. No economic charts can show the extent of these changes, which, running through the million secret channels of mind and heart, can remake a whole nation's will to resist or survive. The greatest achievement of the Marshall Plan will never be recorded in figures and statistics, but humanity will recall how the American people came to a turning point in history and there made a great and creative choice.

The profound political significance of the Marshall experiment thus lies in its general effects—in the revival of hope in Europe and in the assumption of authority and responsibility in the United States. The details of the Plan have, however, been to a great extent economic. The starting point was the decision to give Europe the dollar aid necessary to wipe out the consequences of the war and thus achieve balance in its accounts with the United States. But the more people reflected upon the second aim—the closing of the dollar gap—the more they realized that a simple restoration of Europe's economic capacity would hardly be sufficient. Europe's weakness was not so much caused by war as aggravated by it. The roots of the trouble lay in the rigidity of Europe's divided national economies, in the disorganization of Europe's old markets in the East and in the secular tendency of the United States to become a creditor, yet behave like a debtor. Any plan for equilibrium would have to include all these factors. However, in the first two years of the Marshall Plan, the main emphasis was placed on two only—the restoration of European production and a greater measure of economic unity in Europe. The other factors—the expansion of non-European markets and the adoption by the United States of long-term policies compatible with its new creditor position—were only beginning to be discussed in 1950 when the Korean war came to alter the whole trend and tempo of Western policy.

The first aim—that of restoring European production—has been brilliantly successful. Within eighteen months of the Plan's start, European levels of industrial production were in many cases 25 per cent higher than they had been before the war and agricultural production had recovered almost to its 1938 level. The chief instrument of this remarkably speedy recovery was the direct allocation of large dollar grants to each European government. In 1948, 1949 and 1950, congress voted global sums—roughly $6 billion, $4 billion and $3 billion respectively—and left it to the European governments themselves to devise an equitable basis for sharing the funds. The Organization for European Economic Cooperation (the OEEC) was set up to accomplish this task and to be the general planning instrument of the nineteen Marshall nations. The division of aid was certainly not made without difficulty and often with considerable heat and disagreement. But it never became necessary to refer the actual allocation of aid to Washington. The European group continued in each case to cajole and bully each other into acceptance, although their wranglings were a reminder that national separatism was still a dominant mood in Europe.

The Marshall Plan was not many months old before the realization became general that a simple restoration of European production would not suffice to balance Europe's books. An infinitely harder task faced the member-nations—that of breaking down the innumerable obstacles to freer trade that were impeding expansion at every turn. The war had exacerbated all the old tendencies to economic nationalism and self-sufficiency. Even the degree of freedom prevailing before 1939 in sterling-dollar trade had disappeared and this fact was an additional blow to Western Europe since, before the war, sterling had been the traditional channel by which dollars flowed into Europe. Western Europe had tended to sell to Britain more than Britain sold in return and the sterling balance had been converted into dollars. The whole process turned naturally on Britain possessing surplus dollars. Now there were none.

The aim behind all the protective devices bristling on

practically every European frontier in 1947 was old and familiar—to preserve each nation's reserves of gold and foreign exchange and to keep up local production and employment. If anything can prove the continuity of the European problem, it is that the crisis of 1947 was to so large an extent a repetition of the difficulties of the thirties. The chief difference was the disappearance at last of Britain's ability to pursue free trade. As we have seen, nations do not dare to free their trade and abandon their protective devices if the consequence will be to drain away all their reserves or leave them with pockets of depression and unemployment. A system of freely convertible currencies works only if no one state is a universal debtor or universal creditor. If lire can be converted into marks and marks into sterling and sterling into dollars and dollars back again into lire, the circuit is complete and exchanges can continue to run freely through the whole system. But if at any point, one currency cannot be converted into another because no one has any reserve of it, the circuit stops at that point. Equally it stops if everyone has too much of a currency. It becomes a glut on the market. Traders have enough already and will not exchange other currencies for it. Once again, the circuit comes to a full stop and at that point nations begin to demand payment either in gold or in gold's postwar equivalent, the dollar. If, therefore, in any group of nations, the balance of demand and supply is completely out of line, if the supplies of one currency are universally scarce and of another universally excessive, the haunting fear of loss of reserves remains at the back of every government policy and the search for methods of freeing trade, removing barriers and securing unity thus takes place under the most difficult conditions it is possible to devise. Yet this was the background to the pursuit of unity in Europe after 1947.

With the exception of Switzerland, every nation in the Marshall group was short of dollars. This, in itself, made exchange control universally necessary. No government was prepared to incur debts with its neighbors which could be automatically converted into dollars. From this followed, too, the preference for bilateral trading agreements designed to balance trade absolutely between pairs of nations so as to leave no surplus on either side and thus to prevent dollars from seeping away through chinks in the system of exchange control. Progress toward unity between 1948 and 1950 was also hampered by the repetition inside Europe—on a very much more modest scale—of the phenomenon of a universal creditor, Belgium.

The reasons for Belgium's special position were complex. The country was hardly damaged by the war and could begin producing and exporting on the first day of the armistice. Its dollar and gold reserves were also intact, since it had been unable to use them under the German occupation. It enjoyed a number of windfalls in the shape of British and American payments for the stationing of their forces in Belgium. All these advantages gave the Belgian exporters a flying start and they began supplying their war-devastated neighbors with the essential tools of recovery. The advantage would not have turned so completely in Belgium's favor, however, had it not been for a shrewd piece of economic planning on the part of Belgium's business and financial leaders. The export prices of Belgian goods were raised to well over double their prewar level. Although Belgian production and Belgian productivity remained lower than before the war, the earnings of foreign currency were sufficient to permit a larger percentage of local production to remain in the home market and at the same time to enable the economy to earn general surpluses in European trade.

In and after 1947, this capacity to earn surpluses abroad was intensified by a policy of monetary deflation inside Belgium. War, as we have already seen, is an infallible inflater of currencies and all Europe came out of the war with an aftermath of inflation. In Belgium, however, this problem was tackled more speedily and radically than elsewhere. The "*Plan Gutt*" cut down excessive purchasing power drastically in 1945 and thereafter government spending was reduced and the borrowing of capital by private investors was made more difficult. In this way, much of the surplus purchasing power was withdrawn from circulation and prices began to fall. In 1948, the process began to lead to the creation of some unemployment. Since government spending on public works was exceedingly small and industries could not expand their activities by new investment, a number of workers found themselves without work. In 1949, the general demand for exports also slackened and the number of unemployed increased. By the end of the year, the official figure was about 11 per cent of the labor force. In practice, it was probably not more than 7 per cent. Even so, it represented a level of unemployment which was, apart from the exceptional cases of Italy and Western Germany, the highest in Europe.

When the efforts to cure inflation begin to produce the opposite state of deflation—the creation of a level of monetary demand too low to absorb all the goods and services available—the results, as we have seen, make themselves felt not only in the domestic market but in foreign trade as well. The Belgian example has proved no exception. As Belgian purchases fell off, less Belgian currency was available to other nations. They tended to maintain their demand and continue to buy Belgian goods, and in this way the demand for Belgian francs to settle debts with Belgium began to outstrip the supply of Belgian francs made available by Belgium's foreign purchases. Provided one or two other European nations had still been earning surplus Belgian francs, a deficit here or there would not have mattered since, for instance, France's deficit with Belgium could have been paid with France's surplus of other currencies.

But by 1948, nearly every nation in Europe began to run a deficit with Belgium, the circuit could not be completed and at the end of the balancing of deficits and credits, some nations were found to be owing Belgium more francs than they could procure by trade or borrowing. The debt had then to be paid in gold or dollars, the only two universally acceptable means of payment in the postwar world, but at the same time, the two with which all governments were most determined not to part. If international trade were to mean a steady transfer of gold to Belgium, the enthusiasm of all its neighbors was bound to wane.

Belgium's position as a general creditor made particularly difficult the position of other European nations—such as Norway and Austria and Greece, and, in 1948, France—which had become almost universal debtors. It has already been pointed out that if one nation is a general creditor and another a general debtor, other countries will use the currency of the debtor country to settle their debts with the creditor. If everyone has Norwegian kroner and everyone needs Belgian francs, they will try to convert kroner into francs and finally Norway will find itself saddled with the obligation to pay Belgium not only its own debts, but most of the other debts as well. In such conditions, the transfer of some gold and dollars becomes inevitable and, indeed, in 1948 and 1949, Belgium did contrive to secure a large part of other people's Marshall aid by maintaining trade surpluses with all of them. This was particularly galling to countries such as Norway and Holland who wished to maintain a high level of employment and economic activity and tended to regard Belgian deflation as an attack on their standard of living.

Europe's most general debtor between 1947 and 1950 (with a brief spell of equilibrium in 1948) was, however, Britain. Something has already been said of the delicacy of Britain's political relations with the Continent and of the problems created by Britain's membership in three different communities of nations. Much of the same problem has dogged its economic relations with other members of the Marshall Plan. The British Government brought into the financial working of the scheme not only its own market but the whole sterling area as well. The dollars allotted to Britain went into the dollar pool of the sterling area. The sterling which turned up in the various accounts of other Marshall countries might have been earned in Singapore or Australia or Iraq. No other European currency fulfilled a comparable rôle. Even the French franc—the currency of the French Union—served a group of nations all under the political control of Paris. But the sterling area included not only Britain and its dependent countries, but sovereign Dominions such as Australia and New Zealand, India and Ceylon, and independent nations such as Iraq and Burma. The basis of their association was a voluntary agreement to keep their dollars in a central pool and spend them only on essential purposes, while sterling was used to settle outstanding debts and credits. In addition to this group, other nations joined the sterling area with varying degrees of membership. For instance, a number of countries agreed to limit their demand for debt settlements in dollars (or other "hard" currencies) and were permitted to use sterling to balance their trade with all other nations ready to accept the same limitations. This so-called "transferable account" group included some European nations, among them, Holland and Italy. All in all, the system based on sterling covered in 1949, and 1950, about 50 per cent of the international trade done in the world.

The existence and working of this sterling area—and its inclusion in the Marshall Plan—have been criticized from many sides. For instance, it has been called a device for restricting dollar trade. This, certainly, it has never been. All dollars made available by American purchases, loans and gifts went into the dollar pool and went out again all round the world to finance not simply Britain's trade with America but India's purchases of American wheat, Australia's supplies of American petroleum, New Zealand's purchases of American tractors, Iraq's purchases of refrigerators and Coca-Colas. No extra-American body can create dollars and put them into circulation. The amount of dollars made available by the United States will always set the limits to dollar trading. The sterling area mechanism only restricts this trade in that the Australians and the Iraquis and the Italians and the Latin Americans cannot turn in all their sterling and demand dollars in return. If they did, the result would be a run on British reserves such as occurred in 1947, the collapse of British trade, the end of the sterling area—but not one cent more of dollar trade.

Nor has the existence of the sterling area harmed Europe's trading interests. On the contrary, many of the raw materials vital to European recovery could be bought in the sterling area and the industrialized nations of Western Europe have steadily increased their purchases of raw materials in sterling countries in Africa and in Asia. This they could not have done if sterling had been as scarce as dollars. But Britain's massive purchases abroad, its loans to Dominions and Colonies, its releases of sterling balances in Asia have kept floods of sterling pouring through the trading world. As a result, Europe's trade with the overseas sterling area in 1948 and 1949 was as great—and infinitely more balanced—than its trade with the United States.

Asia, too, has profited from the availability of sterling. Before the war, the non-European members of the sterling area tended to be dollar earners. But between 1947 and 1950, they became hungry and insistent consumers of dollars. Nearly 30 per cent of India's supplies of grain had, for instance, to be paid for in dollars. The sterling area and its dollar pool provided them with a flexible mechanism for keeping their general trade steady and issuing them with dollars for their essential purposes. One can only speculate how much more disturbed conditions in Asia would have become if some £750 million had not been released there through the workings of the sterling area.

None of these advantages can be denied nor should the sterling area be underestimated as a means of stabilizing and facilitating a great mass of multilateral trade in the world. Equally, however, the fact must be recognized that its existence has complicated the narrower task of freeing trade and currencies inside Europe.

Norway and Denmark, Eire and Greece, the Netherlands and Austria, and for a time France, were all debtors in inter-European trade. But their range and volume of trade were relatively small, their difficulties created inconveniences but not insuperable obstacles to the working out of plans for free trade, lower barriers and greater convertibility. But Britain was one of the largest traders in the world. Any lack of balance in its accounts would affect any conceivable system that might be devised and the fact that sterling was in almost universal surplus meant that there was a constant nagging pressure on Britain's reserves and that the British Government, as a result, was exceedingly cautious and wary in acceding to any plan that might make the transfer of gold or dollars more likely. The extent to which Belgium, by judicious deflation, was continuing to channel a large part of Europe's dollars into Brussels increased British caution. One should say at once that Britain was not alone in these restrictions. The fear of losing reserves was universal among the European debtors, but the various governments soon discovered that their fears were expressed more effectively and more vigorously by the British delegation to OEEC and they therefore often found it convenient to leave defensive action to the British team. Often the British found themselves refusing practically alone some measure of liberalization while fellow governments kept silent and seemed prepared to accept the risk, knowing full well that British opposition could be relied on to prevent its realization. It was thus the British who acquired the reputation for "dragging their feet."

An experiment to restore greater flexibility and unity to the European community had, thus, to overcome a fundamental difficulty—the deep disequilibrium in the nations' balance of payments. The circuit of multilateral exchange in the world was broken by one universal creditor—the United States—and one universal debtor—Britain. Inside Europe, Belgium had become a general creditor and three or four other nations were as generally in debt. Yet, as we have seen, no multilateral system of exchange can work without some underlying balance between the trading members. Nor was this disequilibrium the only problem. It was fostered and reinforced by another—that of differing levels of economic activity. It was no coincidence that in Europe those nations which tended to become debtors were all pursuing full employment at home, whereas Belgium, the general creditor, was permitting its level of production to fall and, with it, local demand and employment. Then, in 1949, came more ominous evidence of the intimate connection between domestic activity and stable international trade. This was the year of slight recession in the United States. The decline was ludicrously small, compared with the scale of American production and trade. It amounted as we have seen to no more than 5 per cent of the national income. Yet, within three months, the amount of dollars flowing into the world fell by $500 million. The slackening of American demand created, here and there, for the first time since the war, surpluses of goods and materials. It began to look as though the tremendous boom of postwar demand was coming to an end.

This general slackening in trade had two immediate consequences. The nations' need for dollars had not diminished but their chances of earning them by trade fell away. Britain's need to go on buying was not diminished but its ability to sell goods abroad declined. In the summer of 1949, a greater need for dollars coincided with a decreased demand for sterling. The result was a new run on London's reserves which was brought to an end only when, on September 17, 1949, the pound sterling was devalued from $4 to $2.80. With the exception of Switzerland, Belgium, and Italy, all Europe and a large part of the outside world followed Britain in a 30 per cent devaluation.

We do not know what would have been the consequences of this act if the American recession had continued. Devaluation is a double-edged weapon. It cheapens a nation's goods and makes its exports better able to compete with other suppliers. But it makes imports more expensive and more exports have to be sold to cover their increased cost. It also intensifies the risk of internal inflation since the greater volume of exports must be drained away from the home market and costlier imports may send prices up. One thing is clear, however. Devaluation cannot of itself secure bigger markets for exports if the general level of world trade is declining fast. Had the American recession deepened and general demand continued to slacken, had the free nations plunged down into a depression—as the Communists so devoutly hoped and gleefully announced—the 1949 devaluation would have done little or nothing to check the process. Fortunately, the American economy recovered its upward momentum within a very few months and by the spring of 1950 had reached new heights of productive activity. The world swung up with it and devaluation proved not a temporary and ineffective expedient but a genuine recognition of an economic reality—that almost no currency had the intrinsic value and buying power of the American dollar. On the basis of new, more competitive prices and of the American economy's renewed hunger for raw materials, the sterling area reached for the first time since the war a general balance in its accounts even with the dollar world. The greatest debtor had, temporarily at least, pulled level with the greatest creditor. A measure of equilibrium seemed to be in sight—so much so that in the autumn of 1950, the American Government took the initiative in suggesting a sizable reduction in Britain's share of Marshall aid. Fortunately, however, for any real understanding of the world economy, the reduction was suggested as potentially a temporary expedient which could be revised if the fantastic rise in world prices or a new falling off in American strategic purchases once again exposed Britain to a severe shortage of dollars.

This, then, is the disturbed and fluctuating background that must be borne in mind in examining the various efforts made within the framework of the Marshall Plan to achieve greater European unity. Each experiment has been conditioned by influences and events far beyond its control—by the balance and unbalance in international exchanges, by the slackening and intensifying of world demand, by the policies of nations either wholly or partly outside the European orbit. Both the successes and the disappointments have to be measured against the fact that the stability of world trade cannot be assured through any separate European action. On the contrary, Europe's stability depends upon the actions and reactions of world trade.

# 18

## *Experiments in Unity*

◇◇◇◇◇◇◇◇◇◇◇◇◇◇◇◇◇◇◇◇◇◇◇◇◇◇◇◇◇◇◇◇◇◇◇◇◇◇◇◇◇◇◇◇◇◇◇◇◇

IN THE first two years of the Marshall Plan, the nineteen nations in Europe made a number of different attacks upon the problem of unity. Each represented an attempt to set the law of comparative advantage working again by way of the freer movement of goods and the restoration of competition between the various European economies. Each inevitably came up against the protective instincts of the various governments which were as alive as ever to the risk of domestic unemployment and of national bankruptcy. One of the first means considered was a full customs union. A joint committee was set up to look into the possibilities, but the intricacies and the complications presented by a general frontal attack upon all tariffs were found to be such that three years later the committee had still presented no report.

One or two more limited experiments were attempted, but they, too, ran into difficulties. The French and Italian Governments opened negotiations in 1948 but it did not take much discussion to bring the fundamental difficulty to the surface. If any economic advantage is to flow from a customs union some sacrifices will occur on each side of the frontier. The rationalizing of production means that some enterprises must be abandoned to the more efficient producer and while the general interest gains, local interests may suffer. This they are not prepared to do. In the circumstances of 1948, with over 2 million men unemployed and perhaps 2 million more working short time, no Italian Government could have permitted the free entry of French goods which might have shut down more Italian industries. The Italian motor industry, in particular, fought any greater entry of foreign cars. The producers of Italian wine and fruit were equally hostile. It should be remarked that, once the tariff negotiations began, it became clear that the obstacle to free Franco-Italian trade was not tariffs, but quotas. Italy did not rely upon tariffs to keep out foreign goods and competition. It had inherited from Fascism a system of import licensing whereby only a certain amount of any import from any country was allowed into Italy. Once this "quota" was exhausted, no more imports were permitted. The effect, however, was the same and whether tariffs or quotas were the obstacle, they prevented the flow of international trade.

Rather more success attended the efforts of Holland, Belgium and Luxembourg—the Benelux group—to achieve complete economic union. In 1948, a common set of tariffs was established around the new union and most of the trade barriers between the Netherlands and the Belgium-Luxembourg economic union were removed. Yet even here, progress toward the complete economic union first proposed proved slower and more painful than had been imagined originally. Agricultural Holland and industrial Belgium have economies which are reasonably complementary. The standards of living in the two countries, in spite of Holland's greater sufferings in the war and subsequent loss of the Netherlands East Indies, were not widely dissimilar. The obstacle which held them apart even after the completion of a nominal customs union was above all the question of their different currencies.

As we have seen, in 1948 and 1949 the Belgian franc was scarce compared with the demand for it in Europe. It was a "hard" currency. The supply of Dutch guilders, on the other hand, was somewhat inflated. The Netherlands had been compelled to finance a war in Indonesia, it had tried to make good the damages of war quickly and at the same time keep its population fully employed and provided with social welfare. The result of many claims upon the Dutch Exchequer had been a tendency for more guilders to get into circulation than could be balanced by output and imports.

The Dutch guilder was thus "soft" while the Belgian franc remained "hard." A fusion of the two economies at such a moment would have meant either the flooding of the Belgian market with Dutch demand or the flight of Dutch capital to the Belgian market. So long, therefore, as the two currencies remained in disequilibrium, hopes of a full union had to be postponed. In 1950, after the creation of a general instrument of European convertibility—the European Payments Union—it seemed likely that the Benelux experiment could be completed.

The various discussions and negotiations on customs union did, at least, have the result of showing that in 1948 and 1949, tariffs were less of an obstacle to the revival of free trade and competition than the immense battery of quotas and licensing systems whereby most European governments tried to control the absolute amount of goods they would take in imports from abroad. In 1949, therefore, the British Government took the lead in suggesting that the best immediate method of unshackling trade would be to remove all quantitative restrictions. In the following months 40 per cent of private trade was freed. In the course of 1950, the percentage was raised to 60 per cent. The liberalization of 75 per cent of private trade should have been realized early in 1951, but such developments as Germany's sudden disequilibrium in foreign trade have delayed this development.

This really important step toward a greater freedom in trade would, however, have meant little if all the restrictions on the movement of foreign exchange had remained. Merchants who had seen the import restrictions removed from an attractive market abroad might still find themselves unable to sell there because their government was not prepared to make currency available to finance the transaction. The essential complement of the scheme to remove quantitative restrictions has therefore been a progressive attempt to restore convertibility to Europe's currencies. There could, naturally, be no question of extending convertibility to the dollar. Europe's general dollar shortage was shrinking steadily, but in 1949 it was over $4 billion and over $3 billion in 1950. Moreover, the world's general deficit of dollars still exercised its pressure on the exchanges. In 1949, the United States still had a surplus with every area in the world. Any attempt to make currencies generally convertible into dollars would therefore have drained every government of its precious reserves.

Although general convertibility was not at issue, the problem of the nations' reserves of gold and dollars nevertheless hung over every discussion for making European currencies convertible into each other. The reasons have been explained in a previous chapter. Many European governments had come to fear Belgium's position as general creditor. Britain was handicapped by the oversupply of sterling to the world. The result was that in the first two European payments schemes, the checks on free convertibility were at a maximum.

The first payments scheme of 1948 was strictly bilateral. Each nation received, in Marshall aid dollars, the equivalent of its direct deficit with the United States. If, in addition, it had a surplus with another Marshall country, it extended a credit to it in its own currency (a so-called "drawing right") and received another grant of dollars equal to the credit it had made itself. Under this scheme France, for instance, in addition to direct dollar aid from America, received grants in practically every other European currency, since it appeared to have a deficit with all of them. In 1949, the scheme was amended to make it a little less bilateral. Under the old scheme, the grants in local currency (the drawing rights) could be used only in the country by which they were extended. In 1949, a quarter of them became transferable. In other words, France could use one quarter of its grant from Britain not to buy goods in the sterling area but, for example, to settle a debt with Belgium.

In 1950, a much more ambitious scheme was introduced. Inter-European trade would be conducted entirely through a new clearing union—the European Payments Union—backed by credits from the Marshall countries and a dollar grant from Marshall aid of about $400 million. This Union would be the clearing-house of the Marshall countries' debts and credits and would, in the manner of an ordinary bank, cancel surpluses against deficits. Each nation would begin with a quota of EPU units (one unit, in fact, equals a gold dollar) and these quotas would be used to finance inter-European trade, the net creditors receiving increased allocations from the Union's fund, the debtors drawing on it to finance further trade. When a certain degree of debt had been reached, however, debtors would be compelled to begin to pay dollars or gold into the pool and these would be allotted to the creditors.

In the discussion of the scheme, one of the chief points at issue between Britain and Belgium was the moment at which these gold payments would be introduced. The Belgian Government sought to make this moment as early, the British as late, as possible. European opinion, in its usual cautious and inexplicit way, probably preferred on the whole the British approach, but the decisive factor was undoubtedly a growing impatience in the ECA headquarters with Belgium's apparently insatiable desire for gold and its preference for "hard money" rather than economic expansion. The British, too, were in a stronger position to urge the postponement of gold payments. As a result of devaluation, British exports to Europe increased markedly in 1950 and in any current transactions, the British might have acquired a considerable amount of gold if they had agreed to early gold payments. But they at least showed their consistency by being as ready to postpone the transfer of gold when postponement was *not* in their immediate interests as they had been when early gold payments worked to their disadvantage. In the event, a compromise was reached which postponed the point at which gold would need to be used to settle debts but which retained the eventual obligation to pay out gold in order to keep some check on inveterate debtors.

With the coming into force of the scheme in July, 1950, the Marshall countries reached a freer flow of trade and payments than had been known since the war and—if Germany be included—possibly since the Great Depression. The chief reason for inter-European import quotas and discrimination which had been based on the "hardness" and "softness" of the different currencies now vanished. Indeed, the members of the new Union undertook from January 1, 1951, "to avoid any discrimination in respect of imports of any products as between one member and another." Even so, the scheme depended from the outset upon three factors—direct American support to the Union and continued dollar allocations to bridge the gap in each Marshall country's account with the United States, the ability of Britain to prevent an excessive flow of sterling into the new European Union and the readiness of the "deflationary" states—Belgium and, to a lesser extent, Italy—to modify their policy of limiting home demand and, with it, imports. Nor could the scheme do away completely with exchange control, since the dollar area was not a party to the agreements and the world continued to have an all but universal deficit in its American trade.

It must also be admitted that although a return to freer payments and freer trade is an essential preliminary to unity in the European economy and begins to undo some of the worst protective devices of the last two decades—quotas, import licenses, bilateral trading, inconvertible currencies—it leaves others intact and these, too, are severe obstacles to full economic union and the most effective deployment of resources which such a union can make possible. As we have seen, the obstacles to the free flow of competition do not all lie along national frontiers. Even within national economies, labor and capital seek to defend themselves against competitive pressure and to prevent changes in the country's economic pattern from impinging on their vested interests. In prewar Europe, cartels co-existed with perfectly free arrangements for the movement of imports and currencies. The protection of different firms and trades was organized across frontiers as well as behind them. The leaders in various businesses agreed upon a certain price level and upon the division of the European and world market and these agreements were quite as effective in undoing the advantages of the "single market" as any of the battery of protective devices at the disposal of national governments. But how were they to be undone? The "vested interests" were after all not negligible. The amount of capital invested in many heavy industries is such that any authority would hesitate before refusing it a measure of protection. And the more the community comes to regard its labor force as honorable partners and fully endowed citizens, the less inclined it is to see their lives buffeted this way and that by the chance winds of economic change. How then can the mobility that is necessary for a dynamic and expanding economy be combined with the security which is essential to a decent and dignified way of life?

The answer given by Europe's planners has tended to be that national governments are the right authorities both to check the anti-economic character of cartels and monopolies and to provide citizens with reasonable security. The difficulty here, however, is that the national economies of Europe are not the optimum size for this type of planning. The authority of the national planners does not extend beyond their own frontiers, but there is no guarantee that the sum of nineteen separate national plans will add up into a single efficient "master plan" for Western Europe. The attempt was made in the early days of the Marshall Plan to draw up such a scheme and within it to co-ordinate Europe's program of capital expansion. But no government could really be relied upon to see beyond its own nose. Most of them were determined, whatever their neighbors' plans might be, to expand the basis of their industrial strength—steel-making, electrification, oil refining. Plans for new steel mills, for hydroelectric schemes and oil refineries began to proliferate in Europe. The OEEC served a useful purpose in offering private suggestions that Europe was likely to be over-equipped in certain lines of capital goods.[1] But the task of

[1] A report published by the Economic Commission for Europe in 1949 suggested that by 1951 Europe's steel-making capacity would be in the neighborhood of 70 million tons a year; its annual market not more than 62 million.

compelling governments to modify their plans was beyond it. Yet the alternatives—either to leave each government to safeguard its own national interests or to renounce the safeguards in the name of free competition—seemed equally bleak. The former would fix Europe in a rigid pattern of nineteen uncompetitive economies, the latter might bring in communism in the wake of disorganization and unemployment. It was at this point that M. Schuman put forward his scheme for creating a single market in European iron and steel.

The essence of the Schuman Plan was that it attempted to combine proper safeguards for local and national interests with a general restoration of free movement, competitive costs and the old law of comparative advantage to a vital section of European heavy industry. The authority responsible for the scheme would not be made up of national governments whose interests, the French agreed, would always tend to go no further than their own frontiers. Nor would it be a private international cartel whose actions could not be relied upon to be anything but restrictive. Instead, a new High Authority would be set up with the twofold task of removing all tariffs, quotas and local or national restrictions in the sale of coal and steel, yet at the same time ensuring that this creation of a single market did not bear down too heavily upon any one section within it. A single price would be fixed by the Authority for coal and steel produced anywhere in the area under its control. This price would be considerably below the cost of producing coal and steel in some of the less efficient enterprises. They therefore would be forced out of business, production would be centered on the more efficient businesses and Europe as a whole would gain by cheaper coal and steel and hence by a greater demand for both.

The inefficient producer would not, however, be left to face bankruptcy and unemployment. Two funds would be established by the High Authority, both financed by government grants, and by a levy on sales. The first would provide high-cost producers with price subsidies on a diminishing basis so that the impact of the new lower price would not be felt all at once. The second fund would be available to provide less efficient firms with funds for modernization and rationalization. Those firms, however, which, even with technical re-equipment, would not become competitively efficient would be helped by the Fund to move to other types of industrial production and their workers would be retrained for other work.

Such were the essential features of the new scheme. It ingeniously avoided the pitfalls both of purely national and purely interested control. It provided a return of competitive conditions while safeguarding the possible victims of competition. It could be applied equally well to privately or publicly owned industries. Its importance in providing a new pattern of international economic co-operation was so obvious that the Dutch Foreign Minister, Dr. Stikker (who was also the chief political officer of the OEEC), immediately proposed the extension of the same principle to a wider list of European industries. The Italian delegation to OEEC also gave the notion of extending the Schuman principle its vigorous support.

Nevertheless the Schuman concept raised a number of formidable difficulties—for instance, how were wages and working conditions to be more or less equalized so that one country did not secure an unfair advantage by keeping wages down? And how could wages be compared between countries when in some areas lower wages secured a higher standard of living, thanks to relatively low costs in the economy at large? Would differences in taxation prove a severe handicap to some firms and a competitive advantage to others? The intention of the Plan was to secure little by little an equalization of such conditions but the process would take time.

How, too, would the new union look to competitors and producers and potential purchasers outside the ring? It was the intention of the Plan to safeguard the new European price level for coal and steel by preventing cheaper supplies from entering the market. In other words, the tariffs that were to be removed inside the new single market would remain and might be reinforced round it. Such a move might make for greater efficiency and freer competition inside the union, but it could mean a retreat from competition in the wider world market. This risk would be particularly important if the scheme did not cover the main European producers. Yet the whole preliminary negotiations in the summer of 1950 took place without the participation of the British Government. Europe's largest producer of coal and steel stayed outside the crucial experiment.

It is difficult to know how to allot the blame for this unfortunate and, on balance, unnecessary development. Both the French and the British Governments must take responsibility for their really ludicrous handling of M. Schuman's first invitation to Britain to come to Paris and confer on this plan together with representatives from Germany, Italy and the Benelux powers. For France, the political significance of the scheme was undoubtedly more important than the economic. M. Schuman wished to end dramatically the state of antagonism and general ill will into which Franco-German relations had degenerated. For France to propose the joining of the two countries' heavy industries would create a new atmosphere. It could end the secular struggle between the two nations. It could pave the way to closer relations and ultimately to federal union. Such being France's objectives, M. Schuman had careful private preliminary discussions with the Germans who were not in the least surprised when he issued his dramatic invitation on May 25 in which the political objectives of the Plan—the sacrifice of national sovereignty to the new High Authority and the ultimate achievement of federal union—were stressed and were, indeed, made a condition of each government's acceptance of the invitation.

But the British were surprised—and resentful. It was bad enough that no warning should have been given. It was worse that preliminary discussions should have been conducted with Germany and not with Britain. But possibly the worst of it was that Mr. Bevin was ill in the hospital and that no one of sufficient imagination or responsibility was at the Foreign Office to take the obvious next step—a quick visit to Paris to see what the invitation was all about. Instead there took place a fortnight of note-exchanging in the most pompous manner of traditional diplomacy with Ambassadors acting as go-betweens for Ministers who, if they had so decided, could have met within a couple of hours for explanations and consultations face to face. But Paris might have been Bogota and London in the Antipodes and by the time "official channels" had done their worst, the gap between the French and British points of view, which could perhaps have been crossed if jumped at once, had become an unbridgeable chasm. As a display of the anachronism of nine-tenths of normal diplomatic technique, it was unsurpassed. But it left Britain on one side of the chasm and the six powers preparing to negotiate the Schuman Plan on the other.

The gap, itself, was admittedly important since it turned on the issue of national sovereignty. But it was the French and British handling of the gap that turned it from a gap into an abyss. The French must bear the blame for linking the scheme directly to political federal union. Their reply is that the British Government had shown itself in all previous Marshall Plan negotiations so determined not to sacrifice a jot of sovereignty that the issue of sovereignty had to be made clear at once. But this reply is not really convincing. The British have made a great show of never sacrificing sovereignty [2] and both the Labour Party and the Conservatives made statements about "not permitting a foreign authority to close a single British coal mine," but the record of the British Government on the question of practical internationalism is fully as good as that of the French. The EPU Scheme is, as we have seen, a large move toward freeing the exchanges. All the defense arrangements under the Atlantic Pact amount to complete sacrifices of sovereignty. Moreover, in the negotiations with the other Six Powers on the Schuman Plan, the French have since introduced a variety of safeguards for national governments—a Committee of Ministers, for

[2] One has only to recall the devastating effect of the publications of the Labour Party's pamphlet on "European Unity"—the "Dalton Brown Paper"—in the middle of the Schuman controversy.

instance, has been set up to deal with various matters of crucial importance and the Authority will submit reports to an Assembly drawn from the various parliaments which could very well be drawn from the parliamentarians in the Assembly at Strasbourg. Had British negotiators been at Paris these developments would have gone most of the way to meet British hesitations. By ignoring Britain's practical record of international co-operation and hammering the nail of sovereignty repeatedly on the head, the French finally conveyed the impression that they really did not want British participation at all.

The shortsightedness of the British Government in this matter has been economic rather than political. Its reaction has shown one consistent fallacy—that a nation entirely dependent upon trade can remain complete arbiter of its own economic destiny. One way or another, the competitive tides will beat against Britain's shores and no amount of protection and discrimination can wholly keep them out. If European coal and steel can be produced more cheaply, then nations will buy them, whatever the British Government may do to protect its own market. Coal pits that are exhausted must be closed one day, either by competition or by agreement. High-cost steel will cease to sell, whatever the tariffs that ring it round; or, if its sales are subsidized, it will be sold only at great cost to the British taxpayer. The Schuman Plan is an alternative not to some supposed and illusory British freedom of action but to the inexorable pressure of unchecked and uncontrolled competition. Only a government—and an Opposition—bemused by five years of the postwar sellers' market, could have supposed that, in staying out of the Schuman Plan, they were keeping their "freedom of action." A glance back to 1933 could have told them what such freedom of action can mean—a coal industry ruined by cheap foreign competition and a steel industry about to enter a closed and restrictive international steel cartel. Only an attack of acute economic myopia can explain the failure of British statesmen and their advisers to see the significance of the Schuman Plan as a workable halfway house between the two extremes of the thirties—coal ruined by foreign competition, steel controlled by a foreign cartel.

With this brief survey of the Schuman Plan, we come to the end of Europe's experiments in greater economic unity. They are not negligible. Within two years of the introduction of the Marshall Plan, a measure of freedom in European trade and in European payments has been reached that has reversed not only the consequences of the war but also the tendencies of two or three decades. A vital first step has been taken in recreating the free movement of goods and capital through Europe. At the same time, the Schuman Plan introduces a quite new attempt to overcome the industrial rigidities, both internal and international, in which Europe had been caught fast between the wars. As a two-year balance sheet, the result is impressive. It looks even better when the complete restoration of prewar standards of production is added to it. But most impressive of all, perhaps, are the achievements which cannot be measured so easily—the growth of understanding that has gone on beneath all the tempest on the surface, the growth of knowledge and, between officials, the growth of confidence. In such bodies as the international secretariat of the OEEC there has come into being a potential civil service for Europe as a whole. Such things cannot be entered on a balance sheet but they will be among the most striking consequences of the Marshall Plan.

Nor can it be doubted that the three experiments—of more liberal trade, of freer payments and of single markets for various European branches of production—all point in the right direction, toward a Europe in which national and local barriers to freedom of movement and development have been removed by a combination of free competition and collective planning. Such a Europe would undoubtedly be in the long run a factor making for a productive and expanding world economy. Greater efficiency in the use of its resources would make its goods cheaper and hence more competitive with those of the United States, better methods of producing wealth would encourage a greater accumulation of capital and permit Europe to resume its old rôle of providing the world with capital. In the long run, such a Europe would be a means to bridging the dollar gap, maintaining the world economy at a high level of activity and raising living standards all over the world.

Equally, however, it must be admitted that in the short run, European efforts toward unity contribute little to any of these wider objectives. Far from helping in their realization, European economic unity cannot be achieved without them. That this is the case can easily be proved by asking what would happen to Europe's present schemes for liberalization if dollar aid ceased and the world plunged down into another depression. At present, the dollar gap has been reduced to about $3 billion, but more by the cutting of imports from America than by the expansion of Europe's sales. Even the most optimistic estimates made before the Korean war spoke of a billion-dollar gap after 1952. The extra American assistance given to finance Western rearmament will probably close this gap in the short run but the need to concentrate European production on armaments may, as we have seen, reduce Europe's capacity to export and therefore increase the dollar gap—in the longer run. Yet the present payments scheme is underpinned by the dollar grant both to EPU and to each participant and by a special American safeguard given to Britain limiting the amount of gold it will lose as a result of the workings of the EPU. Remove these dollar props and the whole scheme may fall to the ground. Similarly, the liberalization of European trade has been worked out in a climate created by direct American grants to cover vital European purchases. If the scheme had to work without these grants and with a $2 billion deficit pressing on Europe's exchanges, the temptation to reintroduce bilateral control in order to protect each nation's reserves might be overwhelming.

Moreover, the figure of $2 billion was based on the postulate that the United States would still be producing, exporting and purchasing at a high level of economic activity. Any downward swoop of the entire economy would nullify overnight such a relatively optimistic estimate of the dollar gap. If a slight recession can reduce the world's dollar earnings by $500 million in three months, what havoc might not be played by a more dangerous downward plunge? Not all the experiments in unity that the mind of Europe could conceive would rescue it from disaster under those circumstances. No cheapening of coal and steel under a Schuman Plan, or of electricity, cement, petroleum or agricultural machinery under a Stikker plan would maintain the sale of products for which the demand and the market had vanished. The panic retreat to protection, national and local, would start again.

A national economy during a period of trade depression is like a patient suffering from severe arthritis. The sense of pain and dislocation in every limb of the economy is such that the thought of movement or change of attitude is unthinkable. On the contrary, the economy shrinks in upon itself attempting by complete protection and immobility to prevent a bout of even severer pain. The quotas, the restrictions, the exchange control, with which the Marshall countries have struggled in their efforts to achieve greater integration in Europe were in large part legacies from the collapse of trade, first in the Depression and then in the war. Any new sudden strain upon the structure of European trade would almost automatically undo the degree of liberalization achieved so far and certainly make quite impossible a bolder advance along the path of integration. European unity will not create the expanding world economy. It will be created by it. Vital and hopeful as the various European experiments have been, they depend upon securing a general prosperity and upon bridging the dollar gap.

# 19

# *Tomorrow's World Economy*

◊◊◊◊◊◊◊◊◊◊◊◊◊◊◊◊◊◊◊◊◊◊◊◊◊◊◊◊◊◊◊◊◊◊◊◊◊◊◊◊◊◊◊◊◊◊◊◊

THE United States is sometimes resentful of the fact that other nations tend to lay so much responsibility upon America's action—or inaction. "Why," the Americans ask, "should we be blamed for what happens in the world at large? What is all this, anyway? A plot to make Uncle Sam shoulder everyone else's troubles? We're tired of all this talk about leadership. Why can't someone else do a little leading for a change?" But the outside world is not really attempting a conspiracy. It is simply recognizing a fact—and that fact is the scale of the American economy. It is the largest in the world and the largest in human history. It cannot help affecting everyone else, any more than a very large man can help taking up more room and coming into contact with more people than a small man. There are other sizable economies in the world—that of Britain, for instance —but all of them are dwarfed by the United States. Britain, like every other economy, depends continually and immediately upon the movements of its great neighbor.

These two most powerful economies do, however, by their action and interaction, create the economic climate of the free world. It is a matter of immediate vexation, but possibly of ultimate sanity and balance that they appear at the moment to represent in their outlook and policies two rival principles of economic interest and organization. The

American world view tends to be emotionally more attached to the workings of the law of comparative advantage and to believe that automatic conditions give the law the chance of working to its full effect. Their emphasis therefore tends to be on cutting away obstacles and rigidities and allowing free forces of competition and efficiency to produce the best economic results. The British have come to be more impressed with the need to safeguard national and local interests, to find security for investor and worker and to permit automatic forces to work only when a sufficient degree of protection has been secured. It is no criticism of either outlook to point out that Britain had more faith in competition when its own competitive position was unrivaled—as is America's today.

If there is anything in the facts examined in the last three chapters, it can be said quite categorically that both the United States and Britain are partly right and partly wrong in their outlook and that nothing would be more likely to produce a balanced world economy than that their differing theoretical and emotional outlooks should be made to meet in some workable compromise. The British are surely right in their contention that only an accidental conjunction of historical, social and geographical factors in the nineteenth century made possible an *automatic* expansion of the world economy. Change those underlying factors and automatic forces can begin to contract the economy as certainly as they formerly increased it. Automatic forces will not even out the trade cycle. Automatic forces will not bring a high and stable balance into international trade. On the contrary, in the twentieth century they make the ups and downs more violent and lead to such conditions as those prevailing in Europe in the rigid, quota-ridden, autarkic thirties.

The Americans, however, are surely right in their continued insistence that efficiency, productivity and expansion depend upon these often despised economic forces. The British, in losing confidence in automatic forces, appear all too often to have lost faith in competition and efficiency as well. Every report on industrial productivity brought to Britain from America in the last two years reveals the technical backwardness of much of British industry, the unenterprising management, the opposition of trade unions to technological progress, the extension of the concept of protection until it seems a means of protecting men against the impact of new ideas or the need for better work. If full employment and economic stability are simply other names for freezing the economy in a rigid pattern of obsolescent machines and restrictive practices, the free world may avoid the sudden ruin of depression only to fall into the slow ruin of decay.

But are the British and the American outlooks so fundamentally at variance? Is it beyond the wit of statesmen and economists and business leaders in both countries to work out policies which contain the element of truth in both? Theoretically, at least, it seems possible to envisage a world economy in which certain key positions are maintained by purposive control and governmental action while in the rest of the economy, freedom of movement, action and competition are encouraged and restored. In place of the present pattern which tends to be one of planlessness and unpredictability in the world at large countered at a multitude of particular points by protection and rigidity, one could conceive of an economy whose general pattern was controlled and sustained while real liberty of action returned in the great mass of particular instances. The British concept of stability is not wrong. It is, indeed, inevitable and, under the impact of depression, each government will seek locally and ineffectually to achieve stability, thus chopping up the world into a myriad obstinate, inefficient and indigestible local economies. But if general stability were assured, all excuse for these local rearguard actions on the part of governments would become unnecessary and over a large segment of the economy, the American concept of fluidity and movement could be realized. The essential dynamism would then be restored which the free world needs if it is to achieve the output and the efficiency necessary to a generally expanding economy.

The challenge is thus to translate stability to the general framework of the free economy—to the maintenance of employment, trade and investment—and to restore fluidity and competition to the infinity of particular transactions which take place within the wider framework. It would not seem on the face of it to be a harder task than others the free world has successfully achieved in the past—no more intellectually formidable, surely, than the development of atomic energy, not much more testing physically than the mounting of a war effort, and, in administrative techniques, not very much more complicated than the operations of Mutual Aid or UNRRA or the Marshall Plan. The chief difference is that in all these other objectives, the end was fully willed and accepted. The means therefore followed, not without difficulty, perhaps, but with the success that concentration and determination have usually brought to the efforts of free men. The objective of a stable framework for the free world economy is not yet accepted. Men do not yet see in it the essential condition of a successful struggle against communism. It is therefore still lamentably possible that the free world will lose this struggle, not for lack of means but for lack of aim and will.

Let us suppose, however, that the two decisive economies of the West—America, the senior partner, and its British colleague—agree to give the lead in examining the problem of a stable and lasting framework for world trade. Let us suppose that they take as their starting point the most alarming symptom of instability—the dollar gap—and consider possible policies not with one eye on what divides the American from the British approach but with the sincere intention of adopting what is most valuable in both. What would be the result? A policy requiring an impossibility? One demanding such supreme vision and sacrifice and enlightenment that only seraphs could put it into effect? Or, on the contrary, a policy which demands no more than that self-interest should be as intelligent, determination as genuine and energy as vital as they have been shown to be in the Marshall period? Would a joint strategy demand inconceivably more courage and drive than the nations have shown already? Or would it simply chart a road they can follow with the impetus that is already theirs? In a word, is it a possible or an impossible task?

We have no precise way of estimating what, once the upheaval of rearmament is over, the normal future level of the American surplus will prove to be. In the ten years before the war, the world's shortage of dollars was in the neighborhood of $500 million a year. Those who have therefore estimated that a normal postwar gap might be double that figure do not seem to be making an unreasonable assumption. The strength of the American economy has grown prodigiously since 1939 while that of every other has declined. To double the prewar figure appears a likely enough estimate, erring perhaps on the side of optimism. A solution to the problems posed by this shortage might be drawn wholly from the American philosophy of "automatic" and free expedients. It could be based upon permitting trade to find its level by a judicious devaluation of all non-dollar currencies. The 1949 devaluation appears to have had its effect in making dollar goods less attractive in other markets and encouraging a greater demand for Europe's products. The objection that could have been leveled at such a solution in 1947—that essential goods could only be obtained in the dollar area—is not likely to be true, say, in 1956. There are, however, grave objections to any policy that places complete reliance upon the manipulation of exchange rates. The 1949 experience is not conclusive for, as we have seen, it has been accompanied by a great expansion in American purchases abroad, and a decided improvement in the world economy in the wake of that of the United States. The great risk of devaluation as a general European expedient is that it can constantly widen the competitive gap between the New World and the Old. With each decline in the value of its currency, Europe would be less able to buy American goods and machines and less able to tap the sources of American technology. The competitive efficiency of the United States economy would increase as Europe's sank and devaluation might have to become a progressive expedient, constantly widening the gap between American and European costs. The dollar problem might thus be "solved" in the very short run only by making it more insoluble with each fresh application of the solution.

Unless, moreover, the expedient of devaluation were

accompanied by draconian controls over the movement of capital—and these controls would nullify all hopes of genuinely automatic adjustments—the fall in non-dollar currencies would be the signal for a massive withdrawal of capital from Europe and its transfer to the United States. A large part of the $500 million surplus in the American account in the thirties was made up of refugee capital seeking to escape from the uncertainties of Europe. Since the war, too, illicit transfers of large sums have taken place. If this process were to continue—and under the threat of persistent devaluation it would certainly do so—the free world, which chiefly needs a steady outflow of capital from the United States to fertilize the backward areas of the world, would be faced with the prospect of a movement of capital in exactly the contrary direction. This is not a fanciful picture. It simply represents a projection and acceleration of a process that was beginning to appear before the war.

The unsatisfactory results of such automatic measures have led many critics to swing to the other extreme and to propose a solution in purely "British" terms of control and regulation. "These barriers to trade with America," they say, "cannot be surmounted by ordinary means. All our rules, all our expedients have been designed for a world in which, on balance, nations would need to import as much as they exported and in which some natural flow of interest maintained the circuit of trade. This American phenomenon—that of a great exporting nation under little or no compulsion to import—is too much for us. As for experiments in less restricted trade, more liberal movements of capital and the freer conversion of currency—we throw in our hands. They can perhaps be managed with everyone else, but not with the United States." They, therefore, suggest that the only line of advance open to the free world is to have one set of rules for all non-American nations and a different rule for the United States.

In a sense, they propose that the temporary expedients of Europe's schemes for trade liberalization and inter-convertible currencies should become the rule. Trade would be free everywhere, save with the dollar area. Currencies would be convertible into every currency, except the dollar. These steps, their proposers maintain, do not in any way reduce dollar trade. Every dollar that America makes available by purchases or loans will be eagerly and gratefully spent, but the controls will prevent the drain of European reserves to the United States which, in any uncontrolled system, America's ability to sell and attractiveness to foreign capital, are bound to bring about. The argument has certain attractions and clearly, if there is no way of overcoming the dollar gap save by discrimination and control, it is as well that the area of discrimination should be as limited as possible and should not extend to all currencies and all trade. As we have seen, the danger of the doctrine of non-discrimination in an unstable and unbalanced world is that it automatically makes the instability and the disequilibrium more widespread. If every attempt to reduce imports from the dollar world or to prevent the escape of capital to the United States had, in the name of nondiscrimination, to be extended to every other currency or market, trade would virtually cease. The EPU scheme in Europe recognizes this fact and, as a short term expedient—it is to last two years—it permits the European powers to gain greater freedom within the European market while excluding the dollar from the arrangement.

There are, however, formidable objections to making this the final solution of the dollar gap. In the first place, it would be very difficult, as the last four years have shown, to keep controls on dollar trade and remove them everywhere else. Even through the stringent exchange controls imposed since the war, billions of dollars' worth of European capital has slipped away to America. If the barriers were maintained permanently, it is likely that the experiment of freer trade outside the dollar area would suffer. The efforts of the various governments to restrict and control trade with the rich and plentiful markets of the Americas would almost certainly bedevil every effort—international or local—to return to less restricted patterns of trade.

Another consequence of permanent discrimination could

be a relative impoverishment of the world and a dangerous intensification of Europe's economic problems. The theory of free multilateral trade is, after all, perfectly correct. If trade can move freely in pursuit of the maximum economic efficiency and productivity, the world as a whole profits by the exchange of goods and the division of labor which results. If the free nations resign themselves to a situation in which the New World's capacity to export is permanently lowered and the Old World is thrust back on to reliance upon less efficient and more costly sources of supply, the policy is equivalent to accepting a lower standard of living for Europe permanently. It is not simply a question of reducing Europe's ability to buy American machines and participate in American technical progress. It is sometimes forgotten that the New World has become an increasingly important supplier of raw materials. While exporting communities in the United States —the cotton states and the corn states and the tobacco states, for instance—would be compelled to undertake expensive schemes of agricultural and industrial conversion, the industrial nations of Europe would have to compete with each other to secure higher-cost cotton and tobacco in parts of the world much less well-suited to their production. Such a process would be a direct reversal of the policies most needed in the free world today.

The capacity of the Americas to produce primary products is actually growing. This is the last moment at which to consider cutting them off from the industrial markets of the rest of the world. Outside America, the demand for foodstuffs and raw materials is about to increase enormously with the return to active industrial and exporting life of Germany and Japan. With supplies in the Soviet half of the world an unknown quantity, Europe and Asia must have access to the widest possible sources of primary products elsewhere. This is the last moment at which policies should be considered which threaten to reduce the rôle of the New World as a source of supply. Every argument of economic sanity thus points to a solution of the dollar problem on expansive, not restrictive lines, by a greater flow of dollars, not by a smaller flow of goods. And even if all the economic arguments did not point in the same direction, one political argument would outweigh all the rest—that policies which divide the free nations and sow the seeds of perpetual friction and misunderstanding in the vital sphere of trade will work steadily against the political unity the free world desperately needs to counter Communist pressure.

A dynamic solution to the problem of an expanding world economy cannot lie along restrictionist lines. If reliance is placed either wholly on automatic means or wholly on control and discrimination, the free economy will be split in two. Neither side will advance in step with the other and each will prove an impediment to the other's progress. The solution to which all the evidence seems to point is a marriage of the two methods, control and progressive direction covering only a limited number of key points of the world economy and the free movement of resources returning as far as possible to all other fields. It was good fortune, not necessity, that gave the nineteenth century a system in which the general framework of world trade was automatically upheld by the actions of the British market. Now wayward fortune has reversed its rôle and automatic means upset rather than sustain the expanding economy. The earlier rôle of Britain—that of universal stabilizer—must therefore be "reinvented," like Voltaire's deity, and the responsibility here falls squarely upon the American and British Governments since their actions will be decisive practically through the economy of the free world.

The points to include in the stabilizing sector of their policy can best be determined by deciding which factors have, in the past thirty years, played most havoc with expanding world trade. The immediate answer is that three factors have most undermined stability—the alternation of boom and depression, the failure of trade to balance (of which the dollar gap is the most extreme example) and the virtual ending of international investment. Action in these three spheres would, therefore, go practically all the way to the restoration of reasonable stability and the hope of expansion. The vital first step is each government's readiness to produce a high level of economic activity in its own domestic market. This obligation to pursue full employment need not be restressed at this point, but it should perhaps be repeated that it is or should be as much the official policy of the free governments as collective resistance to aggression or any other United Nations undertaking. All members of the United Nations are formally pledged in the Charter to secure high levels of employment. They have gone further and at the meeting of the Economic and Social Council in the summer of 1950, they undertook to provide the United Nations with full accounts of the steps they proposed to take to economic stability and the information necessary to enable other governments to judge whether they were in fact doing so. The substance of possible policies of domestic full employment were discussed fully in earlier chapters. But it cannot be repeated too often both that expanding world trade is impossible without full employment and that, if there is anything binding in a solemn international undertaking, nations are thoroughly committed to the policy of high domestic activity. To fail on this front is as great a breach of the United Nations Charter as to fail to reinforce the United Nations' forces fighting in Korea—as great and, in the long run, as fatal.

The maintenance of full employment in the United States and Great Britain would go very far to maintain it elsewhere. It would also go a long way toward producing the second element of control—the conscious effort to maintain at the highest possible level of exchange a balance in each nation's accounts and above all in those of the United States. The experience of the upswing of the American economy in 1950 has shown that a thriving, expanding United States draws the world up with it. American industry calls on more of the world's reserves of raw materials, the non-European sterling area becomes again what it was before the war—a dollar earner—and opposition inside the United States to European imports sinks to a minimum (it was above all during the 1949 recession that Mr. Hoffman, then head of the ECA, found he had to listen to the fears felt by American producers in the face of a possible increase in European competition). Moreover, there appears to be a latent tendency in the United States to need greater supplies of external products as its own economy expands and domestic sources of supply are worked out.

Yet even the most optimistic estimates look forward to an American surplus of no less than a billion dollars a year. Is this gap, however, an insuperable difficulty, provided full employment is maintained? It represents no more than one-third of one per cent of what the American national income could become by the middle of this decade. Even if it should prove impossible to lower American tariffs further and reduce this formidable distortion of the world's natural economic flow of trade, there would seem to be an immense variety of expedients whereby so relatively small a sum could be prevented from upsetting the nations' efforts to restore free trade. For instance, might not part of the sum set aside for assistance to backward areas be given in free grants which would not entail repayment in goods or dollars? Within any national economy, it is recognized that some areas are too poverty-stricken to survive and re-adapt themselves without direct grants-in-aid. Within the vast frontiers of the free world, such needs will exist for many decades to come and assistance to them might be a useful way of balancing the dollar account. An even more simple expedient might lie in placing some of the United States regular military orders permanently in the British Commonwealth or in France. The defense bill would not be increased in any way, but part of it could be used to underpin stability in world trade. As these lines are being written, first reports have been published of the inquiry into the problem of the future dollar gap undertaken by Mr. Gordon Gray for President Truman. The report, it seems, suggests that for the next ten years a combination of a billion dollars a year for continuing Marshall aid and $50 million a year for technical assistance under Point IV should cover the dollar gap while a reduction in American tariffs and an increase in American purchases abroad might be the basis of a long term attack on the problem of stability.

Such a program, flexibly administered, should offer a complete solution to the present instability.

Britain's responsibility for stabilizing the world's trade balance would need to take an opposite form. The type of instability Britain has contributed to the world since the war has not been a shortage of its currency, but, on the contrary, a plethora of it. The excuse for all the controls with which Britain has protected its economy, including its maintenance of inconvertible sterling and its periodic releases of sterling to maintain the demand for British goods, has been the existence of the dollar gap and the pressure exerted on the world's exchanges by this dollar shortage. Clearly, however, the excuse would disappear if the American Government undertook to maintain balance in its account. The world shortage of dollars would vanish. The only pressure exercised on Britain then would be of its own creation—if the present oversupply of sterling were allowed to continue. To bring it to an end would be the government's first responsibility. A currency slipping into surplus, which people cease to use as a means of exchange, can be an obstacle to free trade only slightly less damaging than a perennial shortage. The British contribution to balanced trade would, therefore, lie in ending suppressed inflation in Britain and reaching a long-term settlement of the outstanding sterling balances. They should no longer be left to weigh upon the world's exchanges with little certainty as to when and how they may be released. They should be funded and their repayment regulated over the years.

The British sometimes plead that they must continue with a lavish release of the sterling balances in order to meet Asia's claimant needs, but this argument would hold good only if no attempt was made to create the last pivot in the pattern of stability—a revival of overseas lending. In the short run, this move is, as we have seen, purely political. To invest in Asia is as much part of the West's defensive action as to invest in armaments. But its secondary economic advantages should not be neglected. The provision of American loans would increase the flow of dollars and could be a means of covering other nations' deficits with the United States, provided the dollars were "free"—in other words could be spent in any country—and any nation was thus able to compete for the contracts which the fresh capital would make possible. American lending to Asia and Asian purchases of goods in Europe have been thought of as an effective way of reviving the old three-way trade between Europe, America and the Far East. So it might be, provided the United States were also prepared at some point to take more imports in repayment of the Asian credits. This proviso makes American lending an uncertain means of bridging the dollar gap—in the long run. At some point a creditor must behave like a creditor and be ready to accept goods in exchange. Loans cannot be made on the assumption that borrowers will default, but they can hardly do otherwise if their products are not acceptable as means of payment.

The really vital economic significance of Western lending to backward areas is, however, that unless the groundwork of economic stability and the preconditions of development are created by intergovernmental action, neither private nor public investment will ever prosper in these troubled lands. Yet the West needs their development as much as they do themselves. The tremendous capacity to produce capital goods that already exists in the United States and may be recreated with more stable conditions in Europe, will need a market as wide as the world itself to absorb the possible surplus. High consumption and shorter hours will do much to absorb the increases in wealth, but new fields of expansion will also be needed. The world, too, both East and West, must look for a tremendous expansion of primary products—of foodstuffs and raw materials—if men and machines are to be fed in the next fifty years. Unless greater output is achieved, the pressure of demand on world supplies will keep the prices of food and raw materials at its present high level and even drive it higher. But greater output depends upon technological advance and capital investment in the shape of machines and scientific and technical know-how. The East cannot produce its own surplus capital.

Either the Western Powers will come forward with a "bold new program," or Asia and Africa will look to the Communists who, however little they can perform, will not fail in promises.

These, then, are the three key points in an international policy for an expanding economy. Each is essentially a matter for the decision of governments. The maintenance of full employment, positive measures to keep trade balanced, the provision of a steady flow of capital for backward areas lie within the province of each central authority and since governments are for the time being the final arbiters of politics, there is much to be said for leaving responsibility squarely on the only bodies able to exercise it. But if the program of stabilization is to be fully effective and the maximum advantage is to be drawn from it, the Western nations will need to consult and co-operate with each other on every point and harmonize their separate decisions into a single strategy. They will also need the moral support and on occasion, no doubt, the sanction of their neighbors. If, therefore, in the first phase of containment, they decide to set up one or two organs of co-operation and consultation—their Production and Resources Board, for instance, and their Economic Development Board—these bodies can continue to act in the longer run as the economic general staff of the free world. They would already have behind them the experience of joint decisions and joint action—just as the proposed Boards could even now draw on the considerable experience of the ECA and the OEEC. Progress could be organic, the development of responsibility continuous. There would thus be no difficulty in devising the instruments of co-operation, provided the will to create a program of general stability became effective in the West.

# 20

# *Are Common Policies Possible?*

◇◇◇◇◇◇◇◇◇◇◇◇◇◇◇◇◇◇◇◇◇◇◇◇◇◇◇◇◇◇◇◇◇◇◇◇◇◇◇◇◇◇◇◇◇◇

THESE suggestions for combining a certain stability in the general framework of the world economy with the greatest possible freedom of movement and action at all other levels will naturally not go unchallenged. Some critics will be inclined to say that the whole emphasis has been placed on the three elements of control—the maintenance of full employment, the balancing of trade at the highest level and the restoration of international lending—and that they would tend to outweigh all attempts to restore freedom and competition elsewhere. But if one lesson more than any other has been taught by the instabilities of the last thirty years, it is that nations do not restore freedom either internationally or locally when the risk of unemployment and of the loss of trade and foreign reserves hang over them. These fears are always their excuse for the worst and most restrictive forms of regulation. Remove those fears and the excuses vanish as well. A frontal attack could then be made on all forms of economic nationalism and protectionism.

The Western Powers might, indeed, draw up a General Convention specifying on the one hand their acceptance of the three guarantees of stability and on the other outlining the steps each could take toward the removal of trade barriers and the timetable that could be followed in ending these restrictions. For instance, within a year of the coming into force of the General Convention, all currencies would be made convertible. A rather longer period would no doubt be needed to develop the tariff negotiations at present being conducted under the auspices of the General Agreement on Trade and Tariffs. But within the framework of the new Convention it is possible to envisage a much more ambitious stage in which tariffs would be removed altogether over a wide range of products and reduced to uniform low levels on others.

Another agreement, which would probably not take very long to negotiate, might cover the conditions, responsibilities and guarantees involved in the investment of capital in other countries. The treaty signed recently between Uruguay and the United States might be taken as a model. Finally, the Convention would need to include a new and much bolder attack upon the problem of the mobility of labor and the right and the ability of men to cross frontiers in pursuit of work and of new opportunities for advancement. It is absolutely impossible in the long run to restore a dynamic economy in which everything can move except men. If the law of comparative advantage is to work at all, there will be expansions and declines of local prosperity and the more enterprising men must not be hampered if they desire to move out of a declining region and make their fortunes elsewhere. Not all will want to move—many prefer familiarity even at the cost of lower standards. But today, thousands who would move cannot do so. Any exponent of freedom and mobility in the world's economy must be prepared to accept and encourage new movements of immigration.

The General Convention would require both safeguards and sanctions. Groups of nations or groups of industries which wished to soften the local impact of renewed open competition might be encouraged to experiment on the model of the Schuman and Strikker plans. In particular, the British Government should end its misguided determination to hold aloof from the present Schuman proposals. In some cases, the nations' undertaking to maintain general employment and economic activity might not provide sufficient guarantees against severe local maladjustment. A cushioning phase, such as the Schuman Plan envisages, during which workers are retrained and capital diverted to other purposes, would be a useful reinforcement of the wider safeguards.

Sanctions would be needed in case any signatory of the Convention defaulted on its general obligations. If governments permitted either deflation or inflation to continue beyond a certain minimum period and let either begin to exercise an unsettling effect on the world's exchanges, other governments would be permitted to discriminate against the defaulting nations and withdraw from them the benefits of competitive freedom at which the system in general aims. The suggestion of sanctions is not really new. For instance, in the Report on Full Employment presented to the United Nations, the five experts suggest that if a government allows its economy to pass into a deflationary state and as a result its purchases of foreign goods begin to fall, it should be compelled to place with the International Monetary Fund a sum equal to its normal purchases abroad under conditions of normal economic activity. This sum would then be available to finance other nations' imports from the deflating country and thus prevent the creation of a downward spiral in international trade. Some such immediate safeguard might well be introduced into the General Convention and could be administered by the IMF. Moreover, the signatory powers could, through their general economic staff, examine the plight of any economy falling into persistent deflation or inflation and take co-operative measures to bring the country back into balance. Such an examination of the plight of a whole continent took place as a preliminary to the Marshall Plan in 1947. No future disequilibrium is likely to be on such a scale and the measures necessary to restore stability would be much less drastic. The point is that the Western Powers have already used joint consultation and action as a means of restoring equilibrium. There is no reason why they should not do so again. To those who protest that such a proposal would violate national sovereignty, one could perhaps reply that a choice would be left to the defaulting government—either to accept co-operative aid or to take itself out of the Western trading system, with all the consequences in the shape of discrimination and exclusion that such a decision would entail.

There are many critics who, while ready to accept in theory the idea of a world economy part controlled and part free, nevertheless believe that the proposals are not practical politics. "You cannot," they say, "fuse oil and water. Between the exponents of freedom and the supporters of planning, too great a gulf is fixed. This notion of taking something from the American point of view and something from the British presupposes that their views are not in flat contradiction. But suppose they are? What will then become of any joint plan for world trade or stability or expansion?"

That the differences are striking between the believers in planning and the supporters of laisser faire, no sane man will deny, but it is important to remember how much these differences have been blown up and blurred and distorted by the language of the political arena. The epithet "socialist" for the mildest piece of reforming legislation, the accusation of "selfish capitalism" for the least plea for economic independence and variety have been dinned into people's ears through so many electoral campaigns that the supporters of either view stare at each other through a haze of abuse and dislike and misunderstanding. The question here is not whether there are differences but whether they are so absolute that co-operation is impossible. So long as the West is free, the clash of ideas and the struggle of opinions will continue. Freedom is only in peril when all attempts at accommodation and common action become impossible. And, in spite of all the verbal violence, such a pass has not been reached in the West today.

The practical proof of it lies in the actual record of government. If the various types of democratic administration that have existed in the West in the last thirty years were sorted out according to political practice, it would certainly not be found that the result was a series of capitalist governments on the one hand sharply divided from a series of socialist governments on the other. On the contrary, from left to right, the gradations of government would pass into each other like the colors of a spectrum but so gradually that it would be hard to tell where planning ended and laisser faire began. To the left would lie the socialism of the British Government between 1945 and 1950—not by any means complete socialism but nevertheless a program including not only social welfare and planning for full employment but a number of measures of public ownership as well. But by 1950, the British Labour Party was itself moving closer to a variety of experiments in labor government tried at various times in Australia, in New Zealand, in Norway and in Sweden. In these, the emphasis on social welfare has been higher, on nationalization small or nil. Next—somewhere to the left of center—would appear the United States with its New Deal and its Fair Deal, its Tennessee Valley Authority, its public education, its growing social services, but also with the most resoundingly successful free-enterprise system in the world. To the right, one might put some of the postwar regimes in Europe such as the French which, though increasingly devoted to free enterprise, nevertheless plan their industrial development (the Monnet Plan, for instance) and provide generously for social services—the French family allowances are the highest in the West. Belgium, in spite of its full system of social services, must be classified as mainly to the right. Yet, although it officially abhors "planning," its financial planning has probably been the most successful in Europe. Finally, the postwar governments in Western Germany and Italy represent an official return to complete laisser faire, tempered in practice by their inability to ignore the pressing local problem of unemployment. The only complete break in this shaded spectrum of government occurs when freedom is abandoned and political dictatorship takes its place. Then the not altogether surprising result is that whether the break occurs on the extreme right or the extreme left, the types of economy that follow have more in common with each other than with the economies of the free world.

Moreover, the evidence suggests that even within this spectrum, views are not as divided as they were fifteen years ago. Socialism came into being as a protest against manifest social evil—against the misery of the workers working long hours for low wages, against the loss of status felt by the workers as human beings when they were herded into factories in which they had no responsibility and no share, against the irregularities of an economic system that went from slump to boom and could find no steady mechanism for the distribution of the goods it was producing. A man need not be a "socialist" to see that these conditions are evil and a denial of the Western tradition. From the early days of socialism, however, two diverse methods of curing these obvious contradictions and injustices have fought for leadership in the labor movement and among progressives of every class and country. It was from the so-called scientific and dialectical socialism of Marx that the idea of complete state ownership as a "cure-all" of economic evils was derived. Marx himself and Lenin after him did not talk about planning at all and had no concrete suggestions for controlling the trade cycle or stabilizing world trade. They simply said dogmatically that if the state owned everything, these problems would not arise.

No one will deny the disastrous influence of Marxism on the European Left. For a time it captured most of the intellectuals and also the vanguard of the working class in parts of Europe. It seemed to overlay the earlier socialist traditions which were intensely idealist and liberal and also on the whole experimental and undogmatic in method and approach. But in recent years a revulsion has occurred, particularly in the crucial country for socialism, Great Britain. It has in part been created by the spectacle of what tyranny can mean when political and economic power are fused in the single state as they are now from the Elbe eastward. A certain respect for the old idea of "the division of power" has crept back into progressive thinking. But the revulsion has been mainly due to second thoughts about the validity of total state ownership as a general remedy. Changes in ownership leave all the major problems of economic policy unchanged. Nationalized industries have to make profits and sell goods. They have to find capital and make investments. They are dependent upon foreign markets and foreign supplies. In fact the fundamental problems of a "free" economy—how to be both stable and prosperous—would reappear in a state-owned economy and it is these fundamental problems, not the question of ownership as such, that constitute the real challenge to democratic statesmanship.

These new preoccupations do not imply the abandonment by socialists of their aims and ideals. There has been no relaxation in the belief that government can and should be an instrument of welfare. There has been no abandonment of the certainty that free society cannot survive the earlier alternatives of slump and boom and that, above everything else, the worker seeks steady employment. All that has happened is that radical opinion is tending to reconsider some of its presuppositions and to ask whether after all public ownership is the "cure-all" which Marxism promised it would be and whether greater progress, greater freedom, greater flexibility and greater prosperity may not be achieved by other means.

This mood of questioning has not yet crystallized into new thinking and new policy and the lure of Marxism remains as an eminently simple and uncomplicated explanation of everything from the meaning of the universe down to the last detail of the trade cycle. For this reason, it is still impossible to predict where the new emphasis in social democratic thought will be placed. It is even impossible to predict with certainty that there will be a new emphasis. If during these crucial years of examination and reconsideration, the economies of the free world become involved once more in the downward spiral of depression, if the United States' economy were at some time in the future to undergo once again a real slump, then all the rigidities and orthodoxies of Marxist thinking would come flooding back into progressive thought in the West. The chief attraction of Marxism has always lain in the evils it denounced. These have become almost its sole attraction, as the development of Marxist reality in Russia has shown how thoroughly unpleasant a "workers' utopia" can be. But it would be folly to underestimate the mark made on men's minds by the old deadly cycle of depression and unemployment. Should they return, the extremer methods of dealing with them would return to fashion.

It is therefore quite as important for the hope of common policies in the West that the movement in thinking should not be confined to the side of planning and socialism. Have the supporters of laisser faire in all its various forms also looked at the lessons of the last decades? Have they realized that no modern economic system can survive the old fluctuations of boom and slump? Happily for the West, there have been obvious changes of attitude on the side of free enterprise. It is not simply a question of the widespread acceptance of the need for social services and for the redistribution of income through taxation. The last twenty years have seen a steady increase in the interest within private enterprise in the problem of the worker's status, his psychological well being, his participation in the industrial community, the right relations between him and management. Above all, there is a change of attitude toward the crucial problem of full employment and the prevention of violent business fluctuations. No Western government would now argue openly—as was argued by responsible officials only twenty years ago—that between 5 and 8 per cent of the people must be unemployed for the free enterprise system to function properly.

The great significance of Lord Keynes's work was to suggest methods for attacking the problem both of unemployment and of the trade cycle which could be adopted by governments of either right or left. His insistence that the financial mechanisms of the state were the most effective means of dealing with the problem of insufficient demand pointed a way which even the governments least addicted to planning might follow. Few people deny that financial policy is the proper rôle of the state and Lord Keynes's emphasis gave liberal governments an instrument which their instincts did not forbid them to use. It is significant that two more recent studies of the problem of full and stable employment in free society—that of Lord Beveridge in 1944 and of the

United Nations in 1949—also stress the financial aspects of state action to ensure stability and once again demonstrate the fact that their policies can be adopted by socialist or liberal governments alike. In all these matters, the attitude of the United States is naturally decisive, and here the pointers all suggest that the adoption of positive full-employment policies is not entirely inconceivable. Not only has Congress itself passed legislation to make full employment effective, but in the last few months, it has been American officials of the ECA Missions in Europe who have intervened to persuade the "anti-planning" governments in Belgium, Germany and Italy to reverse their policies, end deflation and get more of their unemployed back to work.

If this brief analysis of the changes in thinking on both the right and the left has any validity, it follows that there is a working basis for collaboration between planners and anti-planners, between social democrats and all but the extreme economic liberals. (There are still a few of them, of course; they believe as passionately as Cobden or Bright in the free laws of supply and demand and use the same arguments to prevent state action in the matter of full employment as Bright used to prevent state regulation of hours of work or of child labor in the factory.) Both planners and moderate liberals can agree that it is in everyone's interest that a high domestic level of economic activity shall be maintained. Both sides can agree that this level must be maintained by preserving the highest possible balance between imports and exports supplemented by a judicious use of international investment. Both sides can agree to set up sufficient organs of common economic government to oversee these rules and to take action if, for reasons beyond the control of any individual government, the balance appears to be breaking down. The nations have already set up the International Monetary Fund and the International Bank of Reconstruction. They have also discussed the framework of an International Trade Organization. The work of these bodies could be supplemented and reinforced by the working out of a common Western economic program in the form of the suggested general convention administered and supervised by the West's Production and Resources Board and the Economic Development Board.

Some of the more convinced planners may argue that an international economic policy pared down to such a bare minimum cannot possibly be effective. As a successor to the Marshall Plan, it would fail simply from its generality and its failure to come to grips with the details of international economic stability. But is this really the case? Surely it is a strength and not a weakness in any international policy that it is concerned with nothing but essentials. The complexity of the free world's economy is so great, the span of its interests is so vast, the diversity in economic and social conditions is so bewildering that any planning agency that sought to regulate the details would either be swamped into ineffectiveness or begin to exercise a quite intolerable degree of intervention and control. Even within an economy, it is possible to impede progress, impair flexibility and introduce economic hardening of the arteries if the weight of central planning is too absolute. How much more dangerous could become the control of a world planning agency. Free society is feeling its way in this matter of concerted international action and if its first efforts are not relatively simple and straightforward, the whole experiment may be rejected in disgust and the way thrown open to a return to economic anarchy. For the time being, states and governments must remain the chief executants of policy, while their chosen international agencies act more in the capacity of guides and watchdogs than of actual directors and initiators. To suggest any other course is to condemn the whole effort to evolve a common economic policy to sterility and futility from the start.

# 21

# *Politics of Union*

◇◇◇◇◇◇◇◇◇◇◇◇◇◇◇◇◇◇◇◇◇◇◇◇◇◇◇◇◇◇◇◇◇◇◇◇◇◇◇◇◇◇◇◇◇◇◇◇◇◇◇◇◇

ANY attempt to outline in detail possible policies for the free world always tends to run the risk of emphasizing economics at the expense of everything else. After pages and pages devoted to the discussion of full employment, or free trade or convertible currencies, the reader may easily conclude that perhaps the Marxists are right after all and that the basis of reality is economics and economic issues determine all the rest. The impression is entirely misleading. Economics tend to receive predominant attention because they make up such a large part of the details of policy—once that policy has been decided. For instance, the political decision, "we need fifty divisions in order to contain Russia in Europe," soon turns into the detailed economic argument of what materials, factories and manpower should be used in the defense program, how it is to be financed and what will be its impact upon domestic production and the export trade! The political judgment, "We must maintain internal stability if our people are to support this system of government," turns very quickly into discussions on the best method of keeping the economy at work and living standards attractive. In short, the major decisions are almost invariably political, but their working out involves statesmen and officials in the bread-and-butter problems of daily life. Far and away the two most significant decisions in postwar Europe have been the Marshall Plan and the Atlantic Pact. Both decisions were essentially and entirely political. Yet the negotiations, the expedients, the policies and the problems to which they have given rise have been economic. This obvious fact has nothing to do with the primacy of economies. Economic issues would be paramount only if, as Communists pretend, economic motives had inspired both decisions—if the Marshall Plan had been a means of dumping American surpluses or if the Atlantic Pact had been designed to end an American slump with a rearmament program. Such nonsense is, indeed, talked by Marxists. The truth is, of course, that narrow economic reasoning would have dissuaded the United States from embarking on either. It was a political judgment of Europe's plight and Russia's pressure that led to the American initiative.

There is, however, one field in which both the major decisions and the practical details are concerned with politics. The methods and institutions by which the free world can best express its desire for unity, raise purely political issues. For the last five years the nature and the powers of possible forms of association and of common organs of government have been widely and eagerly discussed and, at one point, the debate has left the sphere of abstract theory and has become an immediate and political issue. In Europe the question of federalism is on the verge of being a genuine issue between states and governments. This controversy is, therefore, a suitable point at which to begin asking whether unity in government is an essential feature in the short run of a policy of containment and, in the long run, of stability and expansion in the free world.

The upholders of the federal ideal, who seem to have most support in France but command a considerable following in Italy and Germany, have as their starting point the anachronism of nationalism. In the modern world it is a dividing force, responsible for century-long feuds and shattering wars. By concentrating all powers in the nation-state and admitting no authority beyond it, Western man has created a battering ram that will shake and crush and smash his civilization to pieces. War is the first menace to human survival, but how can it be outlawed so long as each nation decides to be judge in its own cause? To insist, moreover, on the absolute rights of nationalism may mean before long to be overtaken and left behind by history; the revulsion against nationalism, the federalists claim, has already set in. The sinister fact that Hitler could find quislings in every country and the no less ominous strength of the Communist Fifth Column in Western Europe show that ideology is in the ascendant and nationalism beginning to decay. Wider loyalties are beginning to claim the mass of the people and the Western world will be lost if outmoded nationalism is the only emotional force it can mobilize behind its policies.

These arguments are relevant to the whole field of interstate relations, but they apply with particular force to Europe. In the idea of European civilization, in its incredible achievements, its grandeurs of art and spirit, its creative energy, its capacity century after century to remake the face of the world, there lies an appeal and an ideal for transcending the limited achievement of each European state. There exists a community of culture and tradition crying out for unifying institutions. Separate nationalisms no longer satisfy European man. His political life must come to express what his spiritual and cultural life has long expressed—wider horizons, broader vision, a supernational ideal.

The federalists also argue that the need for European as opposed to purely national administration is borne out by the practical stupidity of the claim to complete national autonomy when put forward by twenty different nations, each of them now completely unable, by their own efforts, to solve the major problems which distract and confuse their citizens' lives. The national governments of Europe cannot meet men's reasonable demands for either military or economic security! What must be said of the pretensions of governments which are unable to provide unaided even the minimum requirements of stability? Should they not, for modesty's sake if for no other reason, transfer their powers to wider institutions which can genuinely perform what they promise? There is not a European government that can defend its country without massive support from outside. Hardly one European country can balance its books, let alone raise its standards, without constant collaboration with other powers. Why, under these circumstances, maintain the right of sovereignty? Every practical reason as well as every argument of idealism and vision points to the establishment of a federal government for Europe and the subordination to it of Europe's separate national sovereignties.

One difficulty in assessing the force of the federalist argument lies in the very great variety of obvious facts and doubtful assumptions upon which it is built up. A critic who finds himself entirely in agreement with one aspect of the argument, may be quite unable to accept the conclusions drawn from it. He may, for instance, find the federalist attitude toward nationalism a most curious amalgam of the true and the false. That wider loyalties could and should temper it, no one will doubt. That the rise of the new secular religions—communism, fascism, nazism—signifies some weakening of the hold of nationalism is also possible. But is it wise to draw from these assumptions the conclusion that nationalism must and can be left behind in political arrangements and, if it shows some recalcitrance, someone must stamp on its head? National feelings and national loyalties are still intensely strong. Europe has recently seen in the spectacle of the royal crisis in Belgium the extent to which within one country, national differences—between Fleming and Walloon—can exacerbate social and political disputes. Yet the two races have lived under a unitary government for over a hundred years. It cannot be assumed that any government, in defending national interests, is neglecting and frustrating the international yearnings of its people. These yearnings, to say the least, are very intermittent and the desire "not to be run by foreigners" is much more constant and widespread. Frontal attacks on national sovereignty may, therefore, arouse suspicions and fears and can actually postpone a supernational solution. The sacrifice of sovereignty appears to be something into which people must be coaxed, not stampeded.

Most sane citizens in any case dislike government. They will not necessarily like it better if it is conducted further off by other people. Those who deprecate nationalism sometimes forget that, stripped of its excesses, it can be an effective safeguard of freedom. The new Soviet imperialism has met no harder obstacle than the inveterate national consciousness of the peoples it is seeking to subdue to its own great Russian national interests. Tito's break with the Cominform was based on pure nationalism. The fortitude of the Finnish people is drawn from it. All hopes that Mao Tse-tung may develop an independent policy must be rooted in it. Nationalism is as essential a force in the world as that of human personality. The great and the small together, molded by history and race and geography and tradition, are real entities, making for richness and variety and resisting the dead-level standardization which, if jargon and policy are any guides, appears to be the fate of those absorbed into Stalin's empire.

None of this is an argument for the exclusive claims of national sovereignty; it is simply a reminder that nationalism is a creative as well as a destructive force. It only becomes destructive—as does human personality—when it admits no claims or responsibilities beyond its own narrow self-interest. Here the federalists have every argument on their side. The self-contained, self-sufficient nation-state is now a complete anachronism. Wider institutions must be found to express men's common purposes, but one may, nevertheless, question whether the conclusion drawn by the European federalists is correct and that these new institutions must necessarily take the form of a European federal government. It is more than a question of the reluctance of electorates—who must be consulted—to set up federal institutions and transfer sovereignty to them. The difficulty goes deeper.

The basis of the federal argument in Europe is that the various European governments, left to themselves, can neither defend themselves nor provide economic stability. For this reason, so the federal argument sensibly runs, other agencies which can provide both military and economic security must take over some of their powers. These agencies, however, to be fully effective, could not be purely European. The last five years have proved conclusively that Europe is not a sufficient base for organizing either the defense or the prosperity of the separate European nations. Two world wars have been won only with massive assistance from the New World. For Britain, in particular, whose sea-borne imports of food depend upon the security of the Atlantic, there can be no thought of defense or even survival unless the United States and Canada are full strategic partners. Nor is Europe's economic plight one that can be solved by Europe alone. Nineteen nations with their accounts in deficit do not lose the deficit by pooling their economies. They produce one very much larger deficit. The overriding obstacle to the achievement of balance—the dollar gap—can, as we have seen, be solved on constructive and expansive lines only if the United States is a partner to the agreement. All the evidence of the Marshall Plan points to the fact that Europe, left to itself, can overcome the difficulty in one way only—by the restrictive method of cutting American imports, a policy which must contradict the hopes of restoring trade on a free and non-discriminatory basis. The expansive and constructive solution demands American participation not in one grand settlement—such a solution is impossible given the continuous and dynamic character of trade—but in a lasting economic partnership designed to counter the ups and downs of trade and secure adjustment by the expansion of the flow of dollars into the world, not by the cutting off of American sales.

Yet if Europe needs this sustained co-operation with North America to achieve genuine security in both defense and in economic life, the argument for a supernational government points not simply to European institutions but to arrangements of Atlantic scope. It should never be forgotten that there is little virtue in government as such. It is an evil, though a necessary one. A government therefore is not "better" simply because it covers a wider area and escapes from pure nationalism. It may indeed be worse and more oppressive and more dangerous. The whole weight of argument against purely national government is that it cannot meet fundamental political and economic needs. But neither can a European government. It is only when the federal area is extended to the whole Atlantic arena that the scope of government becomes genuinely large enough to meet the legitimate needs of Europe's inhabitants. If under these circumstances, purely national government, commanding as it does the familiar support and acceptance of its citizens, is insufficient, how much more insufficient must a European government appear which does not have the hold of national sympathy and traditional obedience and is also unable to satisfy Europe's deep need for security? As an end in itself, it is an illusion created by the mistaken belief that any government is better than national government. The truth is that there is no point in giving up sovereignty unless it is to an effective alternative. To give it up just for the sake of giving it up makes no sense at all.

The institutions which take over power from national governments must be adequate. Otherwise, the average citizen, in whose interests alone the changes are proposed, will be no better off from the point of view of security but will be considerably worse off from the standpoint of feeling in touch with his government and understanding what it is trying to do. In some ways, even national government has become too remote for the satisfactory functioning of the democratic process. It can be argued that if a sorting out of the powers and functions of government is to take place, some should be transferred to organs even smaller and less all-embracing than the state. Powers should be sent upward only if it is clearly and inescapably necessary. Otherwise the degree of government taking place beyond either the reach or understanding of ordinary men will be dangerously increased. And if such a transfer is proved to be absolutely and inescapably necessary —as in the case of defense and economic stability it clearly is—then it must be made to an effective administration, not one that repeats the insufficiencies of national government while lacking its nearness and familiarity.

The balance of argument in the Western world seems,

therefore, to tilt away from purely European institutions to an administrative structure based upon the Atlantic world. Within this framework not only would defense be secure but the chronic unbalance between the deficit countries and the world's universal creditor—the United States—could be solved on the basis of co-operation. An Atlantic community would also meet most of the political, psychological and cultural needs which a purely European union is said to satisfy. If a European federation can solve the problem of restoring freedom to Germany without encouraging resurgent nationalism, how much more might an Atlantic union do so, in which would be included not simply Germany's European peers in power and influence but the overwhelming preponderance of the United States. Again, if the appeal of a European federation is the union of all nations of a common culture, it is purest arrogance to exclude the countrymen of Jefferson and Lincoln and deny to the Americas—or to the English-speaking Dominions—their essential attribute of having re-created the great traditions of the West in new continents overseas. It is an impoverishment, not an enrichment, of Europe to say that it ceased to re-create itself at some point in the middle of the eighteenth century. From the cultural standpoint, the Atlantic is as much the "closed sea" of the West as was the Mediterranean in the heyday of the Roman Empire.

It is also no minor advantage that an Atlantic union would transcend many of the difficulties that are certain to hamper and finally prevent the creation of a purely European structure. There is in many of the aspirations toward European unity a distinct undercurrent of isolationism, a belief that "if only the United States would leave us alone, we could work out our own relations with the Communist half." This mood occasionally receives explicit expression in the French or German press. It is mainly a hidden emotion reaching the surface only in exaggerated criticism of British and American policy or exaggerated belief in the pacific intentions of Russia. A strong repudiation of this idea of the "Third Force" is undoubtedly one of the strands in Britain's—and Scandinavia's—objections to purely European union. They fear that some answering chord of isolationism may be touched to life in the United States. It is true that the realities of the Korean issue have weakened the isolationist appeal—even in France. But containment is not a policy only for today and tomorrow. The institutions it establishes must be capable of expressing Western unity ten years from now when temptation to isolationism may have returned.

The British must also be permitted to support a solution which releases them from the deadlock to which they have been reduced by their membership in three different communities—Europe, the Commonwealth and the Atlantic world. They cannot be accused of being isolationist and anti-federal if they prefer an association which includes all their partners and not just a few of them. Every argument the French put forward for federal union in Europe can be repeated and strengthened by the British in favor of Atlantic union, and the British may be forgiven if they sometimes find it curious that French aspirations are accepted as normal and indeed praiseworthy while British desires are distrusted as yet another demonstration of Albion's perfidiousness. The manner no doubt accounts for much, and it is hard to conceive a more clumsy handling of Britain's European relations than was contrived by the Foreign Office and Mr. Dalton together during the crisis over the Schuman Plan. Yet clumsy diplomacy and bad manners should not altogether obscure what is logical and important in the British—and Scandinavian—case, which is that a union based on Europe is insufficient for either defense or economic stability while a union based on the Atlantic is not.

Yet there are strong arguments for the view that a close Atlantic union, with a federal constitution and government, a pooling of power and a single electorate cannot be an immediate or overriding aim of Western policy. The first and obvious reason is that American public opinion is not prepared for it. The Americans, very understandably, do not feel the compulsion to turn to federal institutions other than their own. If any country in the world is sufficient for its own defense, it is the United States, and although some economic interests might be damaged by failure to reach a co-operative solution of the dollar gap, America would face nothing like the disturbance and impoverishment that would be Europe's lot. The need to pursue co-operative policies is thus far less obvious on the other side of the Atlantic, and the United States today is more easily a patron and sponsor of other people's federal experiments than a participant in them. Britain's unwillingness to join in local and, in its view, insufficient federal experiments has in it, particularly in American eyes, an element of pigheadedness. "Can't those British see that isolationism is dead" the critics ask. "Can't they understand that Britain is not strong enough or self-sufficient enough to stand alone?" No such criticisms can be directed at the United States for, on a practical short-term view, the country is not only able to stand on its own feet but to help everyone else to get on to theirs as well. It takes arguments at once fuller, deeper and more intangible to suggest that America's need of its allies is not much less acute than their need of America. Yet until that conviction grows, there seems no way of demonstrating that Britain's preference for an Atlantic association is no more arbitrary than America's unconscious preference for no association at all. So long as the United States feels, deep in its bones, that no permanent external relations are necessary, just so long will Britain's preference for a partnership including America seem tiresome and unreasonable. One of the great attractions of the "European Solution" in American eyes must be that it involves no permanent American commitment. An Atlantic solution does and, so far, the evidence does not suggest that the United States is yet prepared to accept the idea of a full federal Atlantic union.

This hesitation may, however, possess some very great advantages—at this stage. It may be primarily in Europe that the policy of containment has to be made effective, but the policy also applies far beyond the limits of Europe and, as earlier chapters have suggested, some of the most vulnerable fronts lie in other continents. One of the greatest question marks of the next decade hangs over the relations between

Asia and the Atlantic world and at present those relations are undermined to a fantastic degree by suspicion and distrust. The fear that behind all its protestations the West wishes to reimpose its imperial control is not dead and the Communists do not even let it sleep. Given this degree of uncertainty in the West's relations with Asia, it is possible that the establishment at this stage of a close Atlantic union, creating a federal juggernaut in the West, would have a most unsettling effect upon Asian opinion. The need today is to try by every means to weave a living community of interests between East and West, to quiet doubts and build up by every means organs of co-operation and partnership. A union which of its very essence excluded Asia, set up now at a time when world relationships are still riddled with fear and suspicion, might have the effect of strengthening Western cohesion only at the cost of a most dangerous rift in the free world as a whole.

This possibility is a reminder of the fact that, if the federal argument is pursued to its logical conclusion, any partial union is insufficient. Mankind faces problems today which demand world government for their settlement. Security based on the Atlantic is something, but wars can start in Korea. Economics based on partnership between Europe, the sterling area and the dollar area will be much more stable than the "balkanized" trading system we know today. Yet the great fields of new investment lie in Asia, in Australasia, in Africa. Atomic energy is clearly a force whose only natural frontiers are those of the globe itself. Science, transport, communications are all carrying us in the same direction. Since there is already one great rift in the world—between the Communist half and the free—is it wise to create other barriers and formalize absolutely other possible divisions? Is there not some sense in the argument that on one condition and one condition only can regional arrangements contribute to the stability of human society and that is if they are part of an international system covering the whole world?

# 22

# *Practical Federalism*

OFFICIALLY at least the free nations have already adopted the view that world unity must be their overriding aim. As a result of the experience of two world wars, they have already set up an embryo world government. It is surprising how easy it is, when discussing the proper relations between nation-states and the virtues of this or that form of federalism, to leave out of account mankind's most considerable experiment in practical internationalism—the United Nations. The experiment started perhaps with a freight of hopes too heavy for any human organization to carry and in its first years, it created much disillusion and cynicism. Men listened day after day to the endless dispute in the Security Council, the deadlocks, the vetoes. What they overlooked was the fact that the organization had and held the support of smaller states, Eastern and Western, who found they could meet in its councils and conferences on a basis of complete equality and begin to play some part in the great game of world politics. The failures of the United Nations were sensational and were centered mainly in the Security Council and between the Great Powers. The achievements were more intangible. They occurred in obscure conferences of the Economic Commission for Asia and the Far East, in debates on human rights, in the quiet discussions of the various Specialized Agencies.[1] At a time when no emotion was more sacred to non-European peoples than their newly gained national independence, they found a world organization which was in a real sense theirs.

Such developments of opinion are slow to come and impossible to trace. In the Atlantic world, they were obscured by the tendency toward cynicism and indifference apparent on the European side where the nations had already assisted at the life and death of the old League of Nations. Only in the United States was there genuine popular enthusiasm for the organization. Yet beneath the surface a smouldering fire of support was beginning to spread, waiting for some crisis to fan it from one day to the next into a general conflagration of loyalty and enthusiasm. Such a flashing out of the United Nations' real significance in the world occurred on June 27 when President Truman's decision to send aid, under the Charter, to the South Koreans went round the world. That India and Burma whose "neutrality" had been scrupulous, should now take sides against the Soviet Union, that fifty-two out of the fifty-nine United Nations should associate themselves with an action which, had it been taken without United Nations sanction, would have been as universally criticized—this was the measure of the organization's capacity to move world opinion and evoke world loyalty. Notice was served on the Western Powers that if they wished to exercise effective and creative world leadership, they could not devise a better instrument than the organization they had set up, with such mixed feelings, five years before.

But if the United Nations is to be made the basis of Western co-operation with the free world, there are two formidable hurdles to be overcome. It is certain that the Soviet Union will never again walk out of the Security Council and the Assembly. The cat has been singed too badly to re-

[1] The Specialized Agencies include not only the World Bank and the International Monetary Fund but the International Labour Office, the Food and Agricultural Organization and the World Health Organization.

peat that particular maneuver. How then can the United Nations function at all under the shadow of the Soviet veto? Would it not be wise to set up a new United Nations from which the Soviets and their satellites are excluded? The point can be debated, but there seem formidable arguments in favor of preserving the present United Nations and having one place in the world where the antagonists can meet, even if most of the time they meet only to disagree. Any arrangement that reduces, even by no more than a hairsbreadth, the risk of war is worth preserving and the fact that the Communist nations still come to the United Nations is undoubtedly a steadying factor in an infinitely unstable world.

The right way out of the deadlock in the Security Council has been shown by the General Assembly. In the autumn session of 1950, Mr. Dean Acheson, the American Secretary of State, put forward proposals for strengthening the rôle of the General Assembly as a guardian of peace and international security. The essence of his scheme was that in the event of a veto paralyzing all action in the Security Council, the General Assembly should be summoned at twenty-four-hours notice and that a majority decision in that body should be held to give the nations full authority to go to the aid of a victim of aggression or take such other action as might be called for to prevent a breach of the peace. After a long debate, these proposals were adopted by practically the entire Assembly—the Soviet bloc abstaining—and thus a channel was established, free of the blockage of the veto, to keep the influence and effectiveness of the United Nations flowing into the world. At the same time the nations agreed to explore ways whereby contingents from the various national armies could be made available to the United Nations in such a way that they could be effectively used as a mobile police force.

But to establish flexible, workable machinery in the United Nations is only one small part of a constructive effort needed to make the United Nations work. The crucial question is whether the Atlantic powers really wish to transform it into an instrument of practical internationalism. Their record is on the whole depressing. In America, at least, a great groundswell of popular support for the United Nations has prevented the United States from falling into the extremes of cynicism and indifference which have been only too evident in other lands and perhaps nowhere more so than in Britain. Public statements may have repeatedly proclaimed that British (or French or Scandinavian or even American) policy was rooted in the United Nations but almost every act and every appointment has belied the claim. When governments attach importance to institutions, they are careful to second to them officials of competence and weight. The United Nations has, in its upper levels, all too often been staffed by officials of secondary quality. With the exception of the Security Council, which the veto has made futile from the start, all agencies of the United Nations have tended to be neglected by the Western Powers. No consistent policies have been pursued, no galvanizing lead given. There seems to have been virtually no awareness that the Economic and Social Council and the Specialized Agencies could become, with outstanding officials, a fully thought-out policy and generous financial support, ideal instruments for projecting Western policy into the distrustful Asian world. The foreign offices of Europe may have talked internationalism. They have on the whole devoted themselves to the narrowest pursuit of self-interest. The fact that in June, 1950, the United Nations triumphantly vindicated itself as an instrument of world policy is no credit to them. It happened in spite of their policies, not because of them. Yet one fact is surely clear—that no conceivable United Nations—working with or without the veto, through Security Council or Assembly, through Specialized Agencies or Commissions—can survive indefinitely the fundamental indifference to it of so many of the leading nations in the West. The British Government, which has contrived to show the oldest and tiredest face of British *Realpolitik* at Lake Success, has a special responsibility to prove, by a new policy, fresh support, the seconding of abler officials and the strengthening of the Commonwealth element in the secretariat that the United Nations is an instrument they are prepared to use and an association in which they are determined to become a genuine partner.

The method of approach to international government by way of the United Nations may seem too humdrum and uninspiring for those on whom nationalism has no more hold and who believe that dramatic constitutional changes are the only means of compelling governments to co-operate and of bringing peoples together. They may, indeed, be right. No one can say that the citadel of sovereignty can be taken only by stealth. It may give way to storm and assault. Yet the opposite argument—that sovereignty is more likely to be shuffled off than torn away—cannot be lightly dismissed. In the summer of 1950, there is no doubt that the French Government helped to ensure Britain's absence from the Schuman negotiations by making the sacrifice of sovereignty an essential preliminary to discussion. Even while the exchanges between Paris and London were continuing, the British Government accepted both in the Atlantic defense plans and in the scheme for a European Payments Union notable abrogations of sovereignty. Functional federalism is a working reality in both agreements. But in their negotiation, nobody insisted that sacrifices of sovereignty must take place. The facts were left to speak for themselves. It seems that, in these instances at least, the functional approach has proved more successful than the directly political.

There are, moreover, more ways to the federal solution than the direct road of constitution building. There is an obvious route whereby the United Nations itself can be made to advance steadily in the direction of world government. The representatives who gather in New York can after all claim to speak for their peoples. A universal electorate would produce more *equal* representation, but no *better* representation of local interests. If, on certain issues, the Western Great Powers abandoned the veto and all nations agreed to accept, say, a two-thirds or three-quarters majority in the Assembly, a system would have come into being in which, over a certain field, sovereignty would have been effectively transferred to the United Nations.

Such a voluntary abdication of power may seem unlikely today, but that is because the experiment of an international society is still young. The Great Powers are still jealous of their weight and influence, the smaller powers fearful of being overruled and slighted. These fears and prejudices can only be overcome by steady work and steady example. Inside each national community, the myth of each individual having equal power has made possible the democratic experiment. It is quite true that some men are far more powerful than others and have behind them reserves and resources far beyond those of their neighbors. But little by little, the more powerful groups have agreed to accept common limitations, to abandon special privileges and to co-operate with their less powerful neighbors to make the system work. Happy is the country where this modification of attitude among the powerful has come in time to preserve leadership and social cohesion.

The international scene is not entirely dissimilar. In the free world the preponderence of power lies with the United States and to a lesser extent with the Atlantic community. If they are prepared to forgo domination and practice genuine leadership, if they will accept the judgment of their neighbors and accept the "myth" of equality between states, a federal pattern for the world can emerge not by setting up new and constitutionally perfected institutions but by allowing the existing experiment of the United Nations to develop in that sense.

This practice of co-operation and forbearance by the leaders of the free world is, indeed, an essential preliminary to the achieving of those general sacrifices of sovereignty which our modern closely knit world community demands. The national sovereignty which is beginning to turn sour in the mouths of the old nations of Europe is still an intoxicating wine in the new countries of the East and it is only with the greatest tact and delicacy of touch that the West will persuade them that sacrifices of sovereignty mean genuine progress in the world community and not simply a hidden way of bringing back Western domination and imperialism. The urgency of this problem can best be measured by comparing the need of the new Asiatic governments for outside economic aid and technical assistance with the inability of many of them to make full use of the aid once it is given. The independent governments of such countries as Indonesia or the Philippines lack trained administrators, officials, scientists and technicians. Some governments are even more handicapped by representing, as Chiang Kai-shek once did, a corrupt and indifferent landowning class whose peasantry becomes an easy and instant prey to Asiatic communism. How is aid to be made effective under these conditions? How are land reforms to be introduced and the loyalty of the peasant assured? Must American or British or French or Dutch administrators move in and take over? Such a solution, however effective technically, is politically impossible. If, however, these same administrators were formed into United Nations teams responsible to the Economic and Social Council and their impact upon local conditions could be made in the name of an international organization in which the local government was itself a free and equal member, the fierce nationalism and intense fear of domination might be exorcised. The advice given then would come in the name of the whole United Nations. The reforms proposed would have Asiatic as well as Western opinion behind them. The sanction of cutting off aid if advice was refused would appear not an arbitrary Western act but a considered international judgment. There is, in fact, no other organization than that of the United Nations through which Western plans to develop or stabilize Asia can be carried through without raising the specter of imperialism. The neglect and indifference shown to the potentialities of the United Nations in this field are not by any means the least of the West's mistakes in its dealings with Asia since the war.

Provided a framework of full, confident and equal cooperation is built up between the free nations, there need be no danger in pursuing closer union in any region where special interests and ties draw peoples together. Associations which seem exclusive and even aggressive when they represent the summit of international co-operation lose these disturbing characteristics when they become simply well organized parts of a larger whole. The new nations of Asia, the nations that are growing up in Africa, the whole of Latin America, need not look on an Atlantic Union as a possible menace, if they co-operate daily with the Atlantic powers in the United Nations and have constant experience of their readiness to co-operate and practice give-and-take on a world-wide basis.

In both the Atlantic area and in Europe itself, there are opportunities for even closer co-operation and an even wider transcendence of purely national interests. The policies suggested in earlier chapters—common defense, a common economic strategy, mutual support in the pursuit of domestic full employment—will all be more effective if the Western Powers maintain common organs of consultation, decision and action. An Atlantic Council exists already, an embryo Atlantic Cabinet. If the three other agencies proposed for the immediate needs of containment—a Combined Chiefs of Staff, a Production and Resources Board and an Economic Aid Board—are established as permanent institutions, the Atlantic powers will possess all the organs necessary for an effective measure of regional federalism and here, as in the United Nations, it can be argued that they will reach the goal of political and economic unity more speedily by work and experience and the sacrifices and understanding of daily co-operation than by more grandiose schemes for federal constitution making. "The readiness is all."

Nor do wider schemes—in the world at large or in the Atlantic region—exclude closer local arrangements. The advantage of functional federalism is that it sets natural limits to various forms of intergovernmental co-operation and creates a regional area of action largely eased on a functional need. The course of the river Tennessee, for instance, determines which group of American states need to co-operate in the Tennessee Valley Authority. In Europe, there are a variety of such natural opportunities for functional federalism.[2] The Schuman Plan is a case in point. A European transport authority is another. A third might lie in the construction of a European electricity grid, a fourth in the standardizing and internationalizing of European air transport. In most of these, Britain's concern is obvious and immediate and it can only be hoped that the government will rescind its foolish if understandable decision to abstain from the Schuman Plan.

A secondary advantage of such experiments in "functional federation" is that the governments, in creating new international authorities—such as the High Authority proposed by M. Schuman—begin to unload some of the top heavy powers of national governments and in this way make an added contribution to breaking down Europe's rigid mold of sovereignty.

There is no reason why, in addition to experiments in functional federalism, governments which wish to achieve full federal union should not do so. Holland, Belgium and Luxembourg are attempting an economic union without any federal political structure. Should the French and German Governments decide to move to the creation of federal institutions, their neighbors can only applaud the imagination and courage with which France is ready to stretch out its hand to its old aggressor. Provided no strict constitutional pattern is imposed on unwilling states, there is room for every sort of experiment in greater political unity. For this reason, there is no cause for disappointment or petulance over the failure of the Council of Europe to become a federal government within a year of its establishment. The Council has an essential task to perform in fostering the spirit of Europe. The debates at Strasbourg have already had their effect on the insular British and Scandinavians. A sense of common traditions and a common purpose has begun to emerge. The Council, too, can initiate a number of experiments in "Europeanism." A University of Europe has been

[2] An earlier book, *The West at Bay*, discussed some of these possibilities in greater detail.

discussed. It should be developed at once. The exchange of students and teachers, of artists and works of art, the easing of traveling restrictions, the opening of frontiers, the creation perhaps of a common European passport, the interchangeability of social insurance privileges, the mutual acceptance of qualifications and degrees—all these are means of restoring mobility and freedom to the people of Europe and releasing European men and women, particularly in their youth, from the sense of living behind perpetually closed doors. If, out of this renewed contact and steadily increasing familiarity a sense of European citizenship develops, the full federal solution may well come in time from below from the people themselves.

It can even be argued that institutions without immediate political power—such as the Council of Europe—can exercise a profounder influence than those which are overburdened with executive responsibility. The great task of the Council—and one which no government could carry out—is to recreate the cultural and moral unity of Europe. There can be no profounder responsibility. Through all the accumulation of committees and councils and boards and assemblies, the living spirit of unity and faith must breathe if these "dry bones" are to live. The energies that carry men on and the ideals which inspire them are drawn from deeper sources than fear or necessity. If Europe or the Atlantic nations or the whole free world are to achieve these great goals of unity and strength, it is no small vision that they need to inspire them. But have they such a vision? Is there in the free nations "rational hope" and faith and fortitude enough to withstand the Communist onslaught and remake the world? Without it, they can frame their constitutions and balance their books, expand their economies and man their frontiers. Yet all the same victory will go to the other side.

# PART IV · *Faith*

# 23

# *Faith for Freedom*

ANY human enterprise, even the smallest, needs a measure of faith. Men must believe that what they have undertaken can be carried through. They must believe that their partners will work with them loyally. How much more is faith needed when the enterprise is the building of a free and peaceful world and the partners include all the races of the earth. One of the greatest obstacles to an effective Western policy today is men's uncertainty whether peace can in fact be maintained. Particularly among young people, a future apparently dominated by atomic war cuts off at the roots the rising sap of hope and confidence. Yet the essence of containment is the belief that war is not inevitable and that a combination of strength and patience in the West will deter the Soviets from further aggression and persuade them either to negotiate or at least to live as they did in the twenties and thirties primarily concerned with their own affairs.

An almost equal obstacle to successful containment is distrust between the different partners—the tendency of each to pick out and concentrate on the worst aspects of the other's policy, to rub the sore spots, to put salt in old wounds. Out of a million small reactions of unfamiliarity and misunderstanding, national moods grow up, critical, carping and envenomed. Yet what do the free peoples expect? That their neighbors should be exactly like themselves? That they should escape altogether from the fatality of human weakness and error? That they should be incapable of stupidity or tactlessness or self-interest? No private undertaking, no human enterprise of any sort could be run on such expectations. The Western Allies have to be patient with one another and keep the larger unity of their common purposes alive in their minds to defeat all the day-to-day inconveniences of close alliance. The essence of faith is that it does not depend upon a perpetual renewal of absolute proof. No ally in the West is likely to give its neighbors a daily exhibition of all the virtues necessary for a great undertaking. Let the others therefore give the tolerance they expect. If the concept of American greed, of British duplicity or French cowardice or Italian irresponsibility is brought in over and over again to interpret policies and explain reactions, no common enterprise can possibly succeed. It should be as easy to think the best as to think the worst of an ally, but apparently this is not so and only an effort of faith, constantly renewed, can counter the tendency of men and nations to misunderstand, to recriminate, to grow suspicious and at last permit their alliances to fall apart.

Faith in the enterprise itself and faith in one's partners is, however, no more than the minimum—the least with which free men can hope to survive. The weakness of the phrase "containment" is its negative and defensive ring. The Communists do not make the mistake of thinking that they are simply defending themselves against "Western encirclement." This may be the jargon they use to explain to their own people why they have remained armed and alert. But the essence of their drive, of their propaganda, of their picture of themselves is that they must remake the world according to their own gospel, the single unalterable Marxist-Leninist gospel of salvation.

It is curious that we in the West should tend so uniformly to underestimate or misunderstand the passion that drives communism on. Western critics are never tired of pointing out that it is based upon materialism, that there is no room in the Communist system for mankind's highest aspirations or deepest hopes, that all the power and poetry and inspiration of humanity are banished by communism's fundamental tenet—that the economic structure of society determines all the rest. It may be that, in theory, there is no room in communism for these things, but it is vital to remember that, in practical reality, the Communists hardly give economics a thought. They do not condemn Western society because it is inefficient. On the contrary, they are immensely impressed with the technical achievements of the West. They blame it because it is immoral. They do not extol their own system because it is materially more satisfactory. They extol it because it is a new heaven and a new earth, a transfiguration of the conditions of human existence, the raising up of men's lives to new levels of creativeness and joy. When the tanks pour through the streets of Moscow in a gigantic military parade the radio commentators burst into verse:

> Spring has come. It has come here, it has come in China, in the new streets of Warsaw, in Prague, in the gardens of Bucharest, in the villages of Bulgaria. The banner of victory flies over us. The spring of humanity is with us. It is nearing the workers' suburbs of Paris; it is marching like a master upon the piazzas of Rome. In Calcutta, Karachi and Bombay, it sings of freedom. Our Stalin, whose hand guides the spring of humanity, is leading us to victory.

When a new program of irrigation and public works is announced, the newspapers grow lyrical:

> For centuries the peoples of the East have dreamed of crystal-clear rivers, of fertile gardens in the desert, of a fairyland of happiness. Songs passed down from one generation to the next told of these yearnings. The people were confident that the time would come when clear, transparent rivers and streams would cut through the heart of the desert, when birds would sing in the once-silent stretches of dead sands, when blossoming gardens would flourish under a deep blue sky, when beautiful palaces would appear and crowds of gay people assemble to acclaim with gratitude the conquerors of the desert. Today the Soviet peoples praise in all their tongues the courageous conquerors of the desert

> —the Bolsheviks; and they glorify the Bolshevik Party and the beloved Comrade Stalin, whose genius has opened the path to fulfillment of these age-old aspirations.

The first aspect to strike eye-witnesses of Communist rule in China is the attempt to instill "new thoughts" and "self-criticism" in the unconverted Chinese. Police officers confess on the wall-sheets pinned up in their offices that they have stayed awake until four in the morning wondering in agony of spirit whether their self-criticism has been sufficiently honest and far-reaching; and, lest the cynic should dismiss these wrestlings, it should be said that foreign observers also notice a marked increase in their capacity to recover lost or stolen goods without resorting to bribery.

Long before the technician and the economist and the social engineer begin expounding the economics of communism, the poet and the moralist have fired men's minds with the picture of a moral and inspiring way of life. Whatever the shams of communism—and they are immense—they come clothed in the language of poetry and hope. The dream that has haunted the world from its infancy—of a golden age from which it has been banished and a golden age to which it can return—is repeated in the myth of a primitive communism destroyed by the evil of private property and restored triumphantly in the latter days by the return to communism. The anger and outrage of the prophets of old, denouncing social injustice and considering "the evils that are done under the sun," the promise of the Magnificat, "He hath . . . exalted them of low degree," the exquisite and heartbreaking hope of the Apocalypse "and there shall be no more death, nor sorrow nor crying, neither shall there be any more pain; for the former things are passed away"—all these echoes and intimations which lie deepest in men's hearts are evoked by these so-called materialists, by these men who are supposed to think only in terms of economics and from whose lips the appeal of faith and righteous wrath and world-conquering hope is almost never absent.

It must be admitted that, in comparison with this

apocalyptic vision of the world's warring between Communist good and capitalist evil, Western policy seems, remarkably and inexplicably, to have lost sight of its own vision of the good society or at least to have lost confidence in its powers of explaining what that vision really is. If a visitor from Mars had arrived on earth during 1949 and examined the published statements of East and West, it is not likely that he would have found the "materialists" in the Communist half. The constant preoccupation with economics, the careful calculation of what could and could not be afforded, the ceaseless discussion of the limits of taxation, budgetary equilibrium and the perils of inflation would have met him in almost every capital—until he came to the Iron Curtain. Beyond he would have found himself in a world dominated not by a certain view of economics but by a new—and terrible—view of life. This contrast is all the more extraordinary when one reflects that, on any standard of comparison, the really radical and revolutionary way of life does not lie in the East at all, but in the West. The ideas and aspirations of Western man are still the most startling thing that has ever happened to the human race. Stalin's views of man and society are, by comparison, mortally static and archaic. In fact the world today presents the astonishing spectacle of Western man sleeping unaware on the powder keg of his own revolutionary philosophy and the Stalinists leaping up and down proclaiming as a new revolution a view of man and society which was old when the Pyramids were built.

We know something of the civilizations that have risen and fallen in the long history of mankind. Through all of them two themes of human belief and organization appear to run—the first that man and society are molded by the immense impersonal forces of destiny and circumstance, the second that the state—whether spiritual or temporal—is omnipotent and the source of all meaning. Subjects were no more than shadows of shadows. Reality rested with king and priest and temple. And humankind together, king and peasant, priest and servant, were bound to the "melancholy wheel" of fate, the impersonal and unchanging order of times and seasons, the infinite fatality of history. For thousands upon thousands of years, the great civilizations rose and fell, the people in servitude to the state, state and people alike in servitude to destiny. Behavior, ritual, thought itself were determined collectively. Men and women lived out their lives within the closed circle of omnipotent government and omnipotent fate.

Into this static world with its slow rhythm of rise and fall, exhaustion and renewal, there broke a new force of ideas and vitality which wrought probably the most radical transformation of the human scene since man became recognizably man. Two peoples brought about this transformation, each small in number and vast in energy and fertility—the Jews and the Greeks. It is interesting to speculate what an orthodox Marxist historian would have prophesied for mankind had he lived a few thousand years before Christ and had seen Egypt in its static power, the Hittites building a civilization in Asia Minor, Crete crumbling, the Sumerians a memory and Babylon at its zenith. Which empire would he have chosen as the source of future power and influence? Which ideas would he have foreseen dominating and molding the next age? The guess is permissible that he would have overlooked altogether a pastoral people of Judea who, owing to their curiously indigestible national characteristics, were now sitting in exile by the waters of Babylon and refusing to forget their native land. Nor would this same historian, studying all the barbarian peoples who broke through the barriers of mountain and steppe from the north to settle by the Mediterranean, have recognized in the rude Acheans the predecessors of Aristotle and Socrates. There is, in history a recurring refusal to be bound by the predictors and the analysts. History mocks the men who claim, like Marx, to have mastered its secrets and this infinite unpredictability should be the perennial hope of anyone who believes in the resources of freedom.

With the advent of these two societies—Jewish and Greek—the whole character of human development changed and there entered into history something which we may reasonably call "the Western spirit." The measure of its revolutionary power was that it completely contradicted and annihilated the two dominant themes of the archaic world—the fatality of environment and the omnipotence of the state. There is no space here to set down all that Western man owes to his Jewish and Christian heritage on the one hand and to Greece and Rome on the other. It is a commonplace that our society is grounded to its deepest foundations in classical and Christian antiquity. But of all the riches and diversity, these two entirely revolutionary facts must be remembered for they are the key to the understanding of our own society and to its fundamental divergence from communism. It is only in their light that the radical newness of Western thought and the fundamentally reactionary character of Communist thinking can be fully grasped.

The Greeks and the Jews shared with the older civilizations the idea of a divine order of society, but whereas before this order seemed on the whole to have been made up of the sum of circumstances—the seasons, the days, the cycle of agriculture, the chances of flood and storm, the social order as it existed—in Greek and Jewish thought a gulf opened between the divine order as it existed in the mind of God, and the very human order as it existed on earth. The idea that the sum of things could by human will and action be transformed and remade in the image of the divine took hold of men's imaginations. The static idea of social order began to give way to the revolutionary, to the ideas of a possible perfect society which could be achieved, provided men overcame the irrational and immoral aspects of their own lives and their own institutions. The desire to transform, the desire to create, the desire to seize on material circumstances and change and mold them as an artist transforms the material he works with, this was the immense energy injected into the Western world by the rational vision of the Greeks and the moral vision of the Jews. The divine order ceased to be the sum of things that are and began to become the sum of things as they should be. Try as he would—and to return to the static is always a temptation—Western man could never again drive the fever of creation and transformation and progress out of his blood.

The two streams of thought were equally potent in sweeping away the other principle of ancient society—the acceptance of the omnipotent state. The Greek saw the reflection of the Logos in the rational nature of man. As a creature endowed with reason he acquired inalienable social and political rights, among them the right to self-government. For the Jew, it was the divine image in man that created in him moral responsibility. From the first question of Cain, "Am I my brother's keeper?", flowed out the doctrine of personal responsibility. In the Christian tradition the Greek concept of reason and the Hebrew belief in man's accountability met in the idea of the "free and lawful man," which, in medieval Europe, was the basis of the great constitutional experiment of placing government itself under the law and in the centuries that followed, developed into the full doctrine of representative government and political freedom.

No one will pretend that the progress of these two transforming ideals—of justice and liberty—was regular or complete. The Greek insight into the irrationality of much in man's nature and the institutions he set up has been more than justified. The Hebrew and Christian concept of sin—the pride of the mind and the lust of the heart—has darkened every page of Western history. Yet underneath failure and collapse and defeat, the Western spirit has constantly renewed itself and, in the darkest ages, the voice of the saint and the prophet and the reformer was raised to denounce the things that were and point once again to the things that ought to be. The whole social order could never again be entirely accepted. The state could never again maintain an unquestioned omnipotence. Angry, restless, adventuring, protesting, the reformer fought his way through the thickets of ignorance and prejudice. Pitying, loving, rebuking and consoling, the saint and the mystic sought entrance to the darkest hearts and most wayward lives. Under these pressures, Western society became the most restlessly dynamic and explosive social order the world had ever seen. There could be no rest once these ideals of progress and perfection had been let loose in the mind of Western man.

It is the tragedy of Marxist Communism that it restores the old fetters of fatality and tyranny. Because it borrows the terminology of the West and speaks of true freedom and true democracy and true science, men often overlook the profoundly and terrifyingly reactionary character of its doctrine. The free and morally responsible human being with rights and duties and aspirations which transcend any given social order vanishes. Why? Because there is nothing beyond the social order. Every act of human life, every thought of human minds is entirely conditioned by the general state of material events at that time. History becomes once more the arbiter of all destiny. It is no longer an arena in which men struggle in freedom to remold recalcitrant matter and fashion it to their ideals. Their freedom is an illusion and recalcitrant matter is itself responsible for their ideals. The world of freedom closes. In its place returns the stifling world of necessity in which the childhood of the race was spent. Once again men are bound to the melancholy wheel of their social conditioning. Once again, events mold them, not they events. The collective crust forms once again over the experiment of human freedom. The Western vision fades and in the darkness, there are glimpses of Moloch and Baal and the terrible gods of state and circumstance reasserting their ancient sway.

In such a world, the return to omnipotent government is inevitable. If man is no more than a unit in a social calculation, to what rights and pretensions can he lay claim? It is the total social process, society, the environment as a whole that has significance just as thousands of years ago the apparatus of the state—city or temple—was reality and men no more than its component parts. No one doubts the omnipotent claims of the Soviet state today but some are inclined to overlook the even more omnipotent claims inherent in the prophecy that eventually "the state will wither away." In any conceivable society where variety of claims and interests is admitted, some government must remain as arbiter. The only highly complex societies that can dispense with government are those in which social conditioning has produced such perfect adaptation to circumstance and work that no conflicts are conceivable—and no change and no progress either. We know of such societies. The bees and the ants have reached just such a degree of adaptation to environment. (And if environment is fatality, is reality, is God itself, what greater purpose for humanity can there be than to adapt itself?) Behind the concept of the withering away of the state lies not only the loss of freedom, but the loss of rationality and humanity itself.

These are not idle fears. We know from man's long history that the Western experiment of freedom and responsibility is a flash in the pan, a spark in the longest night, an experiment bounded in space and time and preceded by aeons of collective servitude. To step back into an older environment, to regress, to abandon an experiment at once so testing and so abnormal must be a temptation at the very roots of our being. Communism presents it in a form in which language and propaganda are borrowed from the liberal experiment but fundamental thought and direction lead back into the anonymous tyrannies of antiquity and of primitive mankind. Environment as destiny, the state as omnipotence—these are the principles under whose mastery mankind has spent by far the longest part of its conscious span. The Western phase is a tremendous, a breath-taking experiment. It is not yet certain that it can stay the course.

Yet if the Western experiment is really the most audacious and exhilarating that mankind has ever made, how is it that today, the audacity and the creativeness and the revolutionary zeal so often seem to be on the other side? There is a tremendous paradox here. The crusaders for freedom and progress, for man's ever renewed struggle to build a just and holy society appear to be on the defensive before those who seek to eliminate human freedom and restore the twin tyrannies of fate and government. The real revolutionaries cede ground to the pseudo-revolutionaries. The radicals retreat before the reactionaries, the idealists before the materialists. Indeed, the idealists seem to have turned themselves into materialists and to fight their war of words in calculations and statistics while their adversaries sing of deserts blossoming and spring returning to a resurrected humanity. How have we in the West contrived so to dim our vision that we appear to have lost it? How have we come to do remarkable things in such a totally unremarkable way? When was the initiative lost? How is it that we have yet to recapture it?

There can be only one answer. We have not lost it because the Marxist vision is more potent than ours or because communism offers a more attractive version of society. Indeed, it would be difficult to find anything more unattractive than, say, contemporary Bulgaria, and even if we prefer our communism in idealized form, one searches Marx's pages in vain for a concrete description of what Communist society would be like. No, his strength lay in what he attacked, not in what he promised. And it is still true of communism today that wherever it is not imposed by force, it owes its strength not so much to its own attractiveness as to the weakening of the Western way of life. In the last hundred years, we have seen our grip slacken on those two revolutionary principles upon which the Western experiment has been based. The classical and Christian tradition has grown weaker. In its place, even in the West, the concept of fatality and of almighty circumstance has crept back. The men who founded the Industrial Revolution and believed in unchanging and unaltering economic laws were introducing a god of economic determinism into one sector of their society. It was a savage but appropriate justice that led Marx to turn economic determinism against them in their own industrial stronghold. Workers had been sacrificed to misery and degradation in the name of the "iron laws" of demand and supply. Very well, their employers would now be sacrificed in their turn in the name of economic determinism and dialectical materialism. If matter was to be master, Marx had as good a version of the future to offer as Richard Cobden and John Bright and a much more attractive version from the standpoint of the masses.

Nor was the Manchester School's confidence in the beneficence of laisser faire the only entry point for fatalism and historical materialism. The present reality of God and of an ideal world of law and justice which men should struggle to observe and create even if circumstance drag them the other way, began to fade and the great fatalities—environment, conditioning, heredity, evolution—sapped and weakened the concept of freedom, moral responsibility and will. Unconsciously at first, but with steadily increasing realization and indifference, a vast mass of Western men and women sloughed off their society's traditional idealism and became in practice, if not in belief, materialists as convinced as any on the other side of the Iron Curtain—but with this difference. The materialism preached by Communists was a religion of materialism, materialism raised to a total explanation of life, guide of conduct and spur to action. The materialism of the West was all too often no more than an attitude of "eat, drink and be merry, for tomorrow we die." In a conflict between religious materialism and practical materialism, it seems certain that the religious variety will have the strength to prevail. An idea has never yet in human history been defeated by no idea at all.

Yet although it is true that communism has gained strength by the West's own weaknesses, it may yet be true that the West will learn from the Communists how to recapture its own freedom-loving, transforming and creative spirit. In the first place, men and women in the West can see in Soviet society some of the possible results of their own betrayal of the Western ideal. They see what a society can become which is systematically materialist, godless and "scientific." They see how speedily the safeguards of freedom vanish once the idea of law independent of race or class fades and in its place is put the convenience of the community. They see how terribly human compassion can be maimed if there is no appeal to a higher authority than that of government. They see that science itself, on which the regime is supposedly based, can be perverted if the search for truth gives way to the acceptance of the politically expedient. And reflecting on these things, they are perhaps more ready to reconsider the old safeguards of independence and pity, of justice and of truth. They look perhaps with new interest at an earlier belief—that liberty itself is grounded in the fact that God's authority overrules all others and that, in St. Thomas More's words, a man can be the state's "good servant, but God's first."

But communism does more than provide the Western world with a species of rake's progress of some of its own ideas and assumptions. It is, in a real sense, the conscience of the West. Every pretension, every false claim, every complacency of our Western society is relentlessly exposed by Communist propaganda and all too often our dislike of the critics is rendered a thousand times more bitter by our inner knowledge that their gibes are true. It is infuriating, it is exasperating, it is exhausting for the West to know that every weakness is spied on, every social failure capitalized, every injustice trumpeted abroad, every lack of charity and understanding blown up into a major social crime. But is it certain that without these enraging critics we in the West would be so aware of where we fail ourselves? Might we not drift on in indifference beyond the point at which this weakened institution or that false situation could be repaired? In many ways, we today are paying for the complacency of our grandfathers and great-grandfathers. It was not only the injustice, it was also the appalling smugness of the Victorian possessing classes which put the real vitriol into Marx's pen. Today, at least, no false complacency can hold us back from seeing where are the weaknesses and the shams. Bitterly as a man may resent the shooting pain that warns him of some internal disorder, would he see to curing himself in time without that pain?

Communists today leave us in no doubt where our weaknesses lie. They await in a fever of tension and expectation the coming of another disastrous depression. They seek to exacerbate by every means the gulf between East and West, between Asia and the Atlantic, between developed and backward areas, between rich and poor, slave and free.

They search for every chink in the armor of Western unity. They batten on every national prejudice and try to poison every potential conflict between the Allies of the West. Above all, they preach the decadence and decline of Western ideals, the false pretensions of Western society, the myth of Western religion, the hypocrisy of Western freedom and the certainty of Western collapse. We need therefore have no doubts about the necessary means of Western survival—to be stable, reliable and prosperous ourselves, to share with others our prosperity, to rebuild our defenses, to be patient allies and good friends, to restore our vision and moral purpose, to drive out the gods of fatalism, to restore the "glorious liberty of the sons of God," and in this spirit, to confront our adversaries with a calm fortitude that allays both their fears and their ambitions—these are the main themes for a common policy in the West. Nothing in them is beyond the competence of the Western Powers. Never, indeed, have the material means of fulfilling them been so assured. If there is a doubt at all, it can only be a doubt of the necessary vision and will.

This surely is the crux. In all that they say of the Western world, the Communists are proclaiming the fatal laws of historical necessity. Capitalist society must collapse. The United States must practice selfish imperialism. The Western states must exploit their workers, fight for markets in the world at large, trample down their Asiatic helots and plunge the world into wars of aggression. It follows that every policy of the West that contradicts these fears—every Marshall Plan, every extension of economic aid to backward areas, every increase in social and economic opportunity, every act of justice and reconciliation breaks with the Communists' fundamental gospel—the fatality of history—and restores, triumphantly and creatively, the freedom of the West. We are not bound by collective selfishness. No iron law of economics holds us down. The Western world is a world of freedom and in it, the Western Powers can freely choose and freely act.

# Index

◊◊◊◊◊◊◊◊◊◊◊◊◊◊◊◊◊◊◊◊◊◊◊◊◊◊◊◊◊◊◊◊◊◊◊◊◊◊◊◊◊◊◊◊

# Books that Live

The Norton imprint on a book means that in the publisher's estimation it is a book not for a single season but for the years.

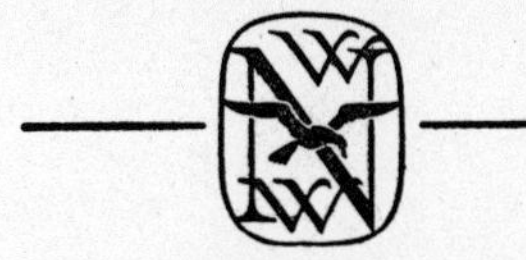